The New Metaphysicals

The New Metaphysicals

Spirituality and the American Religious Imagination

COURTNEY BENDER

The University of Chicago Press   Chicago and London

COURTNEY BENDER is associate professor of religion at
Columbia University and author of *Heaven's Kitchen: Living with
Religion at God's Love We Deliver*, also published by the University of
Chicago Press.

The University of Chicago Press, Chicago 60637
The University of Chicago Press, Ltd., London
© 2010 by The University of Chicago
All rights reserved. Published 2010
Printed in the United States of America
20 19 18 17 16 15 14 13 12 11 10   1 2 3 4 5

ISBN-13: 978-0-226-04279-4 (cloth)
ISBN-13: 978-0-226-04280-0 (paper)
ISBN-10: 0-226-04279-0 (cloth)
ISBN-10: 0-226-04280-4 (paper)

Library of Congress Cataloging-in-Publication Data
Bender, Courtney.
  The new metaphysicals : spirituality and the American religious
imagination / Courtney Bender.
    p. cm.
  Includes bibliographical references and index.
  ISBN-13: 978-0-226-04279-4 (cloth: alk. paper)
  ISBN-10: 0-226-04279-0 (cloth: alk. paper)
  ISBN-13: 978-0-226-04280-0 (pbk.: alk. paper)
  ISBN-10: 0-226-04280-4 (pbk.: alk. paper)
  1. Experience (Religion) 2. Religion and sociology—United
States—Case studies. 3. Spirituality—Massachusetts—
Cambridge. I. Title.
  BL53.B397 2010
  204'.2097444—dc22   2009033208

Contents

Acknowledgments

I am most fortunate to have four good friends who read and thought through major themes of this book with me. Jody Shapiro was my constant conversation partner through the duration of my fieldwork. She conducted a trio of important interviews during the pilot stage of the project and was a constant source of information about the tangle of various yoga groups and alliances in the Boston area. She subsequently read most of the chapters, offering generous comments. As I transitioned from fieldwork into writing and archival work (and continuing into writing), I frequently benefited from my conversations with the nimble-minded Pamela Klassen about things religious and mundane, practical and theoretical, professional and domestic. Her friendship is a true gift, and I hope that we continue to be able to work on future manuscripts in parallel. Closer to home, Erika Dyson provided essential bibliographic suggestions and perceptive commentary on the ideas and theses I floated over many coffees and lunches. And perhaps even more important, she demonstrated through example how it is possible to simultaneously take the metaphysical seriously while retaining (or gaining) a sense of humor about the whole business. Through writing and revisions, David Smilde became a necessary long-distance discussion partner and reader. Our (usually minor) disagreements about cultural sociology have been important grist for the mill; his comments on the manuscript in its penultimate stage were characteristically perceptive.

Many others have offered crucial pieces of advice and commentary when I found myself unable to figure out what to do next. Each of the following people have shaped my thinking in a variety of ways, but when I think back I find that I remember specific conversations that helped me past intellectual culs-de-sac. Henry Goldschmidt offered a vital set of ideas about temporality and nostalgia. John Lardas Modern pushed me to think more about resonance and secularity (and resonating secularity). Tracy Leavelle and Kathryn Lofton both insisted that I pay closer attention to matters of place, though in different ways. Jeff Olick directly and indirectly expanded my understanding of memory and history, and provided a healthy dose of skepticism as I carried on. Christopher White opened up a new (and for me, more interesting) reading of James's writings. Sylvester Johnson pointed me in the direction of some important work on mystical bodies. As the writing progressed, Ann Taves encouraged me to develop my arguments on experience in different directions; our friendly arguments helped me better understand my own position. Wendy Cadge, Dawne Moon, Richard Wood, John Evans, Nancy Ammerman, John Corrigan, Judith Weisenfeld, Rosemary Hicks, and Jodi Eichler-Levine contributed generous and pointed commentary on various portions of the text.

While walking through Harvard Square, on my way to my very first field visit, my path crossed that of Robert Orsi and Leigh Schmidt. We chatted very briefly about the weather, and they politely inquired about my destination. As I answered, my high state of nervous agitation abated somewhat, and I went on my way cheered considerably. I am glad to be able to thank them now for literally sending me on my way, and for their encouragement in our intermittent conversations and correspondence since then.

I have no doubt that had I mentioned this chance meeting to my Cambridge interlocutors, they would have smiled and reminded me (again) that coincidences are never *mere* coincidences. They would have prodded me to elaborate a more meaningful story about that encounter, as they had on many other occasions. It was in such interchanges that my many interlocutors, friends, and circles of respondents taught me how they caught others (and even me) in their webs of significance. I thank each of them for their patient and gentle thoughtfulness in answering my questions, and likewise for their willingness to instruct me as I went along (even when I was an unwilling student). I remain somewhat flabbergasted and humbled by strangers' willingness to talk with me, I admit. But I could not have written this book, or even conceptualized its premises and forms, without their answers to my questions or their attempts to steer me toward "better" ones.

A number of institutions generously supported my research and writing. An initial and important seed grant came from Columbia University's Institute for Social and Economic Research and Policy. Subsequent funding from various Columbia sources allowed me to purchase what is increasingly difficult to purchase: time in the field. And the Warner Fund (University Seminars) provided funds for indexing. In addition, I benefited immensely from the Social Science Research Council's programming on religion and secularism. Jonathan Van-Antwerpen and Craig Calhoun in particular deserve thanks for their invitations to participate in several intellectually expansive and rigorous consultations.

As chapters took shape, I benefited from the probing questions by scholarly audiences at the University of Chicago Divinity School, Harvard University, Princeton University, Yale University, the University of California at San Diego, and Davidson College. I learned an enormous amount from other participants in Princeton University's Cognitive and Textual Methods seminar, organized by Robert Wuthnow. And I am especially grateful for the friendships and intellectual encouragement of my colleagues in Columbia's Department of Religion, including especially Mark Taylor, Gil Anidjar, Michael Como, Wayne Proudfoot, Bernard Faure, Randall Balmer, and John S. Hawley.

At the University of Chicago Press I thank Doug Mitchell, who gleefully recited Pharoah Sanders's line "everything is everything" when I first told him about this project, and then repeated it frequently in our correspondence. (For a while, I had the line taped to the top of my computer screen.) Timothy McGovern saw to it that everything went smoothly at the Press, and Lisa Wehrle that everything in this book reads smoothly. As I revised the manuscript for publication, Rajiv Sicora at Columbia heroically drafted the index.

Finally, Solomon and Hope, my children. I take enormous pleasure in their imaginative and honest dispositions and have tried my hardest to keep this book from intruding too much on our walks in the city or our dinner table conversations. I can look back now over the years I spent with this project and see that its pages encompass hundreds of happy events, both big and small, spent with them, with Jonathan, and with members of my vibrant, life-sustaining extended family. But as I pause to consider these years I always think first of two women who died too soon, and with so much living left to do. My mother

ACKNOWLEDGMENTS

Nancy Shank Bender (1942–2005) and my mother-in-law Susan Brimm Dworkin (1941–2003) were uncommon women: independent thinkers, unyielding in their devotion to their families, and complex in the best possible sense of the term. I have written with them always in mind, and I have acutely missed their counsel. For a long time I thought that I would dedicate this book to their memories. But at the end of the day, this book can be for no one else but Jonathan Dworkin, my love, for all the many reasons.

Long Shadows

I walked quickly down Quincy Street in Harvard Square on a cold night in January 2002, heading toward a meeting of the Mystical Experiences Discussion Group. The group met biweekly at the Swedenborgian Church of the New Jerusalem; I had been attending the group somewhat regularly as part of my research among contemporary mystics and metaphysical practitioners in Cambridge, Massachusetts. My daily routine sent me down Quincy almost every day, and I rarely registered my surroundings, save when the sugar maples were at their full color in the fall or lilacs in bloom in May. On this bitter night, however, I unexpectedly found myself walking with heightened awareness. That day had been a busy one, most of it spent transcribing interviews, including one I had conducted the previous week with Wes, an "energy intuitive," who at the end of our interview had read my energy by placing his hand on my wrist. In the afternoon I had read a student's paper on Jewish-Zen meditation practice and puzzled over a few passages in William James's essay on pragmatism. Now, running late for the meeting, I took note of this particular street's history and its resonance with my research on spiritual life in America. Walking past William James's and Oliver Wendell Holmes's family residences, I realized that those were the very buildings where many of the central ideas and arguments I had been reading about had been first been argued and penned. Despite my tardiness and the bitter wind, I paused for a moment to take in the unobstructed view of the architectural juxtaposition before me. The tidy, gothic chapel sat in the shadows of Harvard

University's brutalist skyscraper, William James Hall, an arrangement that gave metaphorical shape to the ways that Swedenborg's rational scientific mysticism (espoused by William James's father, Henry Sr., and other Cantabrigian luminaries) has been cast in the shadows by liberal definitions of religious experience espoused by James and his contemporaries. Conversations and controversies about religious experience, how or whether it can be pursued, and how union with the divine transforms one's understanding of the self and its relations to others continue nonetheless at the chapel and at myriad other places in Cambridge.

––––––

This is a book about the central presence of individual religious experience in American spiritual cultures and practice. It investigates how this experience is produced, practiced, and articulated in one American city. *The New Metaphysicals* considers how particular cultural, theological, and even scientific legacies make experiencing and touching the divine possible. Religious experiences were a central lingua franca for Cambridge's spiritual practitioners. Numinous, unexpected experiences, mystical experiences of "flow," and daily synchronicities, dreams, and the like shaped the worlds in which spiritual practitioners lived. Their stories were dense with detail and presented occasions for extended, changing, and conflicting interpretations.

When mystics and spiritual practitioners met face to face, their primary focus was often on experience as well. They talked about their meanings and proper interpretation, and together pondered their authenticity. They debated whether experience could be practiced or self-initiated, and how experience changed their bodies. All the while, they worked together to elicit felicitous circumstances for future experiences and drew upon past experiences to evaluate relations with intimates and strangers. And, as they did, they likewise shaped their relations to the past in ways that refigured the traditions of which they were arguably a part. These activities signaled participation in a history that was carried in practice rather than in other forms of memory: the pivotal importance of religious experience in these living articulations positioned practitioners within religious traditions that are indicated through arguments about how experience itself works. These religious practices complicate the importance of traditions, theologies, hierarchies, and institutions, given that they simultaneously reproduce and hide their genealogies.

While this volume focuses throughout on key issues of experience, it began with a set of questions about where (and in fact whether) spiritual identities, practices, and discourses are produced in similar ways to other religious identities, practices, and discourses. I wanted to know how and where people became "spiritual not religious," and what kinds of structures supported their narratives and practices. I thus ventured into an ethnographic study of spirituality in Cambridge, Massachusetts, with the goal of developing a working map of various spiritual practitioners and networks by observing as many settings and interviewing as many leaders and participants as possible.[1] Ethnographic research was necessary, I reasoned, given that most sociological analyses of spirituality focus on individuals and draw almost exclusively on individual-level data (interviews and survey methods) to investigate and evaluate the spiritual.[2] Perhaps as a consequence of these methodological choices, sociological and popular descriptions and analysis have had little to say on the topic of spirituality's production or reproduction. Indeed, most sociological and popular accounts agree that American spirituality is a religious condition that emerges in a new way in the crucible of late twentieth-century social dislocations. New levels of religious seeking and increasing numbers of unaffiliated individuals are indicative of (or the consequence of) ongoing social fragmentation and weakening social ties, increased social mobility, and growing education levels.[3] These studies present spirituality as an individual project, brought forth by the conditions of a society that values the individual.

It quickly became clear to me that the popular and sociological visions of contemporary spiritual seekers as cultural and theological orphans adrift in fragmented, post-religious worlds miss the mark. My work proceeded apace, and as I became familiar with the various networks and internal distinctions within the spiritual networks of Cambridge, I also began to pay more careful attention to the city's spiritual pasts. These pasts were first evident in architecture, as my walk down Quincy Street on that bitterly cold night suggests, but they were also evident in practice. The Swedenborgian Chapel and the Theosophical Society were important centers for a large range of spiritual groups (as were other religious organizations, the local library, an adult education center, and a spiritual bookstore). The city is proud of its record of harboring religious and secular freethinkers, progressives, and experimenters.

Locating my study in Cambridge thus demanded that I think about the location of contemporary spirituality not just in organizational terms but also in geographical and historical terms.[4] Indeed, historians of American religion regularly present a portrait of American spirituality that contrasts strongly with the sociological. In these narratives, the new age and "contemporary spirituality" are emanations of other religious forms, including American metaphysical and harmonial traditions[5] that increasingly serve as the cultural lodestones through which they reimagine the nineteenth century's transnational intellectual networks and engagements with the contradictions of modernity. Although the majority of these historical studies remain focused on the nineteenth century, they evocatively suggest that such connections continue.[6] Cambridge itself plays an important, if not a central, role in these narratives. Prominent figures in Transcendentalism, Spiritualism, Christian Science, mind cure, Theosophy, and Vedanta have important Cambridge chapters: Emerson's famous speech to the Harvard Divinity School, Sarah Bull's turn-of-the-century comparative religion "salon" on Brattle Street, and Henry James's depictions of social reformers and mediums in *The Bostonians*, and others come to mind.[7] In addition, Cambridge has been the setting for ongoing interactions between Americans and "Asian religions," and of many groundbreaking experiments into religious consciousness and experience.

As I went about my research increasingly intrigued by these narratives of historical continuity, I nonetheless began to wonder in earnest whether such histories mattered at all to the people I met at the Seven Stars bookshop or whom I witnessed "soul singing" at a local arts festival. For whom did it matter that hundreds of mesmerists practiced in and around Boston in the 1800s or that William James had taken to the stand to defend their right to practice?[8] Did the people who attended an occasional lecture at the Spiritualist Temple or who enrolled at yoga classes at the Theosophical Society think about these places or about why the events they pursued were so frequently lodged in these settings? Many of the people I met in Cambridge were wholly uninterested in these pasts, and while some were aware of such figures and knew a bit about them, the labors of past Cantabrigians were quite incidental to their pursuits. When on the rare occasion a spiritual practitioner in Cambridge mentioned a Phineas Parkhurst Quimby or a William James, it was to call attention to a shared and timeless quest for knowledge, and not to place themselves within a conventional historical trajectory that included earlier figures such as these.

The histories of Cambridge's metaphysical pasts and their resonance within the present continued to raise and reframe theoretical questions about how religious traditions are carried through space and time, and how these processes shape their felt qualities in the present.[9] How is a tradition felt and carried when its very practice and theology claim a different reading of history and the past than what we generally understand to be carried in traditions? How do practices central to metaphysical and mystical traditions work within the stories that both practitioners and scholars tell about spirituality? While Cambridge's role in answering these questions is particular and peculiar, it is not my intent to restore a forgotten historical narrative to either "spirituality" or "Cambridge."[10] Rather, it is to use both within an inquiry about how forgetting and remembering are linked to practices of various kinds, including practices of experiencing, writing, reading, and speaking.[11] In studying the space and texture of spirituality in Cambridge, I became more attuned to the ways that particular metaphysical, mystical, and harmonial traditions thrive within and through practices that locate and dislocate, historicize and dehistoricize, spiritualize and secularize, embody and offer escape from embodiment.[12]

Spiritual, Metaphysical, and Mystical: Entanglements

Defining spirituality and locating it within social life is notoriously difficult. Much like religion or experience, spirituality is bedeviled not by a lack of definitions but by an almost endless proliferation of them. Most definitions—including those that are historical or genealogical, as well as those that are psychological, perennial, or neurological—have served to protect, defend, debunk, or claim certain territory for the spiritual; these definitions confound more than they illuminate. When we look closely at this proliferation of definitions, we see that each articulates claims about the truth and veracity of spirituality (or religion). But most of these distinctions, particularly those that describe spirituality as a category distinct from religion, are relatively new. As I hope to make clear, the fuzziness, indistinctness, and multiplicity of definitions suggest that we have more to gain by observing how the term "spirituality" is used, and how distinctions within it make some practices and engagements more or less possible.

I begin thus with the view that spirituality, whatever it is and however it is defined, is *entangled* in social life, in history, and in our academic and nonacademic imaginations. Most definitions of recent vintage suffer by defining spirituality as a distinct category of action or activity (or mental state); they likewise seek to extract something essential from it, often trying to find the common denominator of spirituality that exists within the various social locations where it is encountered. But these entanglements at least partly constitute spirituality's framework and shape the paths through which people engage it. Given this, extracting spirituality or mysticism from the institutions where it is lived out both distorts and mischaracterizes the phenomenon, and draws attention away from the conundrums it poses and the possibilities it allows. It is necessary to engage spirituality, historically, institutionally, and imaginatively without pulling it completely together into a single thing. Our way into such inquiry is aided in this respect by sociological theories that approach cultures and traditions as loosely bounded, heterogeneous, and dynamically changing.[13] From this vantage, we can observe claims to identify pure or authentic religious or spiritual traditions as the labor of specific interests. Such efforts take place within (and likewise have a hand in shaping) the pluralistic, heterogeneous, and nonunified social worlds in which we live.[14]

This perspective has been particularly helpful in placing the spiritual in Cambridge, where few spiritual groups were freestanding alternative religious institutions. Most groups and practices are, rather, connected in one way or another to mainstream religious groups and congregations, to spas or alternative medicine clinics, or to local artists' networks and gallery spaces. Similarly, only a handful of my respondents identified as "spiritual." Most emphasized their practices or commitments to specific modes of engaging the divine that they pursued in some of these social settings, for example, telling me to "write down in your notes that I'm a Reiki teacher," or, as another told me, "I'm a yogi, and an artist, and a singer and a writer, and a mystic—and who knows what else I might be becoming?" While my respondents tended to reject broad labels, they nonetheless recognized that others were fellow travelers, and that a number of groups and institutions promoted similar interests. Everyone I spoke with could identify other spiritual practitioners, groups, and individuals in Cambridge, and their own maps and connections helped to round out my portrait. Some of my respondents hopefully suggested that these groups were "emerging" into a new spiritually enlightened movement that would alter the landscape around them. Despite these desires and hopes, what appeared more evident to me is that "spirituality" was both an identifiable "something" and at the same time shaped by constituent parts and practices that operated and thrived within distinct settings. As I will discuss throughout the volume, but particularly in chapter 1, spiritual forms have thrived and been shaped by entanglements with the secular, including its powerful engagements with modern science and progress.[15]

A second set of entanglements involve questions of history. Thus, in addition to using the term "spiritual practitioner" to talk about the people I met in Cambridge, I also call them "metaphysicals" and "mystics" to call attention to the ways their practices are centrally engaged with and entangled in specific American religious trajectories. In other words, respondents are metaphysicals and mystics insofar as they participate within recognizable, historically meaningful definitions of experience and mysticism, and engage in practices that give these concepts social heft and religious validity. Using these terms alongside the more familiar "spiritual" is thus a reminder that our modern spiritual worlds are shaped as much by developments in American religious thought that took shape at the turn of the last century as by more recent developments in the "me" generation. My approach to understanding spiritual practitioners in this light has been to ask how metaphysical and mystical pasts are reproduced in institutions, language, and practice that make spirituality work.

A third set of entanglements that extend beyond the institutional and the historical requires more attention at the outset, namely the entanglements of "spirituality" and "religious experience" in sociological understandings of religion in America.

Sociology, Religious Experience, and Religious Individualism

My focus on the practices of experience might seem strange from within the sociological tradition, where religious experience receives little attention; at first blush, it may even seem to fall outside of the discipline's purview altogether. In some sense it may be outside of the category of "practice" as well. While sociologists occasionally report on the prevalence of religious experiences in various religious groups, or note the importance of collective rituals and effervescence, little in the last four decades of sociological research on religion has offered either a robust or a critical sociology of religious experience. We might think of this as being merely the result of disciplinary boundary work. In other words, religious experience has largely been understood to be a matter for psychology, science, or perhaps theology, rather than sociology. But why is this the case, and how is it that religious experience has taken on the kinds of attributes that makes it apparently uninteresting to sociologists, or perhaps impervious to sociological method?

One possibility is that religious experience, by its nature, is individual, isolated, unexpected, and thus difficult to study with sociological tools or methods.[16] Yet this answer, which surfaces occasionally in sociological studies, seems less than satisfactory once we recognize that this commonplace understanding of religious experience is a "relatively late and distinctively Western" concept, wherein religious experiences are individually experienced events, occurring by dint of natural, biological, or perhaps divine forces.[17] While the many strains of empirical investigation and philosophical commentary on religious experience make it quite difficult to chart out a single story line of this development, we might say in a brief sketch that our current understandings developed in large measure as ideas that resisted Enlightenment critiques of religion and religious reason. These critiques emphasized the irrationality of belief and prompted theologians to shift the space of religious authority from the head (and reason) to the heart (and experience). Experience, located in the emotions and affect, and in other religious "organs," became the key to marking religion's unique truth. As Martin Jay notes, the transformation shifted a broadly based European notion of religion as "*adherence* to belief, either rational or willed, in certain propositions about God and His creation" to a *property* or *condition* "understood as devotional or pious behavior derived from something akin to an emotionally charged, perceptual experience of divinity or the holy."[18]

Wayne Proudfoot identifies Christian theologian Friedrich Schleiermacher's theological argument for religious experience as establishing the "best case" for this definition of religious experience, and traces Schleiermacher's influence on the hermeneutics of Dilthey, Otto, and others. Proudfoot outlines the logical inconsistencies embedded in Schleiermacher's account, demonstrating how arguments for independent, apprehendable religious experience are better understood as texts that teach the rules of the game through which religious experiences take on particular shape as noncommunicable conditions, protected from various forms of "reductionism."[19] Religious experience "formulated the rules for the identification of the numinous moment of experience in such a way as to prevent the 'reduction' of religious experience by its being subsumed under any explanatory or interpretative scheme. . . . If it can be explained, it is not religious experience. The criterion by which the experience is to be identified precludes certain kinds of explanation. What purports to be a neutral phenomenological description is actually a form designed to evoke or to create a particular sort of experience."[20] While a posteriori accounts of such experiences can be subject to inquiry and evaluation, given that they are mediated by language and the need for communication, the experience "itself" remains outside of this realm of investigation and thus impervious to falsification.

Protective strategies such as these reinforced the distinction between the experience itself and its cultural elaboration. These strategies continue to surface from time to time in sociological treatments of religion. For example, in the *Heretical Imperative,* Peter Berger argues that religious traditions initially derive from individual religious experiences, calling such events "irreducible" and impervious to social and cultural analysis. Berger argues that "religious experience . . . *comes to be* embodied in traditions, which mediate it to those who have not had it themselves and which institutionalize it for them as well as for those who had." The process through which raw, analytically inaccessible religious experiences are translated and domesticated into specific cultural-historical traditions is "a constant in human history," stating further that the socially constructed elements of religion, that is, traditions and cultures, are based upon original experiences. Drawing on Mircea Eliade, Rudolph Otto, and others who also propose a priori experience as a fundamental element of human existence, Berger charts a path for a nonreductionistic approach to religion by drawing on a long sociological and theological tradition that claims that religious experience is fundamentally external to and prior to culture and structure.[21] While sociologists rarely now draw on this distinction directly, it remains in place, reverberating, as we will see, in sociological distinctions between experiences and their accounts.

Thus, even as sociologists might criticize psychology's focus on abnormal and peak experiences and its oversimplification of the role of social groups and cultures in shaping religious experience,[22] many sociological studies of religious narratives preserve the distinction between an experience and its account, its immediate individual feeling and its post hoc social iteration.[23] As one critic has observed, making a theoretical distinction between experience and account continues to free sociologists and others to analyze "the mystical claims of religion in terms of social realities," without requiring sociologists to reduce the claims to their interpretations. In short, it holds out the possibility that the reality of religion remains external to the human sciences.[24]

Thus, while sociologists rarely focus explicitly on these distinctions, the practices that set apart experiences from accounts, and that place sociological expertise only on one side of the divide, not only reinforce a particular understanding of experience but also play a role in reinforcing the natural and given characteristics of individual religious experiences. As historians tell us, the discussions and conceptions of a universally available religious experience that took shape in the late nineteenth and early twentieth centuries provided enormous resources for theologians, laypeople, and social scientists to make the case for a universal religious sentiment. American intellectual elites of the late nineteenth century interpreted the writings of German romantics, Asian philosophical texts, neo-Platonic and hermetic texts, and their own religious encounters as evidence for this universal religious sensibility. As Leigh Schmidt argues, such ideas presented the possibility for a universal religion "of the spirit, not dogmatic, ecclesiastical, sacramental, or sectarian, Protestant as much as post-Protestant." American (as well as European and Asian) academics established practices of comparative religion that were often rooted on phenomenological claims that the "world's religions" shared an underlying core of experience.[25] The "ahistorical, poetic, essential, intuitive, and universal mysticism" served ultraliberal Protestants and liberal secularists well. This newly universal mysticism, far from serving as a privatizing and domesticating belief, instead was used to develop worldly engagement with religious others and to seek out the similar truths of religious experience within non-Christian religious traditions.[26] These understandings of experience also were set into play as modern societies made distinctions between religion and science, Western and Eastern religions, and premodern and modern Christianity.[27]

If religious experience was individual, and in its best sense not only independent of religious traditions but the generator of all religious traditions and cultural forms, then it made sense to investigate experience not with sociological tools but rather with psychological or psychical (or scientific) tools and methods. Modern psychological techniques and apparatuses made it possible to observe and document experiences and frequently also to elicit or prompt similar experiences; a captivated public was enthralled by the new sciences of psychology and medicine that were developing to test and "prove" experiential knowledge of the divine.[28] These forays into the science of experience were far from purely academic, as American religious liberals embraced science and scientific methods, and both argued and hoped for demonstrations that "'true religion' was 'religion in general' and authentic religious experience and naturalistic theories of religion were not incompatible."[29]

We can see that these concepts of religious experience clearly informed and shaped the work of early sociologists of religion, who used religious experience as a constituent part of their typologies of religious social organization. Both Ernst Troeltsch and Joachim Wach identify a type of "mystical" religion that emerges from noetic individual experience and that for this reason has difficulty organizing in robust social forms. Wach notes that mysticism "points to a type of religious experience . . . that concerns the individual and innermost self. . . . We feel justified in stating that 'isolation' is constitutive of mystical religion." Wach cites Rudolph Otto's understanding of numinous religious experiences when he argues that religious experience is "ultimately uncommunicable" and thus "generates" a kind of religion that is not social at its base. Says Wach, "There remain mainly two forms of sociality in which the mystic will participate: human companionship in what concerns all daily life and mutual support in the protest directed against traditional religious forms and institutions." Individual religious experiences as a priori experiences have the ability to regenerate religious organization.[30] Nonetheless, a mysticism that takes shape outside of churchly settings also becomes a rhetorically valuable anti-religion: it is improperly socialized religion.

Neither Troeltsch nor Wach believe that Christians should pursue mystical forms. Indeed, Troeltsch warns that experiential religion often leads to the evaporation of religious collectives. While such views may sound somewhat antique from our current vantage, they continue to circulate (both implicitly and explicitly) in recent scholarship on American spirituality, where the possibility of individual, unmediated religious experience and its presumed dangers to the religious community remain firmly entrenched.[31] Examples of unmediated religious experiences often appear in sociological studies of spirituality, whether in claims about the distinctions between experiences (individual) and accounts (social), in survey data that prompt individuals to recall personal experiences and link them to social processes,[32] or in recent studies that argue that individual experience is a component of "spiritual but not religious" identity.[33] It is particularly this last set of studies that concern us in this volume. It is precisely the individual, abnormal type of religious experience, which has developed within a long set of interactions among sociology, philosophy, hermeneutics, and theology, that provides a space for sociologically meaningful "religious individualism" to emerge and take (changing but definite) shape as a category of religious expression; and it is precisely these conversations that we must investigate before analyzing Americans' spiritual expression.

Without intellectual and social scientific grounding for a self-generated (or divinely generated) religious experience, our current view of the "spiritual but not religious" would take on quite different meaning than it currently does. There is not much distance between Wach's description of mysticism and Bellah and colleagues' critique of Sheila Larson (and Sheila-ism) in *Habits of the Heart*. Among the numerous articles that cite "Sheila-ism" as a shorthand for religious individualism, most agree with Bellah that Sheila's religion and her experience mark her as a *bricoleur* in an indeterminate shopping-mall of faith; personal experience drives to personal selection of religious goods, religious expressions, and self-determination.[34] That said, given that we have reasons to investigate religious experience with a more complicated genealogical and generic understanding of the changing definitions of religious experience in various academic fields, it behooves us to return to the question of individual spirituality as it has developed in relation to these naturalized understandings of experience. Yet if we take a view that religious experience as we currently understand it nonetheless carries its histories at least in part in its practices and the ways that it operates to protect itself and to shape certain subjectivities, then a focus on experiential practice becomes necessary. It also invokes a fourth set of entanglements.

Ethnographic Entanglements: Cambridge, Experience, and the Ivy League Professor

The foregoing passages suggest another possibly disconcerting wrinkle that accompanies writing about contemporary spirituality and religious experience. Namely, the emerging and changing understandings of religious experience that my respondents practice and think with are shaped in conversations and engagements (both imagined and real) with academic and scientific interest in the same. Understanding the role of scholarly activity in the genealogies of religious experience in fact leads us to see that scholars, while not central to metaphysical and mystical pursuits, nonetheless have been far more than spectators on the sidelines of changing understandings. Indeed, for the last one hundred years, scholars, including scholars working in the Boston area, have played important roles in shaping the debates about and the appearance and meaning of religious experience. Consequentially, undertaking a study of religious experience in Cambridge means embarking on a project in which scholarly discourses (including social scientific discourses) about experience are already afforded religious meaning by spiritual practitioners. Researchers and the technical terms they employ are often "caught" in ongoing debates among metaphysicals about the authority and reality of religious experiences, making the study of spirituality entangled in one more respect.

The role of scholarly authority in ongoing struggles over the meaning of religious experience should have been evident to me from the very first evening of my field research, when I ventured into the Swedenborgian Chapel on a gorgeous night in the late spring of 2001. Earlier in the week I had noted a flier on a streetlight in Cambridge's Central Square announcing a lecture to commemorate the one-hundredth anniversary of William James's lectures, *The Varieties of Religious Experience.* I arrived a few minutes early, walked up the left side of the Chapel, and slid into an empty pew directly behind three men. They appeared to all be in their early thirties, perhaps graduate students I thought, as they were passing a bound manuscript back and forth among them and talking about it animatedly. I struggled to catch the direction of their conversation over the ambient chatter, but before I could hear too much, the Chapel's minister stood to introduce the evening's speaker. Professor Eugene Taylor, a researcher, author, professor of psychiatry at Harvard's Saybrook Graduate Center, and former president of the Cambridge Swedenborgian Society took the lectern.

Professor Taylor, a noted interpreter of William James's views on religion and psychology, started his lecture with a biting critique of *The Metaphysical Club*.[35] I had just finished reading Menand's history of pragmatism through the remarkable friendships and connections among William James, Oliver Wendell Holmes, Charles Sanders Peirce, John Dewey, and others, and followed Taylor's chapter-and-verse critique with great interest. Taylor complained at length that Menand had ignored Swedenborg's central influence on James and Peirce, and larded his critique with stories of James's religious yearnings and hints that he had recently discovered a box of James's papers that shed light on these topics.[36] Taylor positioned himself as James's champion (and by extension, Swedenborg's as well) against scholarly work that, like Menand's, ignored James's methodological pluralism and religious ecumenism.[37]

Moving his attention from Menand to James's place in this history, Taylor reiterated the fascinating story of the continued positive force of Emanuel Swedenborg's philosophies and mystical writings on American psychology and philosophy. These histories have been relegated to the shadows, Taylor said, and would remain there so long as scholars view pragmatism as a secular philosophy. The audience followed with full attention as the avuncular professor unfurled this story, familiar to those who had read his more popular volume on the intertwined histories of "psychology and spirituality" in America.[38] Sitting there, however, pen in hand, I couldn't help but wonder if many in the audience wouldn't find his criticisms of Menand's new volume pedantic. The book was hardly well read at that point, and, beyond that, Taylor focused almost exclusively on internecine academic arguments about James's intellectual influences and methods. It was not until much later that I would come to understand just how religious this talk was; I completely missed the high drama invoked in Taylor's explication of the ongoing, vital struggle over the realities of religious experience and the strengthening claims of experiential reductionism. Likewise, I failed to grasp how Taylor, himself a professor, had marshaled Menand and his book as new players in an unfolding epic familiar to many in the sanctuary.

Contemporary understandings of religion, religious experience, and spirituality are not only "studied by" historians and sociologists, they are also forged in ongoing interactions between groups of scholars and laypeople. Religious actors and groups actively laid claim to the findings of social scientists and experimentalists, sometimes adapting scholarly research for their own purposes. And thus, while ethnographers are sometimes (possibly correctly) criticized for making too much of the effects of their presence on their research sites, it makes sense to inquire into scholars' roles in articulating and legitimating the worlds of experience I moved within during my field research in Cambridge.

One legacy of past social scientific investigations is that the questions about what religious experience was and how it could be studied became a matter for scholars and "experiencers" alike. As the discourse and practices of identifying scientifically valid experiences entered the lay worlds of religious people in the early twentieth century, giving their experiences power in new ways, mainstream social scientists became less actively interested in investigating the experiential through the "methodologically plural" and inductive frames that earlier generations had engaged, and scholars like Taylor still pressed for. Even though few contemporary scholars play by the rules of these earlier investigations, spiritual practitioners in Cambridge often approach the world of research through this lens and, moreover, engage scholars like myself with a very different vision of what a "scholar" is and how she relates to these communities. What I said, what I wrote, and what I heard was actively shaped by apparitions of various past and present scholarly investigators.[39]

The ubiquity of scholarly observers and collaborators in these worlds was clear at every turn. Spiritual practitioners and mystics were academic name droppers and eager to elaborate their own academic pedigrees (or apologize for their lack thereof). Many told me that they collaborated with local scientists and professors who were researching (for example) alchemical anti-aging remedies and energetically produced music. A spiritual belly dancer talked to me at great length about published anthropological studies documenting women's spiritual practices in Northern Africa, and gave me the names of professors whom I should contact to learn more. Christian Scientists and alternative healers kept close watch on (and sometimes participated in) the research of Herbert Benson's mind-body research group at the Harvard Medical School. Almost everyone knew about other scholars who were actively at work, continuing the traditions of investigation that my respondents understood to validate and authorize their practices, projects, and truths.

In this field scholars were not unusual figures, but rather had particular roles, and perhaps privileges and duties, when it came to investigating spiritual matters. In ways that I did not expect or quickly realize, I was "caught," as Jeanne Favret-Saada suggests, in a web of relations. Many have noted that ethnographic work is a type of barter or exchange, usually unequal. Favret-Saada extends this further, noting how she became caught up in the structures of relations among witches, bewitched, and unwitchers during fieldwork in rural France merely by employing good ethnographic practices of "listening." She notes, "It is always the other person who decides how to interpret what you say." "Just as a peasant must hear the words of the annunciator, if he is to confess that he is indeed bewitched, so it was my interlocutors who decided what my position was . . . by interpreting unguarded clues in my speech."[40] As an outsider to the local dialect and customs, Favret-Saada believed that she shared with her respondents a perception that she was fully outside of the bounded world of hexes and curses, but as she comes to understand, there is no position *for* an outsider in this system. The only positions within the world of witchcraft she entered were those of the bewitched, witches, and unwitchers: what she learned about witchcraft in the region was ultimately shaped through others' positioning, and "catching" of her academic self.[41]

Favret-Saada writes that her failure to recognize that her respondents were talking to her as if she were an unwitcher was exacerbated by what she believed was a profound disconnection between her academic world and that of her respondents. In contrast, I found myself "caught" as a consequence of my unexamined presumption that my respondents and I shared the same sense of the world. After all, we more-or-less shared language, education, geographical proximity, and so on. I expected that we likewise shared a basic understanding of the various positions that we inhabited: that we (for example) shared an understanding of what professors and researchers did, and thus how I would go about my work and what this would mean. And it was indeed unquestionable that my respondents recognized me as a professor and researcher. What they understood that researchers did however, particularly within the orbits of metaphysical networks, was highly inflected by the books they read, the institutions they engaged, and the practices embedded within contemporary spirituality.[42]

As I have already noted, dominant social scientific understandings of contemporary spirituality suggest that it has no culture to speak of, that is, that it is an individual rather than a collective phenomenon. Depicting metaphysicals as people without a past suggests that the cultures that metaphysicals are connected to do not strongly shape them nor demand much from them. They come under scrutiny for being suspect, inauthentic, purchased, mediated through the market and other corrupted influences. Reinforced by individual-level surveys, uncritical reviews of "shopper" and "seeker" spirituality, and so on, it is easy to imagine that there is no culture that might catch a researcher.[43] There are no witches or bewitched. But as my own and others' engagements with spiritual and metaphysical practitioners make evident, there are in fact cultures that catch people in relations to each other. And, as I learned, professors and researchers are caught in particular ways by these imaginative webs. Had I listened differently to Taylor's lecture, some of these structures and the role that scholars play within Cambridge's particular mystical communities may have been more evident. But in my early field research, I was not so aware.

Although I eventually began to understand the peculiar and special roles that religious studies scholars, and social scientists in particular, continue to play in shaping the worlds of experience that I encountered and lived within, I found it both illuminating and somewhat comforting, late in my fieldwork, to come upon an account of Hugo Münsterberg's visit to Edgar Cayce in Thomas Sugrue's hagiography of the trance channeler. This popular account opens with a cold day in 1912 when a stranger steps "off the Pullman." The stranger "spoke quickly, and with a thick German accent," demanding to see Cayce. Four pages later, he introduces himself to the psychic as "Dr. Hugo Münsterberg, of Harvard. I have come here to expose you. There has been entirely too much written about you in the newspapers lately." Münsterberg's impertinent questions, gruff manner, and general rudeness (he dumps all of Cayce's books on the floor) are met at every turn by friendliness, even though the denizens of the small Kentucky town find Münsterberg insufferable. One quips, "You've got to expect that sort of thing from Yankees. They don't know any better, poor souls." Cayce's wife, ever sighing, then asks, "Why don't you get some decent school to investigate you. . . . Harvard is just a pesthole of Republicans."[44]

As amusing as Münsterberg's comeuppance might sound at this remove, Sugrue's set piece has a more serious purpose, namely to bring readers who might share Münsterberg's critical position into Cayce's world and to redeem such skepticism in service of metaphysical inquiry. Sugrue recounts how Münsterberg watches Cayce treat a patient through a doorway that connects two rooms, one large, one small. At the end of one such session, the psychologist traverses the boundary between the rooms and, to everyone's surprise, entreats the patient to follow Cayce's suggested treatment. "If I were you I would do exactly as he says. From what I have heard, and from what the people I have talked with who claim his readings have helped them I would say that some extraordinary benefits have come from these experiences." Münsterberg then addresses Cayce, who is tying his shoes. "Young man, I would like to know more about this. I have never encountered anything quite like it. I would hesitate to pass any opinion without a long and thorough examination. But if it is a trick, I am convinced you are not yourself aware of it." Cayce spiritedly answers that he, too, would like to know more. "If it is a trick, doctor, I would like to know about it before I go too far and cause some harm."[45] Münsterberg shakes Cayce's hands, turns on his heel, and leaves on the next train, the scholar's manners found but his certainty lost. The skeptical, antagonistic Ivy League professor has become a man who is just as bewildered by Cayce as the others.

Sugrue never paints Münsterberg as a convert. The Harvard professor is a powerful figure in this narrative precisely because of his continued skepticism, which Sugrue expertly marshals to the side of the scientific claims for the realities of mystical experience. The aging Ivy League professor who stands in the doorway becomes a broker between pure belief and pure science. He opens up an imaginative space where rational skeptics in pursuit of the truth find not belief but "realities." These realities baffle the explanatory power of scientific paradigms and thus demand the development of new research techniques that will get to the bottom of things. Sugrue's Münsterberg and Eugene Taylor occupy a similar position, where commitments to scientific inquiry and to such a conception of truth point beyond what is currently known, and "beyond" the tools we have to assess them.

Münsterberg is a most unlikely character to stand in as a messenger in any of these respects. A German-born émigré hired by James to the Harvard psychology faculty, Münsterberg explored the power of "suggestion" in his research and commented on its power of healing in his "immensely popular" *Psychology and Life*. Münsterberg argues that healing can take place through mechanisms of "suggestion" that tap into a physiologically sourced unconscious that prior generations incorrectly believed stemmed from divine agents. It seems unlikely that Cayce's abilities would have been particularly interesting to Münsterberg, given that his research focused almost exclusively on the mechanics of the healed rather than of those of the healer. As he noted, "for the man who believes in the metaphysical cure, it may be quite unimportant whether the love curer at his bedside thinks of the psychical Absolute or of the spring hat she will buy with the fee for her metaphysical healing."[46]

Münsterberg is a familiar stock type in spiritual and metaphysical literature: Sugrue is trading heavily within a genre where the voice of learned men (and occasionally women) and other scholarly adepts are marshaled to testify to spiritual truths. Whatever Münsterberg's actual purpose for traveling to Kentucky, Sugrue transforms them into a familiar metaphysical morality play wherein a researcher confronted by the fruits of spiritual activities begins to ponder anew what he really knows. Although scholars rarely notice that they have been appropriated in these ways, when they do, they do not find it enjoyable to have the tables turned. When a psychic reported that she had heard from Münsterberg after his death, and that his word from beyond the grave was that "Spirit return is a truth," his biographer wrote in dismay that the good psychologist "was appropriated . . . by the public to meet its own needs."[47] "Appropriation" might be too strong a word, however, given that even though religious experiencers, mediums, and mystics were "catching" scholars, it likewise remains the case that scholars continue to "catch" metaphysical believers in our own developing webs of significance. The study of contemporary spirituality is made more difficult by the fact that the practice and self-understanding of many spiritual practitioners is already engaged at some level with scholarship and scientific research projects. Recognizing these practices, however, will move us a long way toward better understanding the social and cultural positions of these religious forms.

Looking Forward

The following chapters address various ways that metaphysical cultures and religious experiences are produced and practiced in contemporary Cambridge. The chapters focus, in turn, on *institutions* (fields of production), *language* (discourse), and the practices of *bodies, times,* and *spaces.* "Shamans in the Meetinghouse" addresses the social location of spirituality and experience in various institutional fields, and asks if we might understand spirituality as religion that is produced in secular institutions or settings. "Becoming Mystics" focuses on the discursive power of forming authoritative accounts of religious experience, first demonstrating how formal testimonies shape and occlude social ties, and then demonstrating how the lived practices of experiential accounting transforms and challenges sociological distinctions between experience and account. "Tuning the Body" investigates metaphysicals' two (or more) bodies, one visible and one invisible, that they seek to encounter and train in order to hold constant, powerful contact with the divine. The following chapters, "Karmic Laundry" and "Zooming Around," address, in turn, how metaphysicals understand their place in space and time, through the practices of reincarnation and various other kinds of time and space travel. These chapters in addition demonstrate how spiritual practitioners live within metaphysical realities (experiential realities) that expand their orientations toward the world and to their place in it, through articulating and placing them in perennial, universal histories. In each of the chapters, I am attentive to the ways contemporary practices resonate with the perennialist and universal aspirations of earlier metaphysicals and mystics, and likewise consider how these resonances unravel the claims that the past might otherwise make on the present, thus shaping contemporary spirituality as new rather than old, emergent and free rather than indebted in any way to what has come before.

With these themes in mind, I return briefly in the conclusion to some of the issues I raise here, including the entanglements that sociologists of religion might fruitfully engage in historically sensitive analyses of contemporary spiritual practice. Sociologists might come to better engage American religions in all of their breadth and scope by identifying the varying genealogies of religious experience that recombine within it. Such an analytical project will undoubtedly require thoughtful engagement with the contributing role of social scientific evaluations of religious experience, both in sociology's understanding of religion's place in modern society and (to a lesser degree) in spiritual practitioners' self-understandings. Likewise, such an analytical project will demand that social scientists engage directly with what appears at first blush as uncomfortable parallels in many scholarly and religious imaginations of modern American religion.

This book's opening vignette condenses many of the thematic tensions that I elaborate in the chapters ahead. In ways that I came to appreciate only recently, but that I imagine many of my Cambridge respondents have long understood, something happens in those brief moments when I tell a story about a cold winter's night on Quincy Street. History, landscape, emotion, and intellect converge in a way that still feels new and unique, and that points toward something that has yet to be said. As this book demonstrates, my metaphysical acquaintances and I found similar stories to have quite different powers. Nonetheless, we each in our own way imagine that such stories properly told will elicit new questions about the allure of divine experience for modern Americans.

ONE

Shamans in the Meetinghouse: Locating Contemporary Spirituality

Representing the Spiritual

It is hard to miss the twelve-foot long, eight-foot high "Community Bulletin Board" at the entrance of the Harvest Cooperative Supermarket in Cambridge's Central Square. The board displays a changing drift of flyers and notices, two or three deep, for upcoming political rallies and local arts shows and fairs, Chinese tutors and vegan cooks, and various religious, spiritual, and "mind-body" classes, lectures, and performances. Passersby are encouraged to sign up for a new semester of yoga classes, attend esoteric astrology lectures, drop in on spiritual writers' book readings and spiritual writers' workshops. While the bulletin board at the Coop is the largest of its kind in Cambridge, there are at least a dozen smaller bulletin boards in the city where one can find a similar set of announcements. Even in the age of the Internet, many spiritual teachers and healers spend time "flyering" every month, walking from the Harvest Coop to the secondhand bookstore up the street, across to a café, to several branches of the public library, and hitting the homeopathic apothecary, the adult education center, and a number of others as well. The Harvest Cooperative bulletin board was the most comprehensive board and thus one of the first stops in my quest to understand the location of spirituality in Cambridge. I would sit in the Coop's café, drinking the requisite fair-trade coffee, as I made lists of contacts and groups. I also regularly read copies of *Spirit of Change* or *Earthstar* magazine, two free regional "mind-body-spirit" tabloids that sat in stacks under the bulletin board, along with other free magazines and flyers.

Looking up from my reading in the Coop's café I would see the stately First Baptist Church, its beautifully proportioned steeple reaching skyward, framed in the picture window. The church and the tabloid offer up a well-rehearsed representational juxtaposition that emerged and reemerged in conversations with both colleagues and local metaphysicals. If religion in America is represented by First Baptist's bricks and mortar buildings, institutional stability, and continued community presence, then spirituality is represented by the bulletin board, with its proliferating disorganized practices and programs, appearing and disappearing, jostling with advertisements for all sorts of for-profit services. Spirituality emerges for both scholars and laypeople as distinct and different from religion. It is individual, unorganized by institutions or structures. And while individuals might dip into such institutional "religious" places to find spiritual sustenance, what organizes spirituality appears to be a "market" and choice, where each individual consumer and seeker confronts a marketplace of undifferentiated and changing goods.[1]

In order to understand the shape and the structure of spirituality, we need to disabuse ourselves of the idea that these surface representations are adequate. At the same time, we need to consider the work that they do to shape the ways that we apprehend spirituality in modern America. In this chapter, I discuss the settings where spirituality is learned and practiced in various groups and organizations, focusing on the institutional aspects of spirituality and the ways that group and leaders understand and practically go about producing spirituality.[2] Even my initial forays into spiritual groups and organizations yielded interesting observations that challenged prior views about spirituality. For example, in asking spiritual leaders where they hold their meetings or teach various types of practices, I learned that many do so in religious settings—and not only in the Theosophical Society and the Swedenborgian Chapel, but also in the Old Cambridge Baptist Church, which in the years prior to my fieldwork opened its doors to the local neo-pagan group; the Friends Meetinghouse, which hosted shamans; and the Congregational Church, which hosted ecstatic drumming and dancing groups. I learned that some of the oldest yoga studios meet in the Protestant churches that encircle Cambridge Commons. While some groups merely rent space, others have more active cooperation with these congregations, suggesting more symbiotic and connected relationships between what we consider the religious and the spiritual. Further forays into spiritual organization and groups in Cambridge elicited further examples of relationships between spiritual and other organizations.

The stories and understandings that spiritual leaders presented to me, and their explanations of the ways that they gain legitimacy and understand their work to be most valuable to others, show that what we think of as the spiritual is actively produced within medical, religious, and arts institutions, among others. It is not unorganized or disorganized, but rather organized in different ways, within and adjacent to a variety of religious and secular institutional fields that inflect and shape various spiritual practices. Against the view that people learn to be spiritual practitioners on their own, or purely through the mediations of books and literature or as shoppers in some kind of undifferentiated market, we can observe that spiritual practitioners, metaphysicals, and mystics engage the spiritual in different institutional settings, including some that are usually considered secular. Spirituality's development within these fields is, furthermore, not random. We can trace spirituality's connections to medicine, to certain religious groups, and to the arts (and likely other institutional fields as well) by understanding the trajectories of metaphysical religions in the twentieth century.[3]

Observing the settings where people learn to be spiritual in Cambridge furthermore raises questions about the adequacy of those depictions of contemporary spirituality as an emergent or nascent movement on the cusp of rising into the mainstream culture, to challenge its presuppositions and its structures and forms.[4] Studies that argue that spirituality is a movement, an "emergent network," or a "shadow culture" are frequently more attentive to the range of groups and sites shaping spiritual activity. But they nonetheless share the perspective that spiritual groups are weakly organized in comparison to religious ones: spiritual groups are cast as either being on the verge of emerging into a major cultural force or as occupying an important but continuing subaltern position in relation to mainstream, dominant religious groups. All of these representations circulate in the lived worlds of contemporary Cambridge. Spiritual practitioners draw on these narratives, using them to articulate their place in what they observe to be a burgeoning movement, avant garde, or counterculture (if not all three). At the same time, these narratives of emergence or an existing movement exist in clear tension with the organizational structures that spiritual practitioners work within, and thus obscure some of the characteristics of spiritual practices and organization that contribute to its ongoing strength.

The strength of contemporary spirituality's organization is evident when we observe that its practices, ideas, idioms, understandings of experience, and so on are shaped and reproduced in several institutional fields. Practitioners and teachers gain legitimacy and strength as they are able to participate within these. Spirituality, then, is not its own field, but this does not mean that it is not organized except through the market, nor does it mean that it is "emerging" into a field of its own. It is, rather, entangled. It is buoyed by and learned in recognizable settings, wherein the spiritual is organized and legitimated in different (yet often overlapping) ways. While spiritual practitioners and metaphysicals travel within these various settings (and some more than others),[5] the cultural logics, internal relations, and practices that shape any particular setting are often field specific.[6] Sustained within a number of institutional fields, including some that we frequently understand to be secular, metaphysical religion thrives, "endorsing its major presuppositions and prejudices even as it seems to be outside them; capturing its anxieties even as it seems to explode them in something new and different; resonating with its past in a sympathy that metaphysicians would often occlude and hide."[7] These observations offer new possibilities for tracing the reproduction of religious life in America and suggest a new way of thinking about the formation of our understanding of the secular.

Spirituality in the Fields

Cambridge's spiritual practitioners and teachers most frequently identify themselves by the practices that they teach or pursue. While they might speak about the power of coming together or of common cause with various other practitioners, they position themselves as "artists" or "healers," or perhaps "teachers" or "writers." The self-identity of teachers and their descriptions of what they do, how they make choices about where to teach, how to identify their students, and what they hope their students might gain from them illuminate some of the ways that spirituality is produced. In the following pages, I focus on the organization and production of spirituality in three organizational fields.

Spirituality in Alternative Health Organizations

Over half of the groups and leaders I met with expressed spiritual identities and practices within alternative health modalities as diverse as homeopathy, herbal and flower-essence therapies, Reiki, therapeutic touch, reflexology, and acupuncture. And, indeed, there were plenty of sites through which Cambridge's residents could pursue these various health modalities. In 2002–3, Cambridge boasted a half-dozen alternative or complementary group practices and two "integrative" health groups, three prominent alternative health schools (one each for massage therapy, acupuncture, and shiatsu massage). By my count over one hundred independent alternative health practitioners advertised their numerous modalities and worked in private practices throughout the city.

Not all alternative health practices and offices in Cambridge are explicitly spiritual, yet given that alternative medicine in Cambridge is oriented toward "mind-body connections" that emphasize the scientific reality of invisible energetic forces, most contain some element of what my respondents identified as the spiritual. Kate, a shiatsu massage therapist who has a private practice located just outside of Harvard Square, talked with me at great length about her training to become a licensed shiatsu therapist, the knowledge she gained about anatomy and science, and also what she learned about the meridians and the energy flow through a properly balanced body. When I asked Kate if she had a spiritual aspect to her practice, she explained that the energy flow was the same as the spiritual. *"Spirituality is very much connected to healing . . . in terms of it being important when I'm treating somebody to recognize that the healing is not coming from me. I'm facilitating it, I'm involved in it, [and] the client is [also] involved with it. It's coming partly from universal chi, and I believe it's partly coming from God. I consider what I'm doing as tapping into universal chi, and transmitting it, [so] I'm a transistor, I'm a transmitter, so I'm gaining as I'm giving. . . . Most of the time I am more energized at the end of treatment than I am at the beginning, and that's because . . . if I ease into this chi that's outside of me, while I'm healing, it protects me."* [8]

Tess, a homeopathic healer and licensed practical nurse, similarly told me her remedies connect her and her clients to higher spiritual truths. Homeopathic remedies release *"patterns of energy that are stuck in people's lives in ways that are no longer working well . . . [to] release those so that people can live up to their full potential as they perceive it, and as they want it. . . . A remedy is addressing ways in which their energy leakages, or energies that are distorted or not really working for them, that they then use in a more creative way. You know, it's very fatiguing to have an energy pattern that doesn't work. And it's very freeing to open up, to have it all going— like the light waves in a laser beam—to have everything going in the same direction. It's very powerful."* The language of "receiving messages" and "channeling energy" constitute an important part of alternative health practices in Cambridge. While each practitioner I met is devoted to a particular technique and technologies for channeling divine energy, they agree that they are tapping into the same vital forces or energies that scientific researchers are studying. Disease and sickness are therefore the result of lives out of balance: healing is a process of continual alignment of body, soul, spirit, and emotion with this underlying force.[9]

That alternative health practitioners use this language of energetic and vital forces will be no surprise to those familiar with the histories of alternative healing and medicine in the United States. In the struggles to define American medicine, various medical systems were placed at the margins, including mind cure, mesmerism, and homeopathy. Indeed, in many states it became illegal to claim that such systems could cure, and in others it became illegal to practice at all.[10] While some of these practices dwindled and died away, others shifted the terms and settings in which they were practiced. Insofar as Americans enjoyed medical pluralism, they did so by participating in irregular medical and vitalistic practices transformed into spiritual and religious healing. While not all religious healing modes were protected equally, and Christian Scientists and others came under increasing scrutiny, some enjoyed uneasy protection from legislative acts that fined, prosecuted, and jailed those who continued to practice.

While alternative medicine remained on the sidelines for decades, it is now evident that Americans of all socioeconomic and educational levels use a plurality of practices and technologies in their quests to be healthy, including conventional biomedicine.[11] The dramatic change in the institutional position and legitimacy of alternative medicine (increasingly called "complementary" or "integrative" to denote its developing connections with biomedicine) is the consequence of numerous changes in American polity and culture, including the increased power of health management and insurance entities and the rise of patient-led activist groups.[12] The repositioning of energetic healing within alternative medicine has taken place at the same time that alternative medicine has become increasingly enveloped within mainstream medical practice. Alternative medicine is at present far from countercultural, and its critiques of mainstream medicine have softened in the last decades as alternative practices become more integrated within it. Indeed, the resurgence of many modalities is due in part to the interest of federal and state scientific and medical agencies in understanding these practices as integral, rather than alternative, to regular medicine. In large measure, alternative practitioners have welcomed, if not actively sought, this form of legitimacy.

Examples abound. The National Institutes of Health Center for Alternative Medicine defines and organizes numerous complementary modalities and provides federal funds to measure and evaluate their effectiveness as treatments for specific ailments (for example, evaluating whether massage therapy relieves chronic back pain or therapeutic touch speeds recovery from major surgery). Likewise, numerous state health agencies, reversing policies that banned the practice of many alternative therapies and subjected their practitioners to heavy fines or jail time, now have licensing procedures in place for many alternative therapies. A national acupuncturists' licensing and accreditation board founded in 1975 is now responsible for accrediting acupuncturists in thirty-nine states. Such accreditation, sought by practitioner groups themselves, arguably alters the ways that teachers and practitioners talk about and understand their practices. For example, acupuncturists learned their skills through hands-on apprenticeships prior to 1975, learning about how to position needles through non-Western body diagrams and through intensive mentoring. Currently, all licensed acupuncturists learn anatomy and physiology, and the links between Chinese acupuncture systems and Western biomedicine in approved teaching centers or schools. Acupuncturists not only are familiar with but also are participating members within biomedical discourses. This is made ever more evident by the number of acupuncturists working with mainstream doctors and the rising number of medical conditions that are now considered treatable by acupuncture and are covered by major medical insurers.[13]

While alternative healing has new space in which to flourish, the move toward mainstream acceptance nonetheless also changes the ways that practitioners talk about the spiritual aspects of their practices. Practitioners conform to state and federal definitions of alternative medicine, and in so doing they are able to legitimately work with others in the field of medicine. In so doing, they also adopt more medicalized ways of describing what they do. Deborah, a fifty-year-old yoga teacher, presents a good example. Deborah is heavily invested in learning Sanskrit so that she can "study the Yoga Sutras" on her own, and emphasized throughout her interview that the form of yoga that she teaches promotes its spiritual qualities. Yet, she also spoke with ease about teaching yoga at a local hospital where she is a part of a team of *"health professionals"* in a *"cardiac lifestyle modification program."* The professionals on the team, Deborah says, include *"an MD, a psychiatrist, a physical therapist, a nutritionist, a nurse—and a yoga teacher, who is me."* Asked what each of the specialists does, Deborah said we *"give them the same message from different points of view. And they do change—you talk about transformation, they change over the year, they change so much!"* After telling me about how important Sanskrit and changing are to understanding yoga as a whole system, Deborah's discussion about modifying the habits of *"high stress, type-A people"* sounded very different. Deborah's comments that yoga, biomedicine, psychology, and others all present the same information to people, albeit from "different points of view," is a common refrain among alternative health professionals who work with allopathic doctors. Said Bruce, one of the founders of the Boston's Integrative Medical Alliance and a shiatsu practitioner, *"there are more similarities than differences between all of these practices, certainly between acupuncture and chiropracty, but also between acupuncture and cutting edge medical techniques."*

Alternative practitioners' claims that they work with the same universal energies not only allows them to argue that they are all doing the same type of thing, despite the strong cultural and historical distinctions among yoga, acupuncture, Reiki, and other healing techniques. It furthermore allows them to claim that what they, and all other healers, are doing is properly scientific. Attention by government-funded scientists to various alternative health modalities presents an enormous measure of real and imagined legitimacy to alternative spiritual healers. Most of the scientific research conducted on alternative therapies focuses narrowly on acceptable use and results for specific ailments (for example, does acupuncture mitigate allergies or does meditation alleviate pain), and does not comment on their underlying theories. Yet most practitioners with whom I spoke understood this scientific attention to be directed toward proving the effects of the universal energetic flows and vitalism that laid at the center of their techniques.[14] In a way, then, medical and scientific attention sustains alternative practitioners' discursive claims to vitalism's legitimacy. It generates and regenerates claims that God or the divine is immanently present in energies that individuals can tap into, with the consequence of healthy revitalization of body, mind, and spirit.

Cathy shared her expectation that Reiki, her favored practice, would one day soon be considered as legitimate and valid as other alternative health practices that science had found viable. She related a conversation she had had with her brother-in-law, who was skeptical of her Reiki practice but expressed interest in acupuncture: *"'Well, Reiki is acupuncture without the needles.' And he said, 'No they're different, because they have research to prove acupuncture. They don't have that for Reiki.' 'But it's energy and meridians, it's the same thing' I tell him. But he won't accept Reiki. He was a biology major, so he has that scientific paradigm too!"* Practitioners like Cathy who do not currently have regulated or licensed practices frequently discussed their hopes that one or more of the competing Reiki training schools would be successful in gaining state accreditation, similar to acupuncture or massage. In the meantime, individual Reiki practitioners often employ other strategies to demonstrate their own legitimacy. Cathy, for example, had decided to begin training in licensed massage therapy.

Regardless of the possibility of gaining legal licensing, alternative practitioners establish work settings and surroundings that closely follow the practices and structures of medical doctors and other health providers. Few of the offices I visited were distinct from those of regular doctors (with the exception, perhaps, of a Buddha statue in the corner of the room). Many alternative practitioners keep regular office hours, hire office managers, and file patient records. Most of the group practices have relatively generic names (for example, "Cambridge Health Associates") and operate within networks of referring practitioners and sometimes doctors. They likewise draw on the rituals, scripts, and symbols of medical legitimacy in their practices to make claims for professionalism in their work. The shifting legitimacy of these practices within the medical field broadly understood nonetheless also shapes the ways that clients of practitioners like Kate, Tess, Deborah, Bruce, or Cathy encounter and understand the divine.

SHAPING EXPERIENCE IN ALTERNATIVE HEALTH The position of spirituality within alternative and complementary medicine influences the discourses and practices of practitioners, orienting their concerns toward those of the field in which they gain legitimacy and are sustained institutionally. The benefits of participating within this field of alternative health are self-evident to those who work within it. Not only are they healing others and developing holistic models of health, they are also on the cutting edge of scientific trends that will yield new information about the power of unseen energetic forces.

But the prominent position of spirituality within the field of alternative health also shapes and forms the settings and conduits through which people learn to practice spirituality. As noted, most of the spiritual practitioners and groups that fall into the field of alternative health follow normative practices in medicine, emphasizing client-practitioner relationships, one-on-one therapies, and classes that teach particular modalities and techniques. As a consequence, those who come to these settings will primarily encounter spiritual practices and discourses that develop in relation to understandings of the scientific legitimacy and rule-bound nature of energetic, vital forces. As we will see in the chapters that follow, the motifs of scientific legitimacy carry into the daily practice and consideration of religious experiences in varying ways, shaping the arc of experiential narratives and the ways that spiritual practitioners understand their bodies as conduits of divine energies.

One further observation, however, follows from the entanglement of spirituality in alternative health and its institutional field, namely that these practices and concepts are also implicitly juxtaposed to what takes place within religious organizations. The activities that take place within these settings are organized around fee-for-service and client-practitioner relationships, and not around group activities, collective worship, or other large events. For this reason, as sociologists have argued on occasion, they slip out of the realm of "religion" into something else, such as magic.[15] Yet, as we see in this case, the one-on-one, client-practitioner shape of spirituality within this field is not the result of something internal to the psyche of an individual seeker or practitioner, or even of metaphysical religious traditions in toto. These structures are, rather, a consequence of the historically shaped relationships among science, medicine, and metaphysical religious understandings. The shape of these settings appears to be less of a result of individualism than a consequence of organizational pressures that develop from the field in which spiritual practitioners gain legitimacy and both learn and teach spirituality.[16] The shaping power of nonspiritual institutional fields becomes even more clear when we look closely at the ways that the religious organizational field shapes contemporary spiritual practice and organization.

Spirituality in Religious Organizations

A second location of the "spiritual" in Cambridge was within the field of religious institutions and groups in the city. Metaphysical, occult, and harmonial religious groups with continuing presence sponsored their own ongoing programs, and opened their doors to a variety of nonaffiliated spiritual groups and practitioners, as did numerous liberal Protestant congregations and one Catholic parish church in Central Square. While some of these religious organizations understood their role in hosting spiritual groups as part of their own mission (even if the groups were independently organized), most understood their relationships with spiritual groups in more straightforward financial terms. At the same time, a spiritual group's decision to meet in a church basement or fellowship hall (or sanctuary) shaped those groups' conceptions of their own mission and their role. The various relations developing between spiritual practitioners and groups, and the religious organizations that hosted them, shaped concepts of experience in relation to sacred space and community that felt quite different than what individuals encountered in client-practitioner relationships.

The architectural prominence of Swedenborgian, Spiritualist, and Unity churches in Cambridge and surrounding towns, and the continued presence of Vedanta and Theosophical societies in nearby Boston, provide testament to the once vibrant presence of alternative and harmonial religious traditions in and around Cambridge. Most of these groups currently have relatively small congregations, however, and do very little overt outreach. The average age of the attendees at the Swedenborgian Chapel's Sunday services appeared to be well into their 60s, although a few young couples also regularly attend. Yet while these groups have small congregations, they often play host or incubator to numerous alternative religious experimenters and spirituality groups.

Cambridge's Swedenborgian minister, a young woman who had grown up in a conservative Protestant denomination and converted while studying at Harvard Divinity School, talked with great pride about her congregation's abilities to foster Cambridge's *spiritual community.* *"Our church is able to do that, where some churches might not be able to, because we have such a broad theology. And, Swedenborgians, although we are Christians and believe that Jesus Christ is God incarnate, believe that people of other religions are learning how to be heavenly beings in their religions as well. They have that opportunity to learn."* The Swedenborg Chapel hosts many activities held on a weekly or ongoing basis, including Kundalini yoga classes (which the minister attends), the mystical experience discussion group, a Tibetan cultural and dance group, local chapters of the Jungian Society and (for a time) the International Association of Near-Death Studies, the biannual "Mystical Arts and Talent Show," a monthly chamber music series, and, just as important, an ongoing reading group on the papers of Emanuel Swedenborg. The Chapel charges rent to most of these groups (with the exception of the reading group and mystical discussion group), as well as to the conservative Anglican congregation that worships in the main sanctuary every Sunday morning before the Swedenborgian service begins.

During my fieldwork, the congregation at the Swedenborgian Chapel came dangerously close to losing its property, which is located on a prime parcel of land surrounded by three Harvard buildings. Its minister was open about the fact that this variety of groups helped maintain what little financial solvency the congregation enjoyed. Nonetheless, she also told me also that the Chapel had a theological mission to open its doors to nontraditional groups. *"People are finding different paths to God, and God is finding people through different paths. And so this gives us an extraordinary opportunity that most Christian churches are not able to be open to. We're not threatened by people of different faiths, or by people having different types of experiences. At the [mystical experiences] group last night, people—I refer to God as God, um, and believe that God is love and wisdom. But I heard, in my mind I heard God referred to as light, as the universe— what was the one guy saying? Oh, God is guidance. You know people have all different ways of talking about this ultimate power, this ultimate source. Being Swedenborgian means that I can respect that, and acknowledge that you or this other person calls God guidance, or the universe, but that's Jesus Christ to me. I don't need you to change your language so that I can understand you, or respect that you're having a genuine spiritual experience. So we have this really unique opportunity, and this unique theology."*

The Theosophical Society's board had a similar perspective on its role. My discussions with several board members elicited comments on their pride in opening the doors and classrooms in its Victorian house headquarters to numerous groups. While the board was primarily made up of individuals who had special interests in Theosophy and who attended and led Helena Petrova Blavatsky, Alice Bailey, and Krishnamurti study groups, these were less well attended than the various yoga classes, astrology classes, transmission meditation groups, weekly screenings of Eckhardt Tolle lectures, *A Course in Miracles* and *The Artist's Way* reading groups, and other regular groups that were listed on the Society's monthly newsletter. Larry, a longtime member and past president, told me, *"We're not really making a lot of money, and some of us would say that we're not even breaking even! We're all really volunteers here, there is no one who makes a salary at the Theosophical Society. We are offering these different programs at very reduced cost, and hopefully we're providing a service to the Boston area."*

The Theosophical Society, the Swedenborgian Chapel, and other groups of this kind give themselves pride of place in Cambridge's spiritual community. These groups have by and large opened their doors for new experimental groups, and have likewise not limited what happens within their walls to projects that might be related to their own theological traditions. In a very real way, then, these historically viable (if numerically marginal) religious groups anchor spiritual activities in Cambridge and present their leaders and groups with a sense of the longer histories of experimentation that have taken place in the area. These connections sometimes compel spiritual individuals to think more explicitly about the history of spiritual experimentation, but do so by promoting perennial and universal ideologies. But views that make groups like the Theosophical Society eager to open their doors nonexclusively to any who seek after the truth appear to curtail members' interests in promoting their particular history and theology, beyond encouraging curious individuals to join a Blavatsky or Krishnamurti reading group.

Metaphysical and nonmainstream religious organizations do not have a lock on defining the relationships between religion and contemporary spirituality, however. Numerous Protestant, Jewish, and Catholic congregations also regularly make room within their buildings for spiritual groups. As noted, shamanic practitioners held their drumming circles in the Friends Meetinghouse, the Earth Drum Council met in the First Congregational Church, and numerous churches doubled as yoga studios or hosted spiritual arts exhibitions or performances. Indeed, groups that met regularly to discuss, worship, or practice a spiritual life together often met in buildings maintained by vibrant Protestant, Jewish, and Catholic congregations.

THE RELIGIOUS SHAPING OF EXPERIENCE   While congregations in Cambridge sponsor all kinds of spiritual exercises and programming for their own members and led by their own ministers and staff, these congregations also played host to groups to which they have little or no ideological or interpersonal connection. Cambridge churches rented their spaces to a variety of groups, including nonreligiously affiliated day-care centers, twelve-step groups such as Alcoholics Anonymous, Internet start-up companies, dance studios, and, in one case, a state-run methadone clinic.

From the standpoint of most hosting congregations, these groups are merely tenants: their programs are not listed in church bulletins or otherwise marked in ways to attract church members. While this is the case from the standpoint of the congregation, many of the groups that met in churches often deliberately and thoughtfully imagined the spaces that they temporarily inhabited as connecting them, in one way or another, to their hosts' religious missions. In addition to conforming in substance and style to their hosting congregations' calendars, these groups and group leaders often stated that they chose to meet in churches because they were, in fact, doing the same thing as religious groups.

Hans, an investment banker and shamanic practitioner, said of the Society of Friends, *"I've never been in any of their services, but the ritual of that group kind of has some similarities to it to shamanism. So one would expect—"* he stopped and paused for a moment, choosing his words. *"—they let us be in there."* I probed a bit, asking what he meant about the similarities between shamanic journeying and the Friends' meeting house where his group met. He responded that he appreciated what he knew about the Friends' not having a minister or an appointed leader, which is similar to his group's practice. He continued, *"We appoint the leader at the end of each circle for the next circle. Leadership is not a—we have really tried to keep that away from any kind of religious practice."* Hans's view here notably links shamanism and Quakerism in terms of community organization, rather than theology or ideas of the divine.

In comparison to the client-practitioner relationships and focus on individual health that shape spirituality within alternative health groups, the spirituality groups meeting in churches frequently emphasize community experience, learning together through discussing spiritual journeys or through reading and interpretation. Yoga teachers who teach in churches were less likely to emphasize health and fitness and more likely to include chanting, extended periods of meditation, and focus on the spiritual aspects of yoga. Lucy, a yoga teacher who has taught in several churches, described her classes at a local Episcopal church. *"It's a beautiful chapel, it has rounded ceilings and rounded windows, so it has a very womblike feeling, and the acoustics are wonderful. When I was teaching there, I would almost in every class go into a deep trance state, and it was very um, very poetic, but not sappy. You know it was really, I mean, it was really authentic and lucid. And, those were the sorts of students that I attracted, who really were in it for their souls not just to reduce stress. And all the classes were taught by candlelight in the evenings, and you know it was very lovely."*

While Lucy loved the space in the church, she remained disappointed that there was *"no real affinity"* between the congregational leadership and her studio, and she started looking for other space. After renting space in another Cambridge church for a year, she started teaching in a third church in Harvard Square, a Lutheran congregation that had just finished renovations of a large open meeting room, with a wall of east-facing windows and a labyrinth embossed in the floor. Lucy uses the labyrinth in her classes, often placing stones and lighted candles at important points on it. Lucy also has high praise for the congregation's staff: *"These guys are wonderful. We have very clear boundaries, and if there are things that come up, and of course there are always things that come up, we talk about them and work them out. It is a very clean relationship. I'm so grateful and happy that I've found a group of people who were also responsible as equal partners."*

Regardless of what the local congregations think of the groups that rent their spaces, it is clear that the types of spiritualities that are articulated and made present within their boundaries share affinities with congregational religion. American religious congregations and "congregationalism" is a historically robust institutional field, marked clearly by its nonprofit status, voluntary characteristic, and (frequently although not exclusively) denominational structure.[17] The spiritual groups that use space within congregations often orient themselves toward "congregational" and "group" projects, including worship, meditation, education, or discussion. They generally view themselves as pursuing similar philosophical, ritual, or communal ends (albeit without a shared theology). In contrast to the types of learning that take place in alternative health's client-practitioner relationships, spiritual groups that regularly meet in church buildings are often free and open to the public (sometimes, attendees are asked to make a donation to defray the costs of renting the space). When people meet together to chant "om" and share their mystical experiences, return every week to discuss the finer points of Blavatsky's treatises, join together to listen to lectures on esoteric astrology or to participate in group-guided visualizations or meditations, they are participating in activities that are hardly distinguishable from what regularly happens in those religious spaces, save the content of their discussions and the day of the week.

SPIRITUALITY IN CONGREGATIONS An additional wrinkle within this picture, however, is the fact that American congregational leaders are also deeply invested in developing their members' spiritual passions, albeit usually by drawing on their own traditions' spiritual practices and exemplars to cultivate them. Indeed, it would be strange to imagine that Protestant, Jewish, and Catholic religious institutions have not taken seriously the growing interest among many religious people in individual experiences with the divine, cultivating a spiritual practice, hearing stories of miraculous or mystical events, and investigating what all of these practices and experiences mean.[18]

Liberal Protestant congregations in Cambridge feature lay-led or clergy-led healing circles, labyrinth walks, Zen and vipassana meditation groups, and the like. Many of these programs seem to be experimental and take place outside of the normal routine of the congregation's worship and meetings, for example, during a Friday afternoon vespers or as part of an adult Sunday school class retreat. Introducing non-Christian or other practices of questionable provenance is still troubling for many congregations, and the ministers who might be most open to doing so often expressed that they were constantly feeling their way through the thicket of possible responses to such introductions. One United Church of Christ minister told me that she felt called to the Christian ministry after attending workshops with Rosalyn Bruyere, a nationally known energy healer. She subsequently chose her seminary because of its elective Reiki training course and its openness to bringing the power of energetic healing into "a variety of ministry situations." Even though she was trained in Reiki in a UCC-affiliated seminary and is open about the role that Bruyere's workshops played in bringing her back into the religious life she had rejected as a child, she remains quiet about her Reiki abilities as she performs her ministerial duties. Her calling as a minister, she says, is not to convince others of the truths of Reiki. Rather, it is to *tell others of God's message to us, the love of Jesus Christ.* While Reiki and other healing techniques *deepened my appreciation of the overwhelming, unconditional love that Jesus brings to us,* she keeps her message on teaching her congregation that they are Jesus's "beloved," and uses the Reiki only in circumstances where she can be sure that she will not offend the sensibility of her congregants.

This minister may have less to worry about than she imagines, however, as it appears that many of my respondents who identify as spiritual (and whom I met as regular participants in spiritual practices and groups) are also regular and active participants in local congregations. Larry, the previous president of the Theosophical Society, was raised a Presbyterian and Theosophist, and regularly attends a liberal Catholic church in Harvard Square with his wife and daughter. Cathy, the Reiki practitioner, sings in the choir at her UCC church and teaches Sunday school. Annette, a young woman who channeled and participated in various mystical groups, also attended the Vineyard Fellowship in Cambridge (a neocharismatic Protestant church). The spiritual practitioners I met in Cambridge have numerous religious options where they can find opportunities and settings to explore and reinforce the viability of their more esoteric and metaphysically articulated understandings. Charles, a shamanic "soul singer," was not alone in stating that his explorations in singing with shamanic groups deepened his awareness of and his love for the Christian traditions he grew up within. He told me that shamanic singing renewed his *"strong connection to core Christianity and the Holy Spirit. Having had a shamanic experience, where you have this direct experience with Spirit, actually gave me a deeper appreciation for Christianity. And where Christianity really began with Pentecost, an incredibly powerful, direct experience of the Spirit, it's really from that that the church began. So, and having had some really spiritual experiences, it's like wow! Now—I can appreciate a Pentecostal faith, you know."* Charles started searching for a church to join in earnest after one of his shamanic instructors suggested that he do so. He attended several congregations where he believed he would find spirit-infused singing to be a regular part of the service. After attending several charismatic Protestant and Catholic congregations, he decided that their *"canned music"* was not to his liking, and he is now a regular participant at a local Catholic church, where, he tells me, he has started to have newfound appreciation for liturgical traditions. He has joined the church's lay choir and sings at every opportunity.

These examples of spiritual practitioners and metaphysicals strongly support the view that spirituality and its varied trajectories are often present within liberal, mainstream Protestant congregations, where spiritual practitioners find themselves at home. In these settings what is marked as spiritual or offbeat becomes less distinct from various liberal Christian perspectives. We might expect as much, given the historical interweaving of liberal Protestant mysticisms and metaphysical theologies.[19] Of course, it remains clear to me that many of my respondents are dabblers and experimenters when it comes to congregational participation. Tina, for example, was a serial attender at various religious groups. Listing her most recent visits, she told me, *"There's the Cambridge Insight Meditation Center—I started going to that in the 1980s and was pretty regular, but haven't been much recently. And the Unitarian church where I worked for a long time. I'm not a member but I'm friendly with a lot of those people and occasionally I'll go to their services. There's a Brazilian church, which is very, it has an esoteric tradition that I'm connected with, and that's Christian, I like to go there when I can."* Tina found inspiration in these group settings, but they did not require her committed, regular participation.[20] Other metaphysicals and mystics in Cambridge attended religious organizations for "social" rather than religious reasons, as did Hans, the shamanic practitioner, who was a member of a prominent Protestant congregation in downtown Boston. He found his activities there to be valuable, but primarily social. He likewise felt it was important that his young daughter was raised within a moral community but stressed that *"I'm more interested in the community part of it than the spiritual—cause that's the thing, doing shamanic work, there is so much spirituality involved already that I can't really think of a religion that would help me in that direction. But again I don't know—maybe it will."*

Hans and Tina both share a view that their engagement with religious groups is external to their own formation as spiritual people. While there is no reason to doubt their experience, their own claims and uses of understandings of the distinctions between the spiritual and the religious (where one is more individually or experientially directed, the other is about the "social" or "community") masks their interpolation and entanglement, as others experience them.

Spirituality in Arts Organizations

The connections between the arts and spirituality are certainly not new to either the cultures of elite visual and performing "arts" or American religious institutional cultures.[21] Nonetheless it is important to note that these spiritualities are more focused on the expressive and aesthetic than those produced in alternative health and religious fields. Although my respondents articulated the ways that they experienced or expressed the spiritual through the arts by drawing on a variety of metaphors and idioms, almost all took for granted the self-evident link between spirituality, inspiration, and artistic, creative experience.[22]

Spiritual arts groups in Cambridge, of which there were many, sustained many of these connections, but spiritual arts groups were one small subset of a larger field of arts groups, dance groups, and various schools and galleries that shaped Cambridge's amateur arts field.[23] Cambridge's wider art worlds are quite robust: several local artists' collectives and galleries regularly display art in their galleries and also place local artists' works in cafes, restaurants, and banks. They also sponsor public artists' talks (and an occasional poetry reading), gallery openings, and artists' mixers where (mostly) amateur artists and photographers mingle. These collectives are not open to all: gallery owners and collectives invite artists through judging and evaluating portfolios. Notably, however, many of my respondents are also present on these rosters. Their artistic statements (posted online on these gallery Web sites) show no clear patterns of presenting the "spiritual" aspects of the artistic endeavors that many expressed during interviews, however.

While many of the artists I met during my fieldwork are actively involved in an array of artistic organizations and groups, they also participate within (or are, at the least, aware of) a number of explicitly spiritual arts programs in the city and surrounding areas. These groups, which focus more specifically on expressive and experiential aspects of art, have lower thresholds for entry and fewer authoritative arbiters of aesthetic criteria. In addition to the spiritual belly dance collective, I learned about "soul singing" groups, a regional "mystical chorus" that holds public concerts, the biannual "Mystical Arts and Talent Show" held at the Swedenborgian Chapel, book and poetry readings and author's signings, "dance nights" at local yoga studios, and numerous other groups such as a local drumming and dancing group, and artists who met to talk about spirituality in their paintings.

While spiritual arts organizations and groups share the formal structures of gallery openings, readings, and performances, many of these groups nonetheless in practice blur the lines between artist and audience, and between aesthetic judgment and divine inspiration that is more clearly evoked in Cambridge's other arts groups. Charles holds a weekly group in his house that is devoted to group and individual ecstatic singing. When I asked him how people learn to soul sing he said, *"I have this little phrase [on the flyers I give to interested people] that says 'listen breathe and sing.' And it really is that simple, being completely in the moment. It's really letting your mind go, your thoughts, your fears, your ego, and this idea of performance, of doing it right, any idea of doing it in a certain way. And just being—you know it's what to the jazz musicians is improv. You know, they have an improv—when you see them performing they may have a song they take off from, but that song may have come from just listening and improving to begin with. In many ways it's just a form of improvisation that for many people has a very sacred, spiritual aspect to it."* Indeed, Charles continued, the improvisation in soul singing comes from listening and *"the music or Spirit or whatever it is that brings the song into you, or that somehow opens you up to it or makes you aware of the song."*

The lines between the "artistic" and the "expressive" are blurred by numerous evocations of the divine spirit working in or through individual artists. At the Fall 2003 Mystical Arts and Talent Show, Eric introduced Charles and his friend Peter, "our first act of the evening," but as the two men came to the stage, Charles was quick to clarify as he picked up his drum and thumped it that their performance was "not rehearsed, it is just what comes." He thumped the drum a few times again, adding, "I'm not sure what the drum is going to do." Not quite performers, Charles and Peter were more appropriately understood as

conduits through which "Spirit" entered into their drumming and singing. Without further introduction Charles started humming to the beat
of his drum. Peter hummed too, harmonizing weakly and without confidence (suggesting to me that Charles was not lying when he said they
had not rehearsed). Both had their eyes closed, and Peter rang a small
bell several times. Charles's humming and drumming grew louder, and
then after a few minutes faded away. The audience clapped.

This humming had been a lead in to the main part of Charles's "act."
He stepped up to the microphone again to tell us, "I am going to recite
a poem now, and then after that, I want to lead us in a chant, and we'll
all participate. The poem is one that I wrote seventeen, eighteen years
ago. I haven't really thought of it since, but today, I remembered it. I
don't know why I did, and it is sort of surprising that I did." Charles
smiled, and then told us, "I live in the top floor of a triple-decker, and
one of my tenants has planted a sunflower. You know how big and
beautiful this is. I don't know why, but this got me thinking about
this poem, that I wrote when I was living in the Midwest, in Nebraska,
growing up. In high school I used to run every day, and one field that
I passed was planted with sunflowers, about forty acres of sunflower.
And if you know how beautiful one sunflower is, with its bright yellow,
you can only imagine what 40 acres filled with them would look like. It
was beautiful, and I ran by it every day. And then, one day, something
had changed. There had been a frost the night before, and instead of
standing up, they were all fallen over, humbled. And I wrote a poem
about this, about the sunflowers." Charles read the short free verse, and
then told us that he wanted us to chant the last two lines with him:

summer is done/
flowers bow to the sun

"I know there are a lot of good singers in the group—so please join
in, if you feel like it, and improvise as it's going. I don't know where
this is going, so we'll just see."

As Charles's strong voice carried over his drum, people started to
sing: after several minutes of repetitive chanting, almost everyone in
the audience was singing or humming along. Several had raised their
hands, most had closed their eyes. As Charles brought the song-chant
to a close in an a cappella chorus, I could not help but reflect how by
positioning this act at the beginning of the program's talent show, Eric
had skillfully blurred the line between performance and participation,

a distinction that would continue to be in play through the rest of the acts as well.

The expressive, often participatory world of spiritual arts in Cambridge suggests that the field of "informal arts" and "community arts" shapes a third field in which spirituality is learned, practiced, and performed. Within this field, distinctions between spiritual and nonspiritual artists are not always distinct, as "secular" arts organizations in Cambridge also include and support artists who evoke spiritual rationales and discourses to explain their endeavors. Nonetheless, some distinctions and fissures do become clear from time to time, as many of the amateur artists who participate in "spiritual arts groups" find the types of judgments and aesthetic evaluations that occur within regular arts groups to work against true spiritual experience and expression through the arts. Eric, the organizer of the Mystical Arts and Talent Show (held biannually at the Swedenborgian Chapel), told me that the first two shows, which he organized with a friend who teaches poetry at a local college, were primarily poetry readings and not well attended. They were *"a little too academic,"* he said, but he soon learned that *"there are enough people who practice the arts in an explicitly spiritual way, that we didn't need to tap into the academic, [those] writers and poets who also just happen to do a fair amount of spiritual material."* Preemptively answering a question that I had not quite formed, he continued, *"And, the quality was there, and the people who were meant to be there were really there."* As Eric "rescued" the mystical from the academic, he also alienated a number of artists who defined spiritual art in ways that went beyond the cathartic and expressive. Lucy, a yoga teacher and accomplished poet, was not terribly surprised when Eric turned down her poetry for his October 2001 program. *"He said what I had given him was too dark, he likes things that are happy, that don't reach to other parts of the spiritual experience,"* she related as we walked along the Charles River one afternoon not long afterward. Lucy remained an important supporter of Eric's endeavors to promote the spiritual arts, but all the same found more than ample resources within her non-mystical arts networks to support her work.

Producing the Spiritual

Alternative health, religious, and arts groups produce and sustain various ideas and practices that constitute the spiritual. We can see how the language, practice, and legitimacy of spirituality is produced in various ways. In each of these fields, practitioners engage and articulate the spiritual in a different way, given each field's different historical trajectory and relation to religion and the spiritual, and given its structural shape as a field. These examples suggest that spirituality is articulated through various oppositions and connections in various fields.

While spirituality is produced within three institutional fields, many of the practices that spiritual persons and mystics in Cambridge pursue are practiced in more than one. Various performances (singing, public readings) are structured differently if they take place in a religious or an artistic context; once performance is incorporated into a healing project, it takes on yet another cast. The practice of yoga is a prime example. We have already heard Deborah's comments on how yoga can be understood as a medical practice or a spiritual one, and this is reflected in the position of yoga in Cambridge. During my field research one could take yoga classes in a variety of settings, including stand-alone yoga studios, gyms and health centers, corporate offices, dance studios, elementary schools and universities, mainstream and alternative health alliances, and Protestant churches and Jewish synagogues. Furthermore, forty of the fifty-two certified yoga teachers I tracked in Cambridge taught in at least two different organizational settings every week.[24] Yoga takes on very different inflections, meanings, and purposes in each of these settings, which we can observe by listening to Marcy, a relatively typical yoga teacher, discuss her weekly schedule. Each week in early 2003 she taught two classes over the lunch hour in corporate offices, two classes at a local wellness and complementary health spa, a local Unitarian church, the Mt. Auburn Fitness Club, and a free-standing yoga center. Despite the range of classes and settings, Marcy likes to think of herself as being more interested in the spiritual than the exercise aspects of yoga. I asked her how she conveys this to her students. She said, *"When I was at Kripalu I got into some pretty esoteric practices, breathing techniques and . . . surrender[ing] to the life force energy and go[ing] with the prana. . . . These things were outspoken at Kripalu: 'We are divine beings, cloaked in human flesh' was the approach. . . . And I love all that stuff. . . . I love to immerse myself in it. But when I get hired to teach at the health club I assume, perhaps correctly, perhaps incorrectly, that the students and the management don't want me to say the word God, or Spirit, or Divine. Or even Essence, which goes in that direction. I've never come out and actually asked—there's the fear of those who hire me and [the question] is it my right to do this in this place? And then, I [worry if] I am going to turn people off, or offend them, or incite them, insult them, arouse their anger.*

So I've held back for those reasons. I have to make my living at this. Now mind you, if I didn't have to make my living, I might be able to advertise my yoga class as a spiritual yoga. And have that be the direction, and to teach it as a path of self-compassion. Instead of saying it's for stress reduction, flexibility, muscle strengthening, and community. Which is all true. And all fine, you know. I censor myself sometimes because I want it to be as palatable as I can to everybody. I want to cast a wide net."

Nonetheless, Marcy told me that she always tried to read a piece of poetry at the beginning of class, often something from Rumi (a Sufi poet), Mary Oliver, or Thomas Merton. She hoped that her classes and this poetry might itself prompt her students to query more deeply into the meaning behind yoga, and she always took literature on Kripalu's Lenox, Massachusetts, training and retreat center with her to her classes. Marcy's weekly schedule provides an example of how a single technique, taught by a single person, takes various shapes, meanings, and legitimacies in various contexts. Rather than seeing yoga as a "health" or "expressive" or "spiritual" pursuit singularly, yoga thus takes on all characteristics, confounding any claims to say that it is one or the other. Many (though by no means all) yoga teachers in Cambridge were comfortable in their movement across these various spaces that defined their practice and its purpose and value in overlapping yet noncomplementary ways. Some indeed found that these overlapping meanings were valuable to sustaining business. Terry, the founder of the Arlington Center, describes it as a place where he and others could *"teach yoga and meditation, and yoga therapy."* As he envisioned it, the center would focus on *"stillness practices."* As the Center got up and running, however, Terry interested several "wellness providers" in renting its treatment rooms, and it now advertises Ayurveda, Reiki, physical therapy, and psychotherapy. The Center's offerings also expanded to include programs on dance and the arts. As Terry told me, *"I am a musician and I realize that this is a place where we can help people awaken through music. So, we have some live music programs. We had an evening just a week ago called '*Love Supreme*: An Ecstatic Meditation on the Music of John Coltrane,' where we screened a film of him playing in 1953, on television. And believe me, the picture wasn't good because it was on television, but it was recorded in a studio with great equipment, and when we showed the DVD with our sound system, it felt like we were standing right in the room with him. It blew people away, it was really great. We turned the lights low and laid back on the floor and listened to* Love Supreme, *so we do things like that, when people can suddenly forget themselves, and awaken a little bit, that's what we're about."*

Marcy's and Terry's experiences with yoga bring two things to our attention: that the position of these practices within different fields illuminates and conceals various aspects that make up their global shape, and that these institutional differences are not barriers to practice. In short, while mystical teachers and practitioners shape their practices in relation to local institutional and organizational parameters that allow them to pursue certain goals, these same practical and daily considerations help to reproduce what scholars and practitioners apprehend as the elusiveness of spiritual organizational structures. Whatever practitioners understand as the spiritual is shaped by their participation in institutional fields that define appropriate ways to encounter and speak of the spiritual, and its religious, aesthetic, and scientific realities. With this in mind, it is fair to ask whether the story of spirituality in America might best be told by analyzing the variety of religious practices that persist and are constantly transforming in relation to numerous secular and religious institutional fields.

Things in Their Entanglements

In *Experience and Nature,* John Dewey cautions philosophers to "begin with things in their complex entanglements" rather than "with simplifications made for the purpose of effective judgment and action." This chapter has drawn attention to institutional entanglements that spirituality practitioners live through, and has sought to provide a brief overview of how these entangled histories and meanings construct not one spirituality but many overlapping spiritualities that relate in different ways to various institutional fields in American society. Our next task is to demonstrate how these entanglements might speak back to complicating sociological distinctions between religion and spirituality.[25]

Viewing things "in their entanglements" prompts us to think further about why spirituality and religion so rarely appear to be entangled at all. Recent studies have made it clear that the spiritual and the religious are not necessarily oppositional: numerous spiritual people belong also to religious groups, and mainstream Protestant, Catholic, and Jewish groups have all become more interested in involving their congregations and members in what they term "spiritual development."[26] How did spirituality become autonomous, and what purposes does its autonomy serve? Such questions are all the more perplexing as we see that spirituality, while appearing as an autonomous social fact, is nonetheless difficult to locate in discrete social processes or groups.[27]

The autonomy of spirituality is built on two notions of religion that are endemic to our conceptions of both religion and modern society: first, the notion that individuals can in fact have socially and culturally unmediated religious experiences, and second, the notion that modern Western societies can be distinguished from other historical periods and regions because they exhibit more differentiation and "rationalization." It is the case that the idea of a nonmediated experience depends not only a notion of the individual who moves between spheres, but also on a perspective that spheres are increasingly organized according to nonoverlapping lines of discourse, rationality, and purpose. The secularization and restriction of religion into the sphere of the religious—a central narrative in the story of sociology—suggests that any religious activity, action, or purpose that is located "outside" of the religious institutional field is the work of "individuals" rather than produced within the discourse, practices, or structures of nonreligious fields.[28] The spiritual, defined as individual acts, make it possible to argue for the secularity of increasingly differentiated fields.

Although the logic that links modernity, religious individualism, and spirituality is apparent within many of the recent treatments of spirituality, we can also find it in Troeltsch's classical formulations of church-sect theory, set down in *The Social Teachings of the Christian Churches*. Troeltsch includes a "third type" of Christian organization, which Troeltsch calls the "mystic." This third type of Christianity is uniquely interesting, and also dangerous and degenerate, largely because of its interests in individual sentiment. Mysticism, Troeltsch writes, "has no impulse towards organization at all."[29]

In Troeltsch's schematic portrait, mysticism and "spiritual idealism" emerge as social movements in the modern world, precisely when individual, inward experience takes precedence over the communal. Troeltsch is highly critical of "individualistic mysticism" and views it as fundamentally antagonistic toward the "real nature of Christianity." This debased form, he argues, develops from the "Romanticism" and other theories favored by the liberal, educated classes.[30] They are reviled not because they emphasize individual experience per se (as many other forms of "Christian mysticism" did through history), but rather because they "possess neither the sense of solidarity nor the faith in authority which this requires."[31] Troeltsch argues that mysticism cannot be sustained unless it is connected to more "robust" organizational forms. "In its depreciation of fellowship, public worship, history and social ethics this type of 'spiritual religion,' in spite of all its depth and spirituality, is still a weakened form of religious life," Troeltsch argues.

It "must be maintained in its concrete fullness of life by churches and sects, if an entirely individualistic mysticism is to spiritualize at all. Thus we are forced to this conclusion: this conception of Christianity . . . assumes the continuance of other and more concrete living forms of Christianity as well."[32]

Troeltsch's concerns about mysticism become more clear when they are seen in light of his understanding that the modern world is simultaneously becoming disenchanted. The receding place of religious and other "irrational" meanings means not only that religious authority loses its privilege in public life but that other fields including law, science, and the arts become "demystified" as they develop their own "rational" bases for verification and legitimacy.[33] This narrative of secularization and disenchantment was helped along by understandings of individual mysticism. We might observe, then, how mystical forms (considered to be "individual" and self-generating) present a way to explain the types of religious and enchanted practices that remained embedded within secularizing fields. That is, it became possible to observe the religious practices that continued to be produced or sustained within secular institutions as mere residue or importations by individuals, rather than as constitutively developed in those secular settings.[34]

When we instead begin with the observation that spirituality in the United States is shaped through and within religious discourses and practices that are produced within numerous institutional fields including the religious and the secular, we move far from the description of spirituality as a perennial product of disconnected individuals. We instead see it as embedded and reproduced within certain contexts, including those we have frequently considered to be secular. If the production of religion within these settings has been neglected, it has frequently been due to the explanatory power of mysticism, individualism, and the spiritual, all of which deflect sociological attention to the continued circulation of religious meanings, yearnings, and imaginations in various fields.[35]

With this in mind, we might ask whether the terrain of religious institutions that sociologists have claimed as a sphere of investigation has been too narrowly drawn. Rethinking the ways that the religious (or what we have herein been calling the spiritual) is not only *lived* but *produced* within nonreligious sectors may suggest numerous settings that actively contribute to the complicated stories of American religious history. Michael Schudson offered a critique of recent investigations of "civil society" (including those of political scientists Robert Putnam and Theda Skocpol), arguing that current concepts of the civil society arena are drawn too narrowly and with too much normative baggage. Schudson argues that the standard view of "civil society" understands civic action only as activities and commitments that are sustained over time, are collective, require work, and are not self-interested. Schudson argues that we might include in our understanding of civic life acts that are transitory, the "individual (and insufficiently collective)," the "cheap and convenient," and the "self-interested." Rather than bemoaning the lack of the civic, in other words, we need to take a closer look at the types of persons and institutions that we expect are necessary for societies like ours to thrive, and compare them closely and in relation to those institutions that may in fact be shaping the civic, albeit in ways that do not conform to our expectations.[36]

Schudson's contrarian argument provokes us to imagine and investigate the spaces where religion is produced that might appear to be outside of what we currently understand to be religious institutions, especially as scholars have long held positive associations between civic and religious life in the United States. Indeed, religious groups are (like civic life) generally understood as sustained and non-self-interested communities, whereas the "spiritual" appears as individual, self-interested, cheap (or at least, for sale), and transitory. Studying spirituality does not require that we embrace individualism or convenience as civic or religious goods. But studying spirituality seriously does raise questions about how social scientific practice distinguishes religion from other kinds of actions and organizations, and how such distinctions have mattered not only to sociological analysis but, more broadly, to scholarly and lay evaluations of what the religious is, and how various forms of religious activity mobilize or should mobilize action in the world.

The Whole Health Expo

While it is one thing to argue that the various scholarly narratives are inadequate to explain how the spiritual is organized, where it is learned, and how it produces spiritual practitioners and metaphysicals, it is another to say that such representations of spirituality do not matter. Indeed, such an argument would be difficult to make: as I have noted at several points, spiritual practitioners draw on language wherein they imagine spirituality as emergent from individual consciousness or experience, while others find claims to personal freedom and seeking to be very effective in articulating spiritual selves.

In Cambridge, these various interpretations intersect and move across the varied locations where spirituality is organized and instituted. The active co-presence of so many interpretations and claims about spirituality is a regular part of the worlds of experience in Cambridge, but perhaps never so much on display than during large yearly festivals and expos, such as the biannual Boston Whole Health Expo. The Expo was independently organized by a national vendor of holistic fairs and expositions and provided a venue for a broad range of spiritual and holistic health groups, artists, and others to present their wares and techniques. It took place in a nineteenth-century stone armory building that now functions as an exhibition hall, and was accompanied by lectures, workshops, hands-on "intensives" and various kinds of "ritual work," and artistic performances at the Park Plaza Hotel across the street.[37] The Expo's June 2001 program book and posters emphasized its role in shaping and bolstering a community. Its theme, "Creating Community, Connection, and a Force of Light!," was spread across the program book and announced on banners and signs draped over the entrances to the former armory building, now nicknamed "the Castle." The program prominently featured opportunities for "networking" and "community building," including a "single's night" on the last evening of the exposition and a ten-minute period on both days for silence and group meditation. As I traveled through the Expo's aisles and talked to vendors, however, what caught my attention was not a single (if loose) culture represented, but the ways that vendors simultaneously gestured to a shared culture and offered competing ideas of what that might be.[38]

Arriving downtown on a rainy Saturday morning, I paid the two-day registration ($25) in the lobby of the Park Plaza Hotel and consulted the program. The lobby was filling to capacity, waiting to enter a lecture hall to hear the Expo's keynote speaker for an extra fee of $15. I was eager to look at the exhibits and talk to vendors in relative quiet, so I crossed the street, walking against foot traffic. More than sixty vendors lined three long aisles in the windowless hall. Some stands were quite spartan, trimmed with little more than photocopied pages and hand-lettered signs; others were elaborately decorated with Persian carpets, ferns, or even small cloth tents that created intimate interior spaces. One crystal salesman played a harp. The Castle's dark stone walls hummed and buzzed with music and conversation of hundreds of attendees and vendors. Many people seemed to be accompanied by a friend and moved through the aisles in small groups, chatting with vendors, and, it seemed, sometimes meeting up with others they knew as they walked along. Many more were on their own: I followed their pattern, walking through the aisles, stopping at booths that looked interesting, and then moving on to the next and the next.

I first stopped at a booth advertising "Kirlian photography and aura color therapy." Helen, the short, dark-haired woman behind the booth, told me that she has a practice and works with a women's health collective in the greater Boston area. She offered to take my photograph with her camera and conduct a reading. I asked her what such a reading would tell me. Helen explained that "people have different color auras, and you can read them and do therapy in a very effective way" as she opened up a photo album and motioned to the pictures inside. "Everything has an aura," she continued. "We all have energy, every living thing has an energy field around it, and it takes on different colors depending . . . " she did not say on what. Pointing to various pictures, she explained that the glowing field around each subject's head was an aura. Smiling children had bright and bold auras, and adults with various diseases had darker, dimmer auras. She flipped to a page that held six pictures of a single woman, her aura a different color in each photograph. Helen told me that the subject was going through "stages of healing" and that the shift in color was evidence that she was getting better.

A man walked up to the table and wanted to know more about Helen's camera. It was a regular camera, she said, and the technology was not such a big deal. The process had developed in Russia and Germany. The photographer's subject places her hand on a metal plate connected to the camera. Helen showed us the set-up on the camera behind her. "The head is just the light bulb, the aura reading comes through the hand," she offered as way of explanation. "We're mainly interested in healing, and using all of the various techniques that we have at hand to keep people well." I told her that I found what she did very interesting, but would have to think about her offer for an aura reading (which, I noted, cost fifty dollars).

I turned away from the Kirlian photography stand, but before I got my bearings, a short balding man with thick glasses approached me. "Hello, would you like some free meditation? It's by the JohRei Fellowship." Behind him I noted four people sitting on stools with their eyes closed and their hands in their laps. Four women faced them, each with her hands raised in front with thumbs touching middle finger. I wanted to engage him in conversation, which was no problem as he had seen my eyes divert to the meditating women behind him. "JohRei is a form of meditation that—heals you, makes you healthy. Most people who try it say that it really is relaxing and powerful in a hurry. It takes about eight minutes, and most people who come out of it say that it usually feels like they've been meditating for fifteen minutes or more, that's how they feel. When I first tried it here at the Expo, oh, ten or eleven years ago—that's where I first learned of it—it was like things opened up, it was really powerful. But even for those who don't feel that power, it is still really relaxing. I'd say that 99.9999 percent of people who try it say that it is a pleasing experience."

It was hard not to smile at his long litany of "9's," but it sounded intriguing (and it *was* free), so I agreed to sit for some speeded-up meditation. He introduced me to Arlene, a middle-aged woman with long, graying hair, pale skin, and a very soft voice. She sat me down on a stool and explained the process in a quiet voice that I had to strain to hear over the ambient noise in the hall, noise that included the nearby JohRei busker asking another attendee if he would like some meditation. She said, "You can close your eyes, and we will begin by thanking God silently for the opportunity to meditate. Then we will meditate for three or four minutes, and then I will tap your knees. Then you'll turn around, and I'll meditate for another three or four minute period. Then you will turn around again and we will close with a bow of thanks."

I nodded and did as I was told, only to discover noise rushing in to greet me. Closing my eyes heightened my attention to the noisy crowds, including bits of conversations between people in the aisle several feet from me, a harp playing "Edelweiss," and a constant ringing sound that I later learned came from "singing" crystal bowls. I listened intently, forgetting for a minute the purpose of my sitting, until Arlene tapped my knee and I turned around, resolved to concentrate on meditation for the final three minutes. But the man sitting next to me knocked over a small table when he was also instructed to turn around, and the resulting confusion led Arlene to bring my session to an abrupt end. She bowed quickly and softly as I stood, and I thanked her and she replied, a bit formally, "It is a gift to be able to do this."

I pondered the thought that Arlene had gained something from me in this "energy exchange," and wondered what it might be as I stopped to pick up literature at stands touting the powerful healing effects of acupuncture and craniosacral therapy. I walked by a large stand selling crystals and bumper stickers and found myself watching a short woman in purple energetically waving a copper pipe around a man standing in front of her. "No, I still don't feel anything," he told her again, and she replied that it might take some time to feel an effect. I eavesdropped on two older women clad in track suits who were standing in Mondazzi

Book Emporium's occult section. One had a copy of *The Idiot's Guide to Communicating with Spirits* in her hand, and said to her friend, "You see, look here, I knew that I was right!" The other read over her shoulder, nodding without much enthusiasm as she browsed the tarot decks.

I turned the corner of the next vendor aisle and almost walked right past the petite woman sitting by herself at a stand for the Integrative Medicine Alliance. The absence of hubbub around her table, the lack of things for sale, and her sober navy blue suit looked out of place at the Expo, but the woman called out, and I walked over and shook her hand. Trish handed me her card. She was the IMA's executive director. "It is my business to make connections between alternative health and mainstream health communities," she told me. "Doctors know that their patients are doing this stuff," she says, her eyes casting a glance over the room, "But they don't know a thing about what it is."

Trish asked me if I was a "practitioner," which I took to mean someone involved in alternative medicine. I shook my head, and explained my purpose before asking her if she thought that the Expo was a good place to make connections. "There is a lot of interest in making these connections. Most practitioners are so busy with their own clients, though, that they don't have time or energy to do the other kinds of profession building that they need to, so that's where we come in." As she said that, a psychic in a long white dress, covered in lace, walked by and Trish laughed. "I admit, though, that a lot of the stuff here is a lot more out there—a bit off, a bit less mainstream—than I had expected!"

Trish and I agree to meet the following week, and, feeling encouraged at having set up an interview, I joined the line at the Kebab House. The Expo organizers had set up a dozen large round tables and suspended a large banner that said "Meeting Place" above them, and I sat down with a samosa and a bottle of water and tried to strike up a conversation with the young woman sitting next to me. She apologized, somewhat gruffly I thought, that she didn't have time to talk. "I'm here just to do some community hours toward my degree—I'm a student at the shiatsu school," she said, rapidly finishing her plate of curry. I waved goodbye to her and jotted notes before turning to watch a salesman demonstrate singing crystal bowls, which competed with the sounds of the crystal salesman's harp.

A few minutes later a family joined my table, where I was at that point sitting by myself. An elderly mother walked slowly with a cane, grimacing as she sat. Her grown daughter, who appeared to have Down's syndrome, and a son accompanied her, one sitting on either side. They each had a coffee and a cookie. I smiled over at them, and while the women sat mute, John struck up a conversation. He asked if I had been at other Expos, to which I answered no. He told me that they come every year from Chelmsford. "It's always fun, there's always something interesting to see." As if on cue, another brother joined the small group, reaching in to take his sister's program and noting with disappointment that the "gravity machine people" were not present. "Their machines are cool, they spin you all around," he said to no one in particular before darting over to the singing crystal bowl booth. John watched his brother go, and then told me that he was a Reiki master. He had learned the practice to help give some relief to his mother, but also had a few other clients. If I wanted a session, he could make a house call. I thanked him and took his card. Reiterating that it would be no trouble at all to make a house visit, and leaning in a bit further, I smiled and reminded him that Chelmsford was quite a distance from Cambridge and excused myself.

I ambled over to the Theosophical Society table, where a young man was in a heated conversation with a gray-haired woman behind the booth.

"So, where does the energy come from?" the young man asked the graying woman behind the booth.

"The solar system," she answered.

"But what part of it—the sun, the moon, the—"

"The solar system has energy in it, that's what Blavatsky learned from the—"

"Yes, but what part does the energy come from, the sun?"

"Well, yes, the sun, and also the stars, and the zodiac sign—but Larry is really the one who has studied the technicalities," she said, taking a step back to introduce the man standing beside her (she brushes her long hair back with her hand and I see her nametag, "Violet"). Before stepping back she added, "We talk about energy, and where it comes from, and all of those things in our meetings."

Larry, a tall man with wire-rimmed glasses and a thoughtful face, had been listening intently to the interchange and started in without missing a beat. "The chakras, they are part of every religion, not just ours. All religious groups have some idea of them, even Christianity. You can read about them in the book of Revelation."

"Where in the book of Revelation?" the young man asked, looking surprised.

"The seven vials, when you read them, you can take them as an allegory for the chakras," he said. The young man looked skeptical, and asked whether it was possible to read the Bible in this way. Larry answered, "Blavatsky and Cayce and St. John of the Cross say that you can read the book of Revelation as an allegory for the psychological state."

"Who is this Blavatsky, a psychologist?"

"No, not a psychologist, our founder, the founder of the Theosophical Society. But she is not the only one. Also there is St. John, who is a person in the Catholic tradition, a saint, says you can read the Bible from an allegorical perspective. . . . You see, in the Bible, numbers— three, ten, seven, four—are symbolic of things. And one thousand is ten squared, which makes it whole, which means wholeness and completeness, to the greatest degree, which is a different meaning from what most Christians read."

Violet looked on smiling and interjected from time to time, "This is what we talk about at our meetings. We are always interested in learning more." I smiled at her, and she added quietly to me, "We all have interests, and we don't have all the answers. We just come together to discuss these important issues." Violet handed me a schedule for their weekly meetings, and I joined their mailing list before walking away, venturing on to booths for water purifiers, martial arts studios, and the Forum. My energy was flagging when I was brought up short, by a large display of Mary Baker Eddy's *Science and Health*. A petite, middle-aged woman with dark short hair, a black sweater, and gray knit pants stood in front of the pile of books and a large banner for "Spirituality.com." Seeing that I had stopped, she walked over and asked, "Do you know this book? *Time* magazine calls *Science and Health* one of the seventy-five most influential books by women in the twentieth century. Did you know that?"

I nodded. "This is Christian Science, isn't it?" I asked.

Without missing a beat, she said, "The book is not really denominational. This is a book for everyone, no matter what their religion is."

"But it is Christian Science. Mary Baker Eddy founded Christian Science, right?" I asked again, somewhat confused about what Spirituality. com might be.

She shook her head. "She didn't found a religion. It was just that so many people responded to her and they built the church, because they needed somewhere to go after their life had changed."

"And didn't she lead it?" I asked, somewhat bewildered.

"Yes she did, but it really was about the principles and not about the church—she wanted to make sure, after the group started, that they didn't go off the main track."

Fearing that I was beginning to sound too confrontational, and remembering the interchange I had just witnessed, I backed off a bit. "That's really interesting."

Connie started to tell me about how the book changed her life. After "normal" science failed to help her with chronic illness, she finally opened *Science and Health,* which someone had given her years before. "A week after I read this book and started following its principles, my health problems went away," she told me. "You have to read *this,* not the commentaries or biographies," she said emphatically. "There is so much out there that isn't right, about what we are." Connie and I soon discovered that her daughter had attended my alma mater, and we talked about the Christian Science position on vaccines and about the newly reopened Christian Science library downtown. After a few minutes I asked her what she thought of the Expo. Were people interested in Spirituality.com? Was she selling a lot of books?

She laughed. "This is a pretty dense book, hard to read, but people seem very open to it," she said, handing me some materials from one of Harvard Medical School's alternative health centers that confirmed the "power of prayer." People were very receptive, and why shouldn't they be, she added, "after all, we were the ones who started all of this!"

These stories continued to knock around in my mind as I caught a bus home later that afternoon. What was it, exactly, that Connie believed that Christian Science had started? What was it, exactly, that Connie laid claim to, and how did participants like Connie understand the "all" of the Expo? Did she see the wide swath of disparate groups and wares as an emerging movement, as Trish did, or as something altogether different? Connie, Helen (the aura reader), Larry (at the Theosophy table), and others I met comfortably situated themselves in a story about the Expo as unified around "energy," "chakras," or the ubiquitous "light." These words suggested affinity with a central idea about religious energies that developed in particular metaphysical traditions, and were interpreted with particular technologies and tools. Whatever differences might underlie various vendors' ideas about energy were swept aside in easy references to universal truths, and were similarly reinforced through exhibit-goers' generally polite, inquisitive approach to learning what vendors had to offer. The combative interrogations that Larry and Violet responded to at the Theosophy table remained unique in all of my visits to the Expo: people generally kept their skepticism to themselves, or whispered quietly to their friends, politely nodding and moving on.

The journey that an individual could take through the Expo, considering each of the various booths as individual vendors selling something, does not do full justice to the range of distinctions that likewise continued to be "exposed" and "exposited" there. Representatives of religious groups like Larry, Violet, and Connie took a perennial perspective, interpreting the array of booths as expanding outward from their nineteenth-century leaders' pathbreaking forays into the science of health and the esoteric workings of the universe. Trish's somewhat impatient acceptance of the presence of tarot card readers and psychics suggested quite a different view, as her interests in "professionalizing" integrative health and drawing it "back" into medicine showed a concern about the groups whom she thought were too "out there" or "woo woo." And, lest we forget, the family from Chelmsford had a quite different approach to the Expo than any of these: while they expressed hope that they might discover relief from a chronic disease in the midst of the carnival, they were just as happy to be entertained by the objects, claims, and wonders that they encountered.

Part religious event, part professional association meeting, part entertainment, the Expo was all three, simultaneously, and probably more as well. Tangled together or broken apart, they indicate some of the spaces wherein the spiritual is maintained, cultivated, produced, and presented, and furthermore where we might look to understand how the subjectivities of contemporary spiritual practitioners take shape, in social circumstances where they imbibe and apprehend texts, concepts, and experiences. These various distinctions and various social locations that mark them are consequential to the continued presence and reformation of spirituality. Yet they do not necessarily form a strong institutional presence in the stories of spiritual practitioners. They might learn to seek or experience the divine within these settings, but it is within these settings that they learn not to lean on institutions or religious traditions, but rather to look toward the scientific, the experiential, and the self to access the divine. With these entanglements and their absences in mind, we turn in the next chapter to look more closely at the formation of spiritual narratives and spiritual selves through multiple practices of speaking about, writing, and reading experience.

TWO

Becoming Mystics

The sun shone fiercely through the window at Starbucks onto the table where Tina and I were sitting. Mika had told me about Tina and her spiritual belly dance collective, and when I e-mailed she gamely agreed to meet and talk. After ordering our coffees I began with my usual questions about how her group got started, how many people it attracted, and so on. Before too many minutes had passed, however, Tina paused and said, *"It will probably help you a bit to go into my personal history, so that you understand. . . ."* She then launched into a story, beginning with how in the 1960s she discovered *"the only yoga book in town."* Tina taught herself yoga, a practice she said kept her from *"going crazy in the crazy world we were living in."* Skipping ahead several years, she then told me that when she was in her early twenties she began to suffer from extreme joint pain. It was diagnosed as *"arthritis, but I was aware that I was holding a lot of tension in my body."* This pain redoubled her interest in the mind-body connection. At this point, she said, she had the *"good fortune"* to befriend an acupuncturist and from there to a group involved with Reichian bioenergetics. One day during a bioenergetics session, the *"music in the room turned very Oriental"* and a giant serpent entered Tina's body.

"It came up through my body and I wasn't afraid. It just had a very wise look about it, and it took up the whole core of my body, and it came out through my breath, my throat, my mouth. And it undulated me for about an hour and a half, to this music, I was just completely soft and I wasn't forcing it or making it up. It was during that [session] that I realized what belly

dance was about. We'd always heard about the ancient roots of it, but . . . in the '70s there wasn't a lot of emphasis [on that]. It was much more a cabaret, shake it up baby kind of thing." We laughed before she continued. "So, anyway, I made a vow during that session that I would learn about belly dance. And, by the way, after that session I was completely pain free for the next few weeks." Tina received what she took as a serendipitous prompt to make good on her vow several weeks later. "Lo and behold . . . there was a flyer that landed by accident in my mailbox—addressed to somebody down the street—for belly dancing and women's spirituality." Tina joined a class, and many of those students formed a "collective" that promotes dance and women's spirituality.

Tina's story about the serpent distracted me both from the heat and from the fact that her answer had redirected our interview. I eventually learned a great deal about Tina's dancing collective; she was neither unable nor unwilling to talk about her involvement in spiritual and religious collectives. Nonetheless, by telling me her story about her personal experience, she indirectly challenged my line of questioning about organizations and groups, and asserted experience as the primary mover within Cambridge's spiritual worlds. Against the backdrop of my queries (which I had designed in order to elicit information about where people met other spiritual practitioners and where they learned its discourses), Tina reasserted a familiar narrative, where religious experience or some kind of important encounter or yearning propelled individuals toward the divine.[1] At the end of our interview Tina made this assertion explicit: "I think that in your research, what you're finding is that all of this is about direct experience."

Over time I came to agree with Tina that contemporary spirituality was "all about experience," albeit in ways that diverged somewhat from her understanding. Cambridge's spiritual practitioners lived in worlds of experience shaped not so much by the ubiquity of actual direct experiences as by their ongoing, daily engagement with various interpretive and bodily practices. For example, practitioners sought after religious experience through various bodily practices and with techniques that allowed them to live within bodies that were always attuned to an immanent divine (this topic is the subject of the following chapter). More frequently, however, spiritual practitioners talked about, wrote about, and interpreted their experiences. These practices are the object of this chapter. I focus on the discursive practices that shape metaphysical expression in contemporary Cambridge in order to present a more expansive understanding of the ways that people both live and apprehend the world as inflected with divine presence and possibility.

I begin by analyzing experiential accounts that I heard in interviews, where respondents told me about direct experiences with the divine, and sought in the process to make claims for their authenticity and authority as religious experiences. As we will see, the discursive elements that my respondents use to articulate authoritative and authentic experience narratives also produce their self-representations as religious individuals. From this, we might say that experiential accounts are, like other religious self-narratives, highly regulated and shaped by theological norms that they also reproduce. Specifically, they consistently represent and reproduce claims to religious experience as an individual experience. With this in mind, the notion that spiritual narratives reflect an "actual" experience is thrown into doubt, and we can attend more closely to the ways that experiential narratives, like conversion and other religious accounts, position and indicate individuals' abilities to narrate their lives according to shared norms and expectations.

These narratives do not exhaust the ways that metaphysicals draw upon and recount their experiences, however. The second half of this chapter explores additional narrative practices (including writing practices) that shape the ways that metaphysicals and mystics encounter and interpret their experiences. Noting this variety of practices adds further to our understanding of the complex theologies that are articulated and lived in the very act of recounting and eliciting experiences. These practices give voice to a broader set of understandings of the relationship between an experience and its account, some of which confound the claims made in interview settings for a religious experience's closed, finished, and authoritative meaning and authenticity. In daily practice we see authority and authenticity built in different ways, via the activity of writing, through conscious and conscientious attempts to interpret and reinterpret an experience's meaning. Noting the heterogeneity of practices through which authenticity and authority take shape allows us to better understand what it means to live in a metaphysical register, and how it is that one becomes a mystic.

Accounting for Religious Experience

It is primarily through interviews recording spiritual practitioners' accounts of religious experiences and narratives about spiritual awakenings that we have come to understand contemporary spiritual practitioners. Spiritual practitioners' stories are often the most compelling material we have to indicate spiritual seekers' lack of ties to religious traditions, and it is from this material that we have come to recognize spiritual practitioners as seekers rather than dwellers, or as individuals on quests for self-realization.[2] I also begin in this familiar interview milieu, but rather than focusing on the specifics of the stories that practitioners tell about their life trajectories and mining them for social information, I take the narrative patterns as a sign that they are participants within particular theological and cultural frameworks. With this in mind, I focus on the forms of experiential accounts, analyzing the patterns of narrative arc, the implicit questions that their trajectories raise, and the variety of potential criticisms that they seem to preemptively deflect. While the claims that develop in these narratives frequently require that people appear as quite individualistic within their own stories, we can understand these representations as staking out claims and possibilities for a certain kind of authentic and authoritative experience.

In other words, the dominant and culturally normative ways of describing and accounting for religious experience in Cambridge also helped to form metaphysicals' self-expressions as spiritual individualists with limited social ties and tenuous connections to religious groups and traditions. Experiential accounts and stories are no different from other kinds of narratives. Like all stories, they invoke and embed their tellers in social milieu, and we can, arguably, learn something from those narratives about the cultures and structures that they live within. That said, what we can learn from a story must be related to its generic contours and its specific development and use in dialogic contexts. Various elements, including social ties and turning points, can take on new prominence or be foregrounded in new narrative structures, or alternatively drop out of view, depending on religious norms and demands.[3] While we should be cautious in interpreting narrative expressions or experiential accounts as adequate reflections of the lived worlds where people become metaphysicals or mystics, they do indicate much about the social milieu in which certain claims, ties, and accounts can be sustained. We will return to these issues after laying out some of the generic elements of the experiential accounts I heard in interviews.

Eric's account of the mystical experience that led him to believe that he is the reincarnation of the famous mystic Hildegard of Bingen contains many of the common elements that marked experiential narratives I heard in numerous interviews, and thus provides an excellent example with which to observe how experiential authority and religious individualism are co-created.[4] Eric met me at the side door of the

Swedenborgian Chapel on a blustery November night. Unlike prior visits when I had attended lectures, the Chapel was empty and dark, and the musty old church odor more prominent than I had noticed on prior visits. The building was not empty however, as I could hear a group of singers downstairs. Eric told me it was a local group of Tibetan students who used the basement to practice "traditional dances." Eric ushered me into the parlor, a modern addition that held the community's library. True to its name, it also had several groupings of chairs positioned around coffee tables. Eric had turned on a single lamp that illuminated two wingback chairs. The only other light in the room came from the streetlamps on Kirkland Street. Portraits of the Dalai Lama and Emanuel Swedenborg gazed down benevolently from the shadows; I smiled to myself and thought that our tableau seemed almost spooky, except for the loud enthusiastic singing filtering up from downstairs.

As I pulled out my materials Eric drew his own tape recorder out of his backpack and placed it on the table next to mine. He told me that he was writing his spiritual autobiography for publication, and he thought that the interview would be a good way to "get some things out." This surprised me. I had told Eric (via e-mail) that my questions were primarily about his involvement in local spiritual and religious groups and other activities, and when the tapes started playing I began with my regular list of questions. Eric began to tell me about the mystical arts programs that he was developing, but before long he paused and suggested that in order to better understand his spiritual organizing I would need to know a more about his spiritual awakening. *"This is where it gets into the mystical thread of my own life,"* he offered, noting that he was *"guided to have these [arts] shows by a spirit of Hildegard of Bingen."*

Before telling me the story, Eric asked whether I knew who Hildegard was. I nodded uncertainly, so Eric filled in some background. *"She was a nun, a mystical nun. I have forgotten the exact dates now. Her death date was 1098, because 1998 was her 900th anniversary. [She was] a mystical nun who is mostly known for her music. But she was one of these renaissance people who—she wrote music, she wrote a play, she wrote treatises on medicine and healing and such. She had a lot of visions. She had migraines. I used to relate to that, they—I get migraines, but [they've] diminished over the years as I express my path more."* He added, almost as an aside, *"There was a big boom in Hildegard interest in the late [19]90s. But it had really been since the '60s, that a woman in England started researching Hildegard's abbey in Germany and started collecting the musical works, and [Hildegard] started getting academic attention again. So then, [along] with her music* started to come the theology. She has a very Earth-centered, ecological theology, and a lot of it was revived and adopted into the '90s. It's pretty well quieted down now."

Having dispensed with Hildegard's biography Eric began the thread of his narrative again. He had attended a Presbyterian church with his mother when he was young, but even as a child his interests in mystical things surpassed what the church offered. "First it was science fiction and ghost stories, and as a teenager I got into a more romantic mindset, and then, in college, [it was about] getting more interested in philosophy. . . . But after I graduated I had a big mystical awakening that led to being mentored by Lazaris. He's a channeled entity and is a really comprehensive and wise source of information. Some claim that he's deliberately concocted and it's a hodgepodge of stuff you can research anywhere. But each time I would get into some of it, more energy, more inspiration would come to me. So it was like, there was something right about it, and coordinated about it beyond a simple [hodgepodge.]" Nonetheless, this awakening eventually "fizzled out. It just didn't ground itself, I had quit my job and tried to write a book, [exploring] all this weird, prophetic, cosmic overview energy, but I couldn't express it so I went back to work."

"Then, in 1997 I had another spiritual awakening. And, um, things were coming together. I had bought a Kurzweil keyboard, similar to how in the '80s I had bought some electronic equipment, and I was making all this music. Just pouring out this music. And I, I find music is a real herald, for me, of a new phase of life, a new state of connectedness and consciousness. And so in '97 I was writing this music, and got married and divorced very fast, and I was really going on the edge with writing sort of these semi-channeled, reality conjecture kind of poetry and prose—sort of crazy. But I knew my limits, my edge, better than in the late '80s, because the late '80s I felt that I went a little over.

So in '97 I was more careful and I stayed within my limits. I went to the Whole Health Expo, and I rented a booth and I laid out these seven stories, and just wanted it to go somewhere. (I hadn't quit my job yet, and I worked nearby.) I was just posing this question to the universe, like, 'Look, is there something in me to explore here?' And something happened. Well, I met a lot of nice people and they were also sort of out there like I was—exploring. But they weren't crazy, and I felt pretty healthy with them. It felt pretty good. And this one guy did a spirit reading for me. He just said, 'The spirits say you're not listening, and there's something big you need to hear.' At the end of the weekend, I made friends with this woman and her husband. She was a medical illustrator and she helped me break the stuff down and take it back to my office and store it."

"And I'm taking a bus back home from there, and um, there's a—there's in the newspaper there's a preview, explaining that 1998 was going to be the 900th anniversary of Hildegard of Bingen's death, that there were going to be all these kinds of concerts. And something happened inside of me where I just burst into tears and I was just crying and crying, and I just felt like this was the pivotal moment.

And I didn't know what to do with it, but I knew that Hildegard of Bingen was alive and really important to me. And I started to have all these memories of hearing her name at other times in my life, and each time having a reaction, but not enough context to know what to do with it. One time in the '80s I was working in a liquor store and I heard a—somebody on the radio mentioned her name after the song, and I remember going into a trance. And I swear, this room in the liquor store faded away, and what was more real was being in a woman's body and kneeling and praying in this little room, and feeling really confined in this very small room with a little light, a little window high up. And I just kind of dismissed it. It was too weird. But when this happened in '97, then I started tuning into all of this stuff, and I couldn't believe it."

Over the next half hour, Eric used this pivotal moment as the frame through which he reinterpreted his past, as it helped him to trace connections to past events in his life to which he had not previously assigned meaning. For us, this story also presents a clear example of how an experience's authority is built within narrative: its authority arises not within a direct statement about its "truth" but within the space that it takes within the story. Only a handful of my respondents ever made a bold or declarative statement about the reality of their experiences and left it at that. Rather, they used certain narrative elements to dialogically engage and counter arguments or questions about the experience's truth. Some of my respondents placed their own skepticism about their experience at the fore, drawing me through a variety of "tests" or "experiments" to ascertain their validity. Others took a path like Eric's, contrasting what he knew about the difference between a real experience and wishful thinking by relating his own prior "awakenings" that had not amounted to much (they "fizzled out"). To these interspersed discussions and counterstories we can also add three narrative tropes that help to form authoritative narratives: modes of temporal unfolding, the description of social ties within that plot, and the assertion of embodied or emotional knowledge over cognitive knowledge. As we will see, these articulations minimize the role of prior cultural or religious knowledge, as well as social ties and relationships that might challenge the claim to a direct, unmediated experience. While the rhetorical project of articulating an authentic experience suggests that these narratives cannot be simply read to glean information about where people like Tina or Eric learn to be mystics, we can nonetheless detect the traces of prior conversations via the "answers" to various challenges that are preemptively articulated within them. As I discuss at the end of this section, these answers suggest ways to explore their genealogical resonance. Before doing so, we turn to the three elements that shape authentic narratives.

Temporal Ordering

Narratives unfold in linear fashion. The order of events within any narrative plays an important role in shaping an account's authenticity and the teller's authority. As one of the central social scientific explanatory claims against the "reality" of religious experience is that such events arise from a misrecognition of social, cultural, or experiential cues, it is not surprising that the temporal order of experiential narratives work to minimize the possibility of such explanations. This takes shape in a variety of ways. Eric's story, for example, includes a number of "failed" experiences that precede his "true" experience on the bus. These elements simultaneously indicate his long-standing yearning for mystical contact and demonstrate that he is able to distinguish a real experience from one that was the result of mental instability, subconscious yearnings, or other psychological or social origins.

Mystics more frequently organized their narratives so that the elements before the experience are devoid of anything that might be taken as preknowledge about the kind of experience that takes place. For example, Mike (who had experienced out-of-body experiences and two near-death experiences) described his out-of-body experience this way: *"I popped out of myself and kind of ended up kind of in the corner—a typical out-of-body experience. Looking down at the room, down at myself in the bed, removed from the mental thoughts that I would have had while I was in the bed, removed from physical sensations and the pain, that kind of thing."*

Without pausing he added, *"If you go out of your body—if you didn't know the term, I would just say to somebody, you know I went out of my body, it was just an experience that was, OK, well you just called it what it is, without knowing that that may be what someone else might have called it. I never did any research on it, I never read a book about it at that point, and I didn't have any strong desire to. It was just something that happened. I some-*

how came to know it as an out-of-body experience, probably just because, that was like, that's a kind of generic name for that."

Mike was concerned that I understand that his knowledge of these experiences emerged from within the experience itself. His near-death experiences were similar: *"When they took place I was already fairly open. But I don't know—no matter how open you are nothing opens you enough for that experience. It's beautiful, it's private, and the best details you can't—but it is really like getting struck by lightning. It's a huge shock to your whole sense of what life is. Nothing feels important. Nothing. It's like nothing matters—and it's very difficult to focus on the tasks of life, the everyday mundane tasks. . . . When I say it's hard, it's hard enough just about to make you want to go back [to death]. So, actually I don't know how I figured out that I had a near-death experience. I knew what had happened, and I knew—I knew what had happened."* He paused, again posing and answering his own question in his narrative, without my prompting. *"I knew something really big happened. Maybe somewhere along the line I knew the term? I don't recall."*

Doug similarly commented that he did know what out-of-body experiences were when he started having them. *"I hadn't at that point—I hadn't really read anything. Like, I started having these experiences and then I started reading these books, and went 'wow.' I was checking stuff off like, 'yup yup, I had that, yeah that makes a lot of sense.' And then, you know in subsequent years in talking with a lot of other people who have had these experiences, so there is a lot of similar stuff."* In each of these examples, an experience's authenticity is supported by the exposition of a life prior to the experience that holds little direct bearing on the event. Experiential narratives provide few if any social and cultural markers that might suggest social cues that prompted the experience (and thus undercut its singularity). Eric's, for example, mentions a range of prior mystical interests (in a "new age" channeled source, science fiction, and raving) but notes that they were misguided attempts and explorations. They present a stark contrast to the medieval Catholic devotionalism that he encounters on the bus. The spirit guide that told Eric that he had "not been listening" augured this shift in Eric's attention from new age to old age mysticism, and also reinforced his point that despite all of his seeking, he had no preknowledge of Hildegard or preexisting interest in medieval Christianity that could be attributed to his experience.

Reading through my interviews, it is clear that it was only a rare case where mystics described or discussed cultural or social experiences that might destabilize the claims to the "unexpectedness" or "uniqueness" of an experience. Such details might emerge after the experience or be indicated within descriptive (atemporal) clauses. Social contexts are, of course, not utterly missing from these narratives, but it is instructive to note that religious and spiritual groups only become important (or visible) after the experience takes place. It is only *after* Doug's experience that he turns to books to read about them; it is only *after* Tina describes her experience with the divine serpentine that she begins to talk about her involvement in a group. It is only *after* Eric's encounter on the bus that he returns to Cambridge and develops the mystical arts collective.

Social Ties

Mystical accounts like Eric's likewise articulate social ties in such a way to confirm the uniqueness and authentic individuality of an experience, and organize them temporally to reinforce rather than raise questions about the uniqueness of an experience. In most of the narratives I heard, experiencers say very little about long-standing social ties (with close friends, family, or others) until after they describe the experience. The social interactions that emerge in narratives leading up to the experiential moment are frequently interchanges with strangers, who often take on the quality of oracles (foretelling an impending experience). The overall effect of the narratives, however, is to articulate spiritual experiencers as wanderers and seekers, without communities that bolster or shape the experiences as they happen. We see this played out clearly in Eric's narrative. The only people who appear in Eric's account leading up to the experience are unnamed. He meets them at the Boston Health Expo, and their words to him are oracular. They inform him that he is "on the right track," and that the "spirits" are trying to speak to him, thus setting up a spiritually charged environment, where the "Universe" is working through multiple channels to communicate. Most important, in Eric's understanding, was the person of the "former [Benedictine] nun and medical illustrator" who is an oracular presence given her association with Hildegard's order. These people and social interactions are situated as heralds; they are not "instructing" or "suggesting" Eric how to go forward, but rather making space for his own experience to take place. In brief, these ties are, much like the experience that takes place on the bus, unusual and unexpected; they are oriented toward and make sense only in relation to the experience. While the absence of ties within accounts like Eric's heightens the uniqueness of the experience, it also narratively positions Eric and other mystics in solitary, individual worlds.

Family and friends are not absent from these accounts, but in general appear only as post hoc witnesses, reassuring the experiencer that she or he is not crazy or deluded. Mike's near-death experience narrative drew heavily on the testimony of friends and family to reinforce the reality of his experience. He said, "*I started telling some of my friends and my family about it. And what was amazing is, I was never surprised by it. I mean I was shocked by it, but I never thought it was weird. . . . I didn't think I was crazy—I never gave any thought to whether someone would believe me or not, I just assumed they would believe me, because it was true.*" These social ties work both to reinforce the authenticity of the experience in the narrative and instruct the current listener to accept the story as true. As family and friends come to accept the stories and testimonies of these experiences, these familiars become strategic voices through which mystics can make claims to their own sanity. Furthermore, as we have already seen, having an experience becomes the impetus in these stories to joining groups or seeking out fellow travelers.

Feeling Not Knowing

The organization of social ties in these narratives respond to a variety of imagined interlocutors who might pose counterarguments about the narratives' validity and authenticity. The generically organized plots of these experiences make them authentic to both those who tell them and to those who listen, deflecting alternative explanations that might mark the experiencer as momentarily insane, daydreaming, or stimulated by some forgotten or unknown subconscious suggestion. But as we also see, these narrative structures also render the experiencer as a person with limited social or religious ties, cultural influences, or traditions. One further element works to make experiences authoritative, and likewise further protects experiential knowledge from external critique. This element articulates the authority of the experience through its untranslatability, where the moment of experience itself stands outside of normal cognition and in another realm where embodied and emotional (or perhaps spiritual) knowledge rises to the fore. Eric's story, for example, places his "pivotal moment" not only in an isolated, contingent moment on the bus full of strangers, but also sequesters the actual event itself through conveying it as a moment when emotion overcame him: words fail, both literally and figuratively. A common feature of experiential narratives is that it represents the experience itself as beyond representation. Emotions, bodies, and "felt" experience rather than words signal the true experience. Even when mystics don't make the claims of untranslatability, the moment of the experience itself remains vague and lacking in description: words failed Eric as he began to describe what happened to him on the bus. *"Something happened inside of me where I just burst into tears and I was just crying and crying."*

Tears and bodily sensations emerge as signs of pure experience. In the moments where accounts focus attention on emotions, tears, and bodies, words disappear. The moment of experience itself becomes untranslatable to others, and even perhaps to oneself. Description of the experience "itself" is made impossible, it seems, as words give way to representations of the body's visceral reactions. The body's response in fact becomes a sign of divine presence.[5] The narrator's shift from the cognitive (translatable) events to emotive or embodied events suggests both that the value of the experience is beyond words and created culture, and by extension that it is immune from analysis and further investigation. Subtle and not so subtle shifts within the narrative from knowing to feeling reinforces a claim that it is impossible to describe an event, and that it is impossible for anyone to know except through its effects. Not only does this protect the experience from certain kinds of reductive interpretation,[6] it also works to place those who listen within an experiential-discursive milieu where they might come likewise to experience through listening to these accounts. Of course, whether such accounts have this effect on a listener is another matter, but the rhetorical strategies embedded within these genres are nonetheless important to note. Understanding the dialogic and social aspects of experiential accounting makes even more clear the ways that telling experiential accounts embeds speakers and listeners within particular cultural and religious genres and practices.

Experiencers and Listeners

Were out-of-body experiences or miraculous visions attributable to the workings of subliminal consciousness, the reemergence of forgotten childhood events, or the consequence of mental disturbances with origins in the physical body rather than some external source?[7] The generic contours of experiential narratives, which build authority and authenticity by omitting social ties, limiting precultural knowledge, and emphasizing emotion, certainly sought to answer such questions. But these were not *my* questions: not once during the interviews did I suggest that I was interested at all in the source of their experiences or how the speakers knew they were true. As my respondents' narratives appeared to answer questions about their experiences' authority and authenticity that I had not asked (or to my knowledge had even inti-mated), it occurred to me that the space of the interview suggested a particular role and trajectory of social scientific questions that anyone who arrived at a doorstep with recording equipment, forms, and pa-perwork, would ask.[8] As I spent more time in the field, I became more attuned to the peculiarities of the interview format, and in particular to the narrative contours that emerged frequently in interviews yet ir-regularly, if at all, in other contexts. The emphasis on authority and authenticity that took center stage in the interviews did not carry into every setting where metaphysicals talked about experiences.

Before moving on to consider a wider range of contexts and prac-tices where mystics recount their experiences we should consider how the scholarly interview context marks out fertile imaginative space for both spiritual experiencers and social scientists, and gives shape to particular experiential claims. The interview is important for spiritual practitioners to dialogically express the authority of their experiences in relation to a (secular) social science or science. The value of scien-tific authority is undergirded and built within the metaphysical and harmonial traditions, marking out (as I have noted in the introduc-tion) a robust historical entanglement. For social scientists, the space of the interview in contrast has been the site where we have discovered and interpreted individualistic spirituality. The narrative structures of experience within interviews thus reproduce (simultaneously and un-equally) two different notions of scientific authority.

This nonetheless requires that we rethink the context of an inter-view not as unknown territory to spiritual practitioners, but as an op-portunity to present or convince a listener (or a listener that is imagined to be of a particular kind) of a theological point or claim, in this case the validity of religious experiences. This is consistent with approaches to religious narratives as forms that express and reproduce theological and cultural concepts. Individual conversion narratives and other sto-ries, for example, reflect the broader narrative structures of a particular religious group; membership or affiliation with a group means coming to place one's own life story within the structural narrative framework (and its theological or ideological trajectory) recognized by the larger group and, thereby, also by scholars who can link a narrative style to a particular religious community.[9]

The social space where spiritual practitioners learn to engage these narratives is rarely evident from within the experiential narratives themselves. Nonetheless the space of the interview as a context where these particular tropes resonate is nonetheless intriguing, particularly

as the main tropes in these narratives map onto William James's definition of religious experience as the "feelings, acts and experiences of individual men in their solitude, so far as they apprehend themselves to
stand in relation to whatever they may consider the divine."[10] In both,
experiential meaning cannot ever be fully conveyed to others, appropriate feeling and emotions are important markers of authenticity, and
an experience apprehended in solitude trumps social authority. James's
definition, widely repeated within social scientific literature and frequently indicated by the talismanic presence of the *Varieties of Religious
Experience* on Cambridge mystics' bookshelves, suggest that we can also
consider James's volume as teaching both social scientists and religious
individuals what it means to have an experience. The translation and
expansion of certain types of religious experience into the idiom of
psychology and thus into a more scientific register enables the further
expansion of these particular kinds of "religious experiences" into multiple cultural and historical moments. For this reason, interviews can
be considered a peculiarly powerful space wherein spiritual practitioners' desires to scientifically validate their religious experiences takes
on special force and shape.

The fact that the *Varieties* and its definition of experience continues
to be used (albeit in quite different ways) by social scientists and by
spiritual practitioners is particularly interesting given that the volume
was written with multiple audiences in mind. James drew copiously
from the work of his graduate student Edwin Starbuck, who developed
and distributed the first "survey" on religious experience as part of his
graduate work. Together, these accounts arguably both display a scientist's "breadth" of interest in types of experience and (with their multiple repetition) place readers within a textual milieu where various
pedagogical and theological impulses are in play.[11] According to Christopher White, Starbuck's survey asked respondents to describe their experiences in detail in writing; in so doing, it sought to elicit the respondents' renewed connection with God. As people reflected on their past
experiences, Starbuck wrote, they would also "awaken . . . certain immediate reactions, hopeful that 'what came forth spontaneously would
be the most vital and essential elements of the experience.'"[12] Starbuck
believed that revisiting experiences via writing and reading would elicit
"actual feelings of the sense of communion." Experiential accounts of
the type represented in the *Varieties* are not meant to be mere secondhand accounts. In other words, original listeners to the Gifford lectures
and later readers of the same are confronted by a milieu of confession
and testimony in which they can catch the resonance of experience,

recalling with the same frisson their own past experiences. *The Varieties* is thus not only a scientific work that draws on and displays the disciplinary procedures of early American psychologists. It is also a pedagogical textual environment in which it is expected that readers will encounter the residue of others' strongly resonant, singularly authoritative experiences and thereby seek their own. James's textual and social environment spreads outward now into social scientific, popular cultural, and other settings. It creates new conditions for encountering transcendence and finding fullness that are shaped equally by scientific technique and scholarly footnotes.

To draw this out a bit, the foregoing mystical accounts do not work merely to "protect" the experience from a skeptical listener but work to actively draw the listener into the space of the experience itself. Drawing emotions into accounts, and "hiding" the moment of the experience itself through claims to its ineffability, help to rhetorically establish the point that a listener can only know in part, and that full knowledge of an experience comes only to those who experience it firsthand. Yet at the same time, some accounts positioned those who listened in a narrative space where they could "experience" at the very least some of the curiosity or surprise that attended such events, if not gain direct access to their power. Tina and Eric, for example, both stopped the temporal flow of their narratives to present background information about bioenergetics and Hildegard, respectively. The use of such descriptive clauses gave me (their listener) bits of information that could be linked indirectly and then directly to later elements in their developing accounts.[13] Eric's brief, off-the-cuff description of Hildegard's biography thus became a kind of experiential knowledge for me, in the sense that it resonated with the threads of his story even before he drew all the pieces together himself.[14] As experiencers tell their stories to others within specific social milieu, they learn how to better recount or account for their experiences. These practices mark the continued relevance of particular conceptions of religious experience, shared (albeit unequally) by both spiritual practitioners and social scientists.

Speaking Is Experiencing

When I called Mike to set up a time to meet, he warned me that he would not be able to recount his experiences during our interview, adding that speaking about them was such a powerful act that it usually exhausted him completely. He offered instead to send me two videotapes of recent talks he had given, so I could hear them. That was fine with me, I said.

When we sat down a few weeks later at the Whole Foods cafeteria on River Street, I thanked him for loaning me his tapes. He sounded relieved. *"[When I was on my way here I realized again how I didn't] want to tell you the whole story tonight about the NDEs. I truly didn't. I'm not in the place where I could go through it tonight."* Speaking about his experiences had an energetic effect both on him and often on those who listened. Mike told me that he *"actualized"* the divine energy that he had encountered during his near-death experiences whenever he told the stories. *"Each time I spoke I was getting extremely intoxicated by the process, because you can't talk about the Light without experiencing it in a very, very three-dimensional way. And what would happen is, it expands you, and if your body is not really healthy it can just blow your circuits out over and over and over again. So I would go and I would speak, and during one talk that you watched, I had the flu—I had the flu for the week before that, I was really sick. So when I did that talk I had no energy. But I was kind fired up. I was kind of—there was energy in that. But subsequent to that talk, I spent a week in bed."*

We talked instead about how he became involved in speaking in the first place. After two near-death experiences, Mike attended a meeting of the International Association of Near-Death Studies. The Boston chapter, he told me, was partly research oriented and partly a support group. He found it somewhat odd at first that none of the regular participants had actually had an NDE, but it was also for that reason that he was eagerly welcomed into the group. Within a week of his first visit, one of the group leaders asked if he would speak about his experience at a local Spiritualist church. The church was holding a conference on near-death experiences, and it had contacted her to send an "experiencer." *"I was apparently articulate enough so she called and said, 'Mike, there's a Reverend who wants someone to come and talk.' And I said, 'What do you mean, talk about it?' She said, 'You know, your presentation. To tell your story.' And I was like, 'Like in a group?'"* Mike told me that he had not really thought of the experience as something others would want to hear about. To him, it seemed personal and private.

"So that's what happened. When I got up to do it, I was the most recent experiencer [at the conference], so it was the most fresh with me, the energy of it was still very fresh. I was really jazzed up even though I was not feeling well. I felt like I was supposed to do what I was doing. I was sent there to give the word." Mike's talk was a success, and word spread quickly that there was a new dynamic speaker on the circuit. He kept getting calls and *"I just kept saying yes."* Mike gave his talk in churches, on a local

television program, and a nationally broadcast radio show. Telling his story nearly took over his life. After each talk, *"people would come up and they all wanted to touch me. . . . And, there was—I had, some really serious issues, boundary issues. I felt on the one hand that I knew that there was something that I had, that was somehow important or special to the people who I was communicating with. That was one thing. On the other hand, I was feeling physically very drained. I was not well, I wasn't getting money, I was really overwhelmed with this sense of time. Time was against me in my life. And, the people who were approaching me, [some] were seeing things in me that I hadn't yet seen about myself. I wasn't really in full recognition of what I was bringing to them. I didn't really know. I am not certain I do now, but I know more now than I did then. I was putting out an energy that was very, um, different than the energy that I felt I was working with."*

Mike reiterated that his talks were important because of the "energy" they conveyed and not because of the actual words. In opening his mouth he became a conduit for divine energies, and in making this point again and again made it clear to me that the "truth" of an experiential account laid not in the words (or whether they were consistent from one telling to the next) but rather in what he and others felt in the moment of speaking or listening. It was thus not a surprise that Mike was likewise quite reluctant to write down his experiences. *"I never have the desire ever to put anything in writing, I don't like [writing it down] because the way that I describe the experience, each time, is actually slightly different based on what analogy I feel is most in line with how I am feeling that day. So some days I'll describe it one way and some days I'll describe it another way. Sometimes, it's like when you're in the flow of it, it's like—I don' t know. It's like, OK, you try to remember but you're also trying to be in the energy. I'll give you an example. In one of my talks I talk about the tunnel going upward. And I'm doing this with my hand,"* he waved his right hand in the air. *"I know it goes to the left, that's how I saw it. But I'm saying, I'm actually saying, like I'm going to the right with my hand, and saying to the left. And while these details are very insignificant and truly no one even notices, I care, because one of the things that is really important to me is that people understand. I've never sought to prove the experience nor do I want to, but I do want people to know that there's the possibility that these things do happen. So if you have skeptics, and they can find one aspect by which to say, 'Wait a minute, you said this one time and this another time,'"* Mike shook his head as he relayed these imaginary conversations with skeptics. *"It really isn't a contradiction. It's really hard to be immersed in it and relay it the same way [each time]. But the essence of the energy and all the pieces are still there."*

Mike's near-death experiences were among the most dramatic that I encountered, but he was far from alone in suggesting that the act of speaking an experience engaged the speaker and listener in the "powers" of the original experience. The force that emanated from these stories was neither metaphorical nor merely aesthetic, but conveyed rather a sense of the experience itself, and offered the possibility that its power would not just be recalled but activated.[15] This expectation further complicates interpretive presumptions that individual "experience" is not within the purview of sociologists, and that we are left only with dry, secondhand accounts. While this position arguably reminds scholars not to mistake an account for the event to which it refers, the lived claims of experiencers about what their accounts do, and how they relate to their experiences, challenge the clear and fast decision between an event and its narration. Speaking brings the event back to life: what makes a past event authentic in this sense is the power that emanates from the spoken word about it.

While Mike was adamant that the divine vitality conveyed in speaking was not able to carry through into written, textualized renditions, many of my respondents felt quite differently. Many wrote their experiences and invested the practice of writing with the kinds of experiential vitality that Mike experienced in speaking. Writing was also experiencing, and in approaching writing in this way, my respondents further clouded a distinction between an experience and its account. Those respondents who wrote did not view their activity as "merely" recording past experiences, but rather as a practice and site where they tapped into these divine energies. The divine thus moved not only in their memories and in past experiences, but also within the moment of recounting. Mystical practices thus often give power and immediacy to writing that is generally ceded to the sites of voice and speech. These practices, particularly "guided writing" or "free writing," emphasize cathartic or nonfocused writing as a way to get one's "true" meaning (or God's powerful creativity) out into the world.

Writing Experience

Sheila, a homeopathic healer in Harvard Square, reflected on her typical client, saying *"she's a woman in her 40s. . . . I'm lucky that the women that I see here are very self-observing, self aware, articulate, and able to give me a lot of feedback. . . . For intakes, I ask people for a timeline of their lives and they xerox their diaries. I get wheelbarrows full. [Or, they say], I happen to be writing the story of my life, let me download it for you.—Welcome to Cambridge!"*

Sheila was not far from the mark. Almost all of my respondents kept journals, dream diaries, or something of that sort. Many write memoirs, poetry, and stories for real or intended publics. Eric was not the only one who brought a tape recorder to an interview, and a handful of my respondents likewise brought their published work to share. Two respondents brought me signed copies of their books. In writing and revising their experiences mystics also encounter and reengage the divine. Within many of these practices we see a similar desire or understanding to Mike's, in which the divine becomes real, or reinstated, within the act of writing itself. In other practices we see another kind of experiential world take shape as mystical writing practices shape mystical orientations toward the world, so that they can detect and interpret daily life as a series of unfolding serendipitous, divinely organized events. Writing practices, like speaking practices, are expansive both in the ways they articulate experiential meaning and in the ways that they articulate mystics' sense of their own power and abilities to tap into the divine.

In contrast to the narratives I heard during interviews, the "authority" and "authenticity" of textualized accounts were often unclear. In other spaces, a more extensive and humanistic vision of religious experience takes shape. Mystics, it turns out, seem more flexible and open to various competing understandings of inspiration and divine engagement in these accounts than they are in interviews. The relationship between "direct experience" (to use Tina's phrase) and text is an important one in religious worlds; indeed, religious studies scholar Steven Katz argues that while many mystical traditions are shaped via pursuit of some form of experience, "the actual interpretation of sacred texts . . . comprises a substantial part of what mystics actually do and plays a significant role in achieving those ultimate states of experience (and metaexperience) that mystics seek."[16] And while my Cambridge respondents have only marginal connections to the religious-mystical traditions identified by Katz and his colleagues, contemporary practitioners' daily practices are nonetheless also oriented toward texts that offer a variety of possibilities for interpretation and experience.

For contemporary mystics and spiritual practitioners, these practices include interpreting their own stories and experiences as sacred texts of particular kinds. This possibility is perhaps most clearly crystallized in a book that I found in a secondhand book shop one day while I was killing time between interviews. Bobbi Parish's how-to book *Cre-*

ate Your Own Personal Sacred Text offers readers a variety of reading and writing practices with which they might gain direct experience with the divine. Parish begins her book with her own tale of self-discovery, beginning in her early adult life, when she one day realized that "the god I had been raised to believe in was man-made, a façade of doctrine and dogma so thick that his true nature was barely perceivable. My experiences with him had always been through an intermediary. . . . By the time his messages reached me, they were garbled and contorted by someone else's perception or ego." She continued, "Tired of working through intermediaries, I threw out all my conceptions of Spirit and sought to make direct, face-to-face contact."

Parish's quest was initially impeded rather than aided by scripture. She tells her readers that she yearned for the divine wisdom that those texts offered, but found their messages marred or blurred by the "egos" or the specific "cultures" of their writers. Upon failing to find the pure voice of God in the world's wisdom literature, she began to keep a journal of her own. She began to have "face-to-face" contact with God as she began recording her experiences, and likewise realized that she was on the "same journey" as the writers of the world's religious scriptures. This, she said, led her to a deepened appreciation of scripture: she began to read again, this time "meditating upon and contemplating what I was reading," and in so doing learning that she could make "the direct contact with Spirit that I so desired."[17] All stories and all scriptures could become dynamically alive with divine messages, if she meditated on them correctly. She encouraged her readers to follow her path, to create their own texts in this way.

Parish was not the only author to encourage readers to cultivate dynamic reading and writing practices in order to hear God. The voice of the divine and direct experience, Parish suggests, comes through work and attention, meditation, and action. Likewise, she suggests (as did many of my respondents) that texts and narratives do not merely record past events or actions, but are rather dynamic sites that can foster direct encounter. Telling and listening to stories, writing, and interpretation are all practices of religious encounter. Reading and writing were not merely forms of accounting for past events. They were additionally, and perhaps more importantly, activities through which the divine entered into the present. These elements of metaphysical "accounting" became more evident as I moved from interviews into fieldwork, where mystics not only told me their stories but in addition discussed their meanings and proper ways of interpreting them. In these free-flowing conversations I also learned more about their intimate projects of writing and journaling about their experiences, and other practices wherein experiences became part of spiritual practitioners' daily worlds.[18]

The texts that my respondents worked with included occasionally the "sacred texts" of various traditions but more frequently the "sacred texts" of their own experiences. Making one's one experiences and the texts that encapsulated them "sacred" was aided by practices in which mystics learned that their very act of writing was a site of the divine's presence. This is also a very long-standing religious idea, one that many of my respondents introduced to me in formal interviews and informal conversations.

For example, Marcy told me that writing, not yoga, was her primary religious practice. She had learned to cultivate the practice of writing "morning pages" when she took a course on *The Artist's Way,* a best-selling book by Julie Cameron that professes to bring out the artistic side of every person. During a particularly bleak time in her life, Marcy started to take long walks in her neighborhood and, on one such walk, noticed a flyer stuck to a lamppost for an *Artist's Way* workshop on her block. A friend had given her a copy of the book several years before, but she had never opened it. When she saw the sign, however, she remembered how much her friend had encouraged her to read it. So, Marcy told me, she signed up for the course, and soon became a devoted reader and practitioner. *"That book saved my life."*

Cameron tells her readers that in order to regain their creative and core self, they should begin with a simple exercise, writing "morning pages." This exercise consists of daily, solitary writing: Cameron suggests a minimum of three pages of longhand writing. This writing is similar to a diary and not meant for anyone else, or perhaps even the author, to read. Cameron claims that writing in this way every day in a disciplined way is an act of "connecting" with the inner self that is often forgotten or not listened to. Sitting, listening, and putting the hand in motion over a page forges this connection. Cameron further suggests that people not think too much while they write: they should put down whatever comes to mind. "These daily morning meanderings are not meant to be art. Or even writing. . . . Pages are meant to be, simply, the act of moving the hand across the page and writing down *whatever* comes to mind. Nothing is too petty, too silly, too stupid, or too weird to be included." Marcy made this practice part of her daily routine, and now, several years later, still wakes up every morning to her pages. Marcy said *"I would wake up, feed the cat, make some tea, and then do my ritualistic journaling, in what was now my sacred space. . . . It became the ritualistic way that I woke up every day and made myself do my journal writing.*" Cameron calls attention to this ritualistic aspect, noting "It may be useful for you to think of the morning pages as meditation. . . . It is impossible to write morning pages for any extended period of time without coming into contact with an unexpected inner power. Anyone who faithfully writes morning pages will be led to a connection with a source of wisdom from within. When I am stuck in a painful situation or problem that I don't think I know how to handle, I will go to the pages and ask for guidance."[19]

Marcy explained to me that writing morning pages "*is really about the process of excavating, what do I want to do with my life? What can I change in my life?*" At first, Marcy said, she liked writing because it allowed her to "*do something that is completely nonproductive,*" but she soon discovered that it was in fact productively allowing her to "*get back in touch with myself.*" Now, Marcy views her journaling as primarily "*a time of connection. . . . I would pray sometimes, in the writing, sometimes it was prayer that I was writing. It became a sacred practice to me. So I began to embrace sacred ritual—that's really what happened, actually.*" At some point, Marcy told me, she began to ask for and receive "wisdom" about the next steps in her life through her journal. She had decided that she could not continue in her job as a radio announcer and reporter for a regional public radio station, and she eventually gave notice at the station, without another job lined up. She had been journaling for a year, and "*by that point I was pretty much ingrained in a practice of daily journaling, and that's where a lot of truths were being heard. Sometimes it was a laundry list, but often times, answers would come, to questions, things I was dealing with—really answers to prayer. So I journaled for a while about this decision, and, in my mind I was thinking, maybe I would temp or do some more freelance. Within a week I had all this freelance work—all over the place. Stuff was literally falling into my lap—money and work and good co-workers.*"

Marcy's hope that "*answers would come*" in the pages of her notebook resonates with Cameron's claim that the divine appears on the written page. Cameron counsels her readers that they should not see themselves as the authors of their journals, but rather as "the instruments" of divine creativity.[20] The divine becomes present *within* the practice of writing and the texts produced. Texts and stories, perhaps particularly those that are engaged in writing about past religious experiences, thus are alive with the presence of an all-powerful divine force. Writing is a generative site.

Cameron's late-twentieth-century claim on the "divine" as the active source of writers' creative effervescence is far from novel, nor is her view that "divine creativity" is manifest within passive, open-ended flow writing. Writing has long been imagined as a metaphorical and an actual practice through which God speaks, but my respondents seemed particularly attuned to the literal understanding that the divine wrote and was written into the fabric of every act. My respondents liked to repeat a line attributed to Meister Eckhart, "Each creature is a word of God and a book about God." These hopes that something marked as the "divine" moves upon the written page (and moreover, within the written pages that reflect and capture the essence of mystics' lives) resonates with earlier American metaphysical writing practices that verge toward inspirational writing, automatic writing, and mediumship. Cameron's claims about the origins of inspiration place her self-help book in close relation to nineteenth-century writers' fascination with inspiration and divinity, and resonate with ideas that played out in psychological investigations into automatic writing (as "evidence" for the active presence of divine agents, ghostly or spirit presence, or, within the field of psychology, evidence of a "dissociated consciousness").[21]

Cameron's rules for "morning pages," for example, share surprising similarities with Charles Hammond's widely circulated 1852 directions for mediums. Hammond suggests that readers who follow his printed rules will be able to receive messages from the beyond through proper technique. Mediumship can be learned and practiced: it is not a special gift. He writes that to have contact with the dead, one must "sit one hour each day where no noise will attract attention." Calmness and passivity are necessary, for as Hammond writes, the spirit will communicate when it wants to, "without aid." Mediums should not resist or doubt when their hand starts moving, Hammond instructs, because "when mediums resist, nothing reliable can be written." Hammond adds that it is best to meditate on spirits who are "capable of instructing in the knowledge of God," rather than the darker spirits who (presumably) know less about truth. Nonetheless, the emphasis within these rules is clearly for writers to give up attention to their own written pages, to let things "flow," and to not question or resist what comes to the page.[22]

Deceased spirits' messages were not always written, of course, even though written and textualized messages continue to be a part of the practice of twentieth-century Spiritualists and trance channelers.[23] However, Hammond's and others' attention to the passive writer as a medium for the spirits links those who wait for inspiration and those who wait for the spirits in a very similar set of postures and approaches to pen and paper. These postures were also used in laboratory experiments in early psychological experimental labs, and the "planchette," a board on which the arm could rest comfortably, was used in both séances and in scientific laboratories. Psychologists' interests in automatic writing was more focused than that of the psychical writers, for whom automatic writing suggested evidence of extra-personal communication: psychologists instead suggested it presented evidence of "double consciousness," an idea that likewise fell out of favor among mainstream psychologists (although not before a young Gertrude Stein, while still a student at Radcliffe, participated in laboratory experiments and co-authored two academic papers on the phenomenon).[24]

Published in the same year as Stein's first psychology paper, Ralph Waldo Trine's New Thought classic *In Tune with the Infinite* likewise instructs readers that they can become in tune with the divine via writing. To do so, Trine encourages his readers to practice mental discipline and focus solely on the moment at hand. "In order for your higher inspirations to come through . . . you must open your soul, you must open it fully to the Supreme Source of all inspiration," he opines. Criticizing conventional writing that focuses on form, revision, and grammar, he suggests that true inspiration comes from a freedom and an openness. "Be true. Be fearless. Be loyal to the promptings of your own soul. Remember that an author can never write more than he himself is. If he would write more, then he must be more. *He is simply his own amanuensis.*" Yet Trine admits that being one's own amanuensis ultimately means tapping into a larger, extra-individual source. "I had rather be an amanuensis of the Infinite God, as it is my privilege literally to be, than a slave to the formulated rules of any rhetorician, or to the opinions of any critic." The "Breath of God" moves through those who open themselves to these divine powers within, Trine writes. "When you come into the realization of your oneness with the Infinite Life and Power, and open yourself that it might work through you, you will find that you have entered upon an entirely new phase, and that an increasing power will be yours."[25]

Claims to catharsis, to automatic writing, and to tapping into the spirit are all distinct, yet in various twentieth-century texts there is a distinct ambiguity that attends to each. Such ambiguities rest at the core of Jane Revere Burke's 1922 volume *The One Way.* Burke published several volumes of automatic writing in the first decades of the twentieth century, all of which consist of spirit messages from deceased notable men. Burke's book *The One Way* claims to record the spirit-world ruminations of William James, with whom Burke had long "conversations" about the nature of spirit writing and the value of her books. Burke has the great fortune of finding the answers to her questions about automatic writing in her pen: as she tells her readers, she writes questions on the page and then allows James to answer. "Why do I know what the pencil is going to write?" she asked James. The answer came, "You know that the language you and I use is the thought language, and you perceive the thought before the pencil gets it down." Burke continues to dwell on the actual position of the spirit's control, and wonders whether it resides in her body, her pencil, or her mind. She determines that James and the other spirits whom she contacts "think" thoughts to her and that she then translates these unformed words onto the page. "The experience of automatic writing is an absolutely extraordinary one," she writes. "No one who has been through it can question the certainty of a control outside themselves. . . . I feel sure that the contact between the amanuensis and the control can be wholly spiritual, and that though it may be only psychic it is never material."[26]

While the spirits might "think thoughts" and Burke has some ability to choose how to convey them, she nonetheless disavows any authorial role. Instead, she claims for herself the role of medium or channel, and beyond that, claims that it is not James either who is the author of her book. Rather, the "source" of her knowledge is none other than "the one old channel of Jesus Christ." And, had she not encountered the idea of automatic writing (popular given the "particular mood of the world today"), she could have published the book just as she had, "without realizing that it was being done by automatic writing— simply believing that I was inspired."[27] Burke's ambiguous and dialogic depictions of her writing's influence by James (or inspiration, or Jesus Christ) suggests that identifying the "actual" origin and mechanisms of writing are of less interest than her observations that such inspiration is possible. Like Charles Hammond and Ralph Waldo Trine, Jane Revere Burke emphasizes the passivity of writers, and claims authority not through the active work of shaping ideas but rather by letting go, writing (as Trine demands) "from the heart" rather than from convention. Or, as Cameron encourages, writing what comes to mind without thinking it over.[28]

One is unlikely to find much in contemporary writing books that encourages prospective writers to imagine that a dead person or spirit friend dictates the words that appear on a page. Nonetheless "letting go" and refusing to resist continues as the central element and practice to shape inspired writing. Whether one lets go in order to allow the inner voice, one's own divinely inspired creativity, or the divine itself to speak remains ambiguous but, at the same time, generative in these accounts. The emphasis on form contributes to this continued ambiguity, but also reinforces the overall understanding that writing is a primary and active moment of direct experience, even as it might also be a moment of recording or reinterpreting past experience.[29]

Divine inspiration, however, is only one of many writing practices that shapes my respondents' understanding of the relationships between experiences and their (textualized) accounts. As I moved from reading prescriptive literature and learning about journaling practices to talking with and participating in metaphysical worlds in Cambridge, I heard about further complexities of writing and interpretation. Writing creates a record, one that can be consulted and revised. So while Julia Cameron tells her readers to discard their morning pages, my respondents (including Marcy) frequently returned to their morning pages in order reassess and actively reinterpret prior events. In so doing, the tightly organized narratives of experience I encountered in interviews unraveled further.

Interpreting Experience

The open-endedness of mystics' interpretations of mystical experiences is a striking hallmark of their lived practice, and is quite different from the more distinctive and closed meanings that they articulate in the narrative genres used in interviews. In fact, the open possibility, or even expectation, of interpretive uncertainty drives and galvanizes mystics' interests in their stories, and is evident within (and expressed in) their attention to the ways that new experiences, events, and "insights" change not only the meaning of past events but, at times, even their status as religious experiences altogether. Thus Eric continued to return to his experience on the bus. In the process Eric considered numerous events and "connections" that were at least potentially related to his bus experience. At some point later on he told me, *"I was ready to start considering, 'Maybe I'm [Hildegard's] reincarnation.' Enough things were resonant that it was possible—her German connection too, and just so many things felt really profound and really emotional and really right. And I wasn't feeling egotistical to say that I could be her reincarnation, I just [had a] feeling that there is something to be acknowledged there."* A variety of things from his past and several similarities in his biography and Hildegard's suggested to Eric that *"this was the way to go, and so I did quit my job, and for the next nine months just explored this idea: I could be the reincarnation of Hildegard, and if Hildegard, who or what else could I find in my unconscious? And then I did go over the edge a bit, and started conjecturing, I started getting into the ego of it, and conjecturing I might be other famous people. But there was a sense of, 'I'm just sort of experimenting and seeing where it goes,' and it didn't particularly go anywhere. . . . Anyway, sort of to wrap that up, that—following all these synchronicities and ideas, and sort of haunting, dragging myself through my past and going around MIT and all of the places I had been, and revisiting important moments of my life and reconsidering what it might mean in light of sort of this new spiritual awakening, I—ended up coming here to the Swedenborg Chapel."* As he centered back to Cambridge he also met a Harvard Divinity School student who told him that she believed she was the reincarnation of another famous mystic. His chance conversation with this student appeared to act as something of a corrective to this particular conjecture and the hubris that it suggested. Talking with her *"started easing me off [the idea of] literally being Hildegard, and started easing me into [learning about] some of the identities around her."* He grinned as he spoke, saying, *"There was this Elizabeth Chernaux, who was a Hildegard wannabe, in her lifetime, who was a little overly ambitious—and would proclaim things that were a little embarrassing and not true. And I started seeing, maybe I could be her, I've acted like her."*

I met Eric on a number of occasions through the following two years. While his experience on the bus was a central one, he was constantly revising what it meant and, in the process, reshaping the arc of the narrative itself. Eric was in fact the first one to call this to my attention. He had started to take a more active interest in finding out about my spiritual life after I attended the mystical experience group several times, where I had shared some of my dreams. Eric wanted to know more about my dream life. I answered that I frequently remembered my dreams, and he asked if I ever wrote them down. I could tell from the question that he was going to suggest that I do so, and so I answered negatively and added, *"I think of dreams as being very . . . slippery. [I think that writing] them down changes them. If they're just living in my head, then to write them down puts more weight on them. Because the writing of the dream is a different thing than the dream itself."*

"Well you might—" Eric started, but I could hear what he was going to say, and I was all of a sudden worried that he might have been offended, so I added, not quite believing it, *"I'm not saying that one way is better than the other, but they are different things—"*

He didn't let me finish. *"You have to work out the writing style that works for you. Like if you start writing them down, you might go through kind of a painful period. I've gotten good at comfortably writing them down and flowing with the interpreting a bit, and then letting it be part of my day, and it works out more and I make notes as I go along. I like to document a lot. Yeah, you could be expressing the pain of the discomfort of the first phase of, if you were to incorporate writing them down in to your routine."* Eric diagnosed my resistance as not wanting to confront the "pain" in my dreams, a suggestion that I bristled at and that effectively ended our conversation that evening. Eric suggested that I take a look at a paper he had written about dreams.

When I read the paper later on I realized that I had been quite mistaken about Eric. He was quite aware that an account could not capture the dream itself. He did not believe that he was channeling a divine transcript when he wrote. Rather, writing was a site of struggling over a dream's interpretation, and that struggle could ultimately lead to its correct and proper meaning. Drawing on Emanuel Swedenborg as a model of how to document one's own journey to "self-discovery and self-purification," Eric put great emphasis on how Swedenborg had "struggled with dreams' meanings, *in order to reveal*" them.

Eric was similarly explicit about how new experiences forced him to reconsider past experiences' meanings. This process involved remembering or recalling events that until that time had appeared inconsequential. Mystics like Eric often seemed resolved to let the "final" interpretation stand somewhere in the distant future: as such, their experiences remained open for interpretation and even for the possibility that a previous "experience" might be determined in the future to be not an experience at all. While at any given moment a narrative of synchronicity took on the role of an authoritative if provisional interpretation, the practice of inscription and self-making via writing was on the whole more open ended than closed. Mystics sought the experience yet-to-come, which held the possibility of resolving unsolved mysteries or creatively unsettling other previous interpretations. Daily life was thus always possibly revelatory.[30]

Interpretation, Serendipity, and Synchronicity

"Synchronicity" is as much practice as theory. While it is important to note the continued resonance of concepts of correspondence, coincidence, and synchronicity within the expansive spaces of American metaphysical theologies both past and present, it is equally interesting to consider the specific practices of observation, interpretation, and analysis that give rise to meaningful coincidence. As the spirits counseled Eric that he was not listening, spiritualist minister and writer Elizabeth Owen counsels her readers to pay attention to the acts of the divine around them. "Pay attention to synchronistic events. There is no such thing as a coincidence. When we believe in coincidence, we are placing a limit on the capacity of God to manifest what we need."[31] Another spiritual writer avers, "Synchronicity . . . brings into focus our invisible connections to the Big Design . . . and to one another. I have shared in my other books many synchronistic events that were threaded throughout my life. Each synchronistic encounter anchored me to something within myself, and to something greater than myself. These events allowed me to experience the bigger picture—the web of life of which we are all a part."[32]

Metaphysical authors and my respondents claim that synchronous events are self-evident and merely need to be noted or attended to. Yet they also note that they participate within a number of practices that make it easier to detect such connections. In many cases, these practices involve recording daily events: if synchronicity is easy to overlook but always present, then what is required is a close investigation of everyday interactions. Unlike the "flow writing" of Julia Cameron and others, where experience takes place within the act of putting pencil to paper, in metaphysical diary keeping mystics record minor events and daily minutiae with a view to preserving them for the future. In the process, they uncover connections that they would have "otherwise missed." The process, they say, reveals divine presence. Given the emphasis placed on the possibility that any (or every) event can be potentially meaningful, and the simultaneous understanding that an event's meaning is articulated in a relation between it and another event, all recorded events become meaningful through their own *deferral* of significance. All moments can be meaningful, but the meaning of any event is illuminated as it is understood in relation to another event, in the past or in the future.

This divine that takes shape within these practices is likewise much more immanent than "transcendent," as when inspirational writer Squire Rushnell encourages his readers to look for the presence of the divine in everything. He suggests that once we start looking, "God winks" become apparent everywhere: he likewise encourages readers to rethink past events, mining them for signs of God that they have overlooked in the busyness of daily events. "Take the time, before you start to write, to examine your life. Reflect on each question, and then let your thoughts flow." Soon, Rushnell suggests, the writer will be able to "just let your memory, not your rational mind, do the writing. You'll be surprised at what will emerge."[33] Owen also encourages writing as a way to find God's presence: as events are written down, God's presence becomes evident. "[S]ometimes a thought will pop into our minds, the name of a tune, a sound, or we may see a symbol," Owen says. "This may or may not be one of your spirit teachers. . . . Jot down your experiences during meditation in your journal. This way, in a few days you will be able to refer back to a particular question and the answer you received. . . . We can get carried away by interpreting everything . . . as a message from the spirit world. . . . While everything happens for a reason, the 'message' you thought you received may also be a figment of your imagination. . . . That is why recording experiences in your journal is so important. Your journal will tell you how accurate you are, how you are advancing, and when your imagination is getting the better of you."[34]

The world becomes profoundly connected as metaphysicals devote more time to inscribing daily events and seeking the meaning that connects them. For example, John told me that he had been thinking of buying a house, and recently had been shown the house that he "knew" he should buy. He knew this because he had dreamt about that very house a year earlier, before he had been considering such a purchase. *"I'd like to find the spot in my journal, but I know that I had a dream last year about exactly that house. I remember waking up from that dream and thinking, 'That was so realistic! But—I don't want to own a split level ranch in the woods, especially* not *one with an anchor in the front yard. That's weird, I don't think that's ever going to happen.' But—it did. And it's a really nice spot."* John had not found the place in his journal where he had recorded his dream: in this event at least the journal was not an actual point of reference, but a talisman of a memory that could now be joined to his decision about the house. John was comfortable with this understanding of his dream as an oracle without consulting or "proving" his previous dream; likewise, he was not upset that the house did not actually have an anchor in the front yard. Rather, the anchor in the dream signaled the security he would find there. *"It is really going to ground everything for me. . . . The things I need to do are going to happen there."*

John moved to his new house and I did not see him as frequently, but I bumped into him one evening at the Cambridge Center for Adult Education, where he was talking animatedly with a few acquaintances. I waved and he motioned me over and asked if I remembered his house dream. Without waiting for a reply, he told me that a construction crew had uncovered an old ship's anchor in his front yard just that week. "It blew me away," John said, chuckling.

The presence of a real anchor did not suggest to John that his previous (symbolic) interpretation had been wrong. The house was now even more an anchor, but this time with a physical manifestation of that symbol taking center place on his front lawn. John and many others were extremely comfortable with the slippage and changing articulation of where "coincidences" and synchronicities rested, and also somewhat circumspect about their role in shaping these coincidental experiences. Metaphysicals presumed that there were many "anchors" to uncover. At the same time, the notion that "everything" was a meaningful coincident caused some to pause. I met Cathy a few days later at an Indian restaurant, and our discussion turned to the anchor when I noted the prominent image of Ganesh (the Hindu deity with an elephant's head) on the wall above Cathy's head.

"Did you know I have a little elephant on my mantle piece with his trunk up?" Cathy asked as she turned around to get a better look at the Ganesh behind her.

"Is it a Ganesh?"

"It could be," she said, shrugging. "I also have an elephant pillow— it's Ganesh—courtesy of TJ Maxx. I wanted something that would bring some Asian influence into my living room."

I laughed. "What is Ganesh doing in TJ Maxx?"

"I don't know!—Maybe bringing things together for the greater enlightenment?" Now we were both laughing. Cathy continued, "But seriously—I have dreams about a baby elephant. One time, the elephant had me in its trunk, and was trying to keep me from going where I wanted to go. And another time, I was playing with the baby elephant, I was, playing hide and seek, and I was hiding behind a tree and then I became, became the essence of the tree. And this elephant came crashing through the jungle and I jumped out from behind the tree and said, 'Surprise!' I don't know who it is. I thought for a while maybe it was my husband Richard. I wrote a whole bunch of e-mails to John about the dreams, and at the end of them he wrote, 'Well, I better go get some peanuts.'—I don't know why he thought it was him. But that's it. How do you decide when something is meaningful? Or if it is random? That's something that drives me nuts about John. For him, *everything* is deeply meaningful. I accept much more than he does that there is an element of randomness or choice that is functioning. Where every little hair means something? I am not comfortable with that."

Remembering John's dream, I queried, "So, you don't buy the anchor thing?"

"No. I do buy it. That is pretty cool, OK? But not *every* person you run into is a destiny waiting to happen. Not *everybody* you see on the subway has a message especially for you."

"So how do you know?" I wondered out loud.

"I don't know," Cathy answered. "See, thinking about these things brings up more questions than there are answers, and even though one way is to say everything has significance, well—I would be too busy sifting through the minutiae of my life!"

We both took a bite of our curries, reflecting, and then Cathy continued, "But the questions keep coming. It's like shopping. Shopping is minutiae, but for some people it is very important . . . so one person's irrelevance is another's—"

I interjected, "But about coincidence, what if . . . ?"

Cathy cut me off. "Take the day that I went to the fair," she said, recounting a terrible day we had already discussed. She had taken her children to a harvest fair in a nearby town. One child got sick and when they returned to their car, Cathy noticed that it had a flat. Then she discovered that her AAA membership had expired. In frustration she finally called her husband at work to pick them up, and resigned herself to waiting for an hour with a sick child in the hot parking lot. She turned on the A/C and the car radio, and the next song that came on was her favorite "spiritual" song. She immediately felt at peace. She asked me: "Was that meaningful, or was that random? It was really probably random, but it was also *really great*. So perhaps it was the universe telling me it was going to be OK. That's how I took it that day. Now, when I have a dream of a baby elephant, I could look into its eyes with the big lashes and think it was somebody specific. And I could dream about it another night and believe it's someone else. Maybe it's just a theme, not a specific person—maybe with its trunk, maybe it's a metaphor for channeling, not a person. Or, maybe it is just a dream about baby elephants." Cathy was resistant to settling on a single meaning; each might be useful or help her understand some element of her life. "Experience" was not just something that people *had,* but that as Eric, Cathy, and others averred, something that they made again and again. Experiences and their interpretations, their texts and their vital energies shaped and were shaped in various practices that embedded Cambridge's mystics in worlds where everything was, or could be, about direct experience.

Conclusion

In turning to how Cambridge's mystics speak, write, read, and interpret their own (and others') experiences in other settings, we encounter a number of other practices through which religious experiences become things that people can talk about, and that they can interpret and ponder. These practices unsettle any interpretation that suggests that mystical experiential practices depend on *claims* to direct experiences. Even though such claims continue to surface in contexts where mystics imagine or detect the presence of counterarguments, the narratives that result are but one of a number of heterogeneous interpretive practices. As we have seen in this chapter, metaphysical practitioners participate in a range of practices that challenge strict distinctions between religious experiences and accounts that emerge in the protective narratives I discussed in the first half of this chapter.

Once we acknowledge the changing demands and changing articulation of an authentic or authoritative narrative within a broader range of social contexts and spiritual practices, "religious experience" accounts take on a different position within our interpretation of American spiritual expression. Drawing on Katz and others, we can observe that Cambridge's mystics are distinctively religious or spiritual not because they emphasize direct experiences but because of their participation in historically and culturally distinctive practices.

Mystics did not venerate past experiences in ways that close them to interpretation, but rather used them as sources that marked their shifting positions within worlds where the "infinite" and the "divine" are always unfolding, in immanent events throughout daily life. The interpretive practices that circulate in these communities give shape to imaginative worlds where "something else [is] possible . . . [where] while we see what did happen, we also see the image of what else could have happened."[35] Contemporary metaphysical experiences are not mere "images" of the past. They are unfinished, living events and in that respect continue to speak and change.

––––––

Toward the end of my interview with Tina I realized that she hadn't really identified the serpent. Curiosity getting the better of me, I hesitantly asked, "*So, the serpent—what was it? Any thoughts on that?*"

"*Well, I've certainly had thoughts on that!*" she laughed. "*I had already heard of Kundalini, which is the serpent coiled at the base of the spine, but for me it was like many of these things, 'Oh, well that's a metaphor for something, I know nothing direct about that.' Part of this experience of this direct spiritual reality is that you get to see that it's real. And for me it was an experience [where I could say to myself], 'Oh, this is what, this is why they call Kundalini the serpent.' And–"*

Tina paused briefly, and ended not with answers but with questions of her own. *"I don't know. Is it the spirit of this energy, is it the human way that we choose to interpret it, is it the only way? Is it our own mental construct for the experience of energy moving in our body, or is it some spirit that is larger than our own mental construct? It's kind of the old question with any religion. You know, is Christ a separate being from us, or separate from our myth, or is it something there that comes into us, or is it us, you know? Or is it our imagination?"*

There was another pause before she added, *"And where do you make that distinction? I don't know—I don't know."*

Tina's response gestured to the open, creative dynamics in which personal experiences formed the texts of these experiential worlds. Mystical texts do not (always) hark back to a claim to an original meaning ready to be interpreted and reiterated but rather build on practices in which meaning irrupts in the moment of retelling, thus capturing speaker and listener, text and interpretation, experiencer and divine in a new moment filled with transformative power.

THREE

Tuning the Body

To be a body, is to be tied to a certain world . . . our body is not primarily in space: it is of it.[1]

If it be true that the departed spirits exist, only we cannot see them, it is quite probable that there may be hundreds and millions of them about us we can neither see, feel, nor touch. We may be continually passing and repassing through their bodies, and they do not see or feel us.[2]

Experience does not just happen. Cambridge's spiritual practitioners vigorously pursue, cultivate, and develop experience with the divine energy sources that they believe underlie prior experiences and all of life. While mystics would speak about yearning for closer and more vibrant contact with the divine and revel in interpretive practices that shape and reshape their understanding of various experiences and coincidences, their bodily practices and disciplines pointed toward another set of understandings of possibility for constant contact and engagement with the divine and its energetic powers. Mystics' practices focus great attention on the body, and in particular on maintaining proper connection to the universe's divine sources of energy. In so doing, they come to experience their bodies and selves as primarily "energetic." Rather than engage their flesh and blood bodies as the primary site of religious identity, metaphysicals favored language and imagery that highlighted their energetic bodies, manifested by particles of energy. *"We are just bits of energy, moving all the time,"* Crystal reminded me repeatedly. Hans echoed: *"We are all like the energies around us, just like the dust in the air."* He continued, *"You know that usually you don't see it, but when a ray shines on [it], suddenly you see it. I alter my consciousness through drumming—I use drumming [but you could use other techniques]—and I am able to see the energy. What we see in normal life is also forms of energy, that are dense enough for us to see and touch."*

The energetic, particulate bodies to which Hans and Crystal refer are no mere metaphors. They are not soul or spirit in some indeterminate sense, but rather take form and follow particular rules and laws. Nothing made this clearer than the testimony of those who had "gone out of body." Doug described the moment he realized that he was primarily an astral rather than physical entity. Wandering around the room in an out-of-body state, he said, *"I could actually hear the music change. It felt like, I could hear it 20 feet in front of me and then at some point it was on my side, and then at some point it was behind me. Which was great, I thought in retrospect. It totally makes sense. If I was perfectly stationary and I was hearing from my physical ears, the sound, the music would have stayed the same. My radio wasn't moving. So what that means is that I was moving. And that I was actually hearing that music from my spirit body and not my physical body. Because if the music is moving around, and now the music is behind me, that means I was actually hearing it from me. In fact, [during] the first really lucid, really good OBE that I had, this question kind of popped into my head: where am I? And you'd say—what is the answer to that?"*

I answered that I didn't know.

"The answer is always this: 'I am here.' OK? So where am I, I am here. And here is? . . . Well, the conclusion is that I am not there, in my physical body over there, but I am here. So all that is me, and my consciousness and my awareness and my thoughts and everything is here. That was what first made it really clear as to what I am and to where I am. I'm really this spirit body encased in this physical body. It really gave me a sense of this physical body just being this temporary thing. And that, when that passes, I'm still around, because I'm here. Yeah. And I had all my thoughts and all my everything. I was just, in this other [nonphysical] form. Which was very interesting. There were, there were all sorts of interesting experiments and things that I did with the astral body, which is like looking at my arm. That is one of the things that I did see during that first experiment, the first time it happened I was a little bit nervous, but I remember thinking well I know there is no reason to be nervous, it's OK, just—at first I was lying on the couch here, just lying down, and my arms are crossed like that but I had my astral arms out like this. And I was looking at my spirit arms, and they were translucent, they looked like lucite, and you could see the outlines because the light would bend a little bit, you could tell that there was kind of like a glassy type. . . . And I

kind of had this translucent outline of my physical body, and really that's the way it works, actually. Your astral body takes the default shape of your physical body. If you don't think about anything, that's its default shape. Like, it's whatever you are now. If you would go out of your body right now you would look, you would be the same shape and form as you are right now. But you can change that, and those are experiments I have done as well, too. Where, if you've ever seen the cartoon Plastic Man, that's what it's like. So I would squash my head like this, or stretch things out, extend my arms to the wall there. Um, it's—it's very much will. It's directed by what your intentions are, what you want. But—the spirit body is unbelievably flexible and resilient and robust, and you can just do whatever you want."

Few spiritual practitioners in Cambridge regularly travel out of body. Yet most share Doug's understanding that they have two bodies, one energetic and one physical, one lasting and one temporary. The energetic body has a concrete existence, and while it is more flexible than one might suspect, it nonetheless continues through time and retains its own kinds of knowledge, and (as we will see in the following chapters) has its own sort of bodily memory. The nonmaterial body of "particles" is a source of great fascination, as metaphysicals sought to understand how the particulate self might become visible through various practices and in other unexpected exoteric ways.

Metaphysicals' understandings of their energetic bodies drew them to a focus on various bodily disciplines: Cambridge metaphysicals carried on the robust harmonial tradition through which the empowerment of the energetic body became possible through cultivating a physical body that was open and strong. Various bodily practices allowed practitioners to see their energetic bodies and maximize their powers. The possibilities of liberation and freedom that emerged in encountering one's true (energetic) body and self was nonetheless not without its own hazards or concerns.

In Cambridge, metaphysicals speak less of "mind" and "body" than of two kinds of bodies, one physical and material, the other energetic. This suggests a hierarchy of bodies, where one is more free, more powerful, and more pure or true to one's own self. The energetic body is hidden, but seeing it means seeing the true person: the physical body is necessary, but as a tool or a sign rather than a space of its own authentic encounter. This chapter considers what it means for metaphysicals to live within, and discover truth about themselves, through two bodies. As they pursue these truths and their authentic connections, spiritual practitioners' two bodies intertwine: the invisible sometimes reveals itself in the visible, or the visible body can be trained to reveal the invisible. Cambridge practitioners depend on their fleshy bodies to tune, channel, or conduct energy properly. They understand that their physical bodies can impede or channel divine energies, and that their tuned bodies are implements of great power, allowing metaphysicals to tap into the energetic divine at will. The physical and fleshy body can be a "container," but it is also a channel, conduit, or "switch." Meditation, yoga, Reiki, acupuncture, and a variety of other activities provided ways to find and maintain physical bodies that were open, aligned, or relaxed, and therein properly attuned to the energies that simultaneously coursed through them and constituted them.[3]

These bodily practices likewise suggest a different set of questions about the value of direct experiences and peak mystical events. Within the world of bodily control, peak experiences are less valued than a life of constant, controlled connection. Lucy suggested as much when she told me this anecdote. *"There's some guy practicing meditation, and he goes to his guru and he says, 'Oh I have these incredible visions—isn't this wonderful?' And the guru says, 'Don't worry, they'll go away.'"* Lucy told me that as her yoga teaching style matured, it shifted away from the trancelike states she once regularly experienced toward more practical matters of position and concentration. And while she could still *"occasionally teach a poetic class, I can't do that every time. I feel responsible to people's bodies."* Indeed, proper bodily comportment opened up the path to boundless success that would be evident not through visions and peak experiences but through a life organized by the same powers, controlled by rigorous discipline and intention. Through various bodily practices, and indeed through constant attention to the physical body itself, spiritual practitioners seek not a momentary shock but rather a constant, firm connection to the currents that course through them.[4] The emphasis on control (and the potential dangers of uncontrolled energy) caused my respondents in turn to harbor some ambivalence toward their own mystical experiences. Peak experiences, particularly those that take shape early on in their personal narratives, indicate a life out of order, a lack of understanding of the powers of divine energies, or the divine reaching in through a life where one is "not listening" to reveal a higher, more important purpose.

───────

Metaphysicals' practices produce the claims that constant contact with the divine is not only possible but simple. Instructors and guidebooks incessantly encourage novices to put aside the view that alignment is difficult to attain. The greatest barrier to its attainment is one's own doubt and the "society" that expects immediate results and goals. They state in contrast that only openness is necessary to recovering one's natural relations with one's body and divine energy. Finding a way to this body is an issue of subtraction rather than addition. As David, a yoga instructor told me, yoga is particularly suited to this task, as it is a practice that tells people to *"let go of the past—and I don't mean that in some kind of disembodied memory sense, or mental representations. I mean, [let go of] the past as it lives in the present and creates it. Our reactions to things. They act as a veil between us and what is actually happening. A lot of our likes and dislikes are reflexive and limiting. We feel like a self when we have those likes and dislikes honored, we feel happy or successful. And it's totally wrong. What meditation and yoga does is say that the present is happiness now."* Letting go of the past, he furthermore remarked, is a "natural" process that meditation and yoga proffer. *"This natural process of cessation starts happening, you start to clear, you begin to recognize that knowing is a stand-alone clear thing, like clear, still water. . . . When students come to my class, we present them with an opportunity. We say, put your goals aside. Be. Find out who you really are right now."*

Claims that one can come to such embodied knowledge and power through forgetting and literally shedding (bad) routines and habits and emerging into one's "birthright" of a natural body resonates strongly with well-known tropes in twentieth-century American middle-class cultures.[5] Throughout the twentieth century Americans have embraced the view that American society and culture creates nervous conditions and pent-up energies that result in physical illness and a limitation of the self's potentials. Not one of my respondents mentioned what I thought to be a central irony of relaxation, namely that it requires work, discipline, and vigilance. Nor did my respondents wonder in the slightest that the bodily practices that made natural selves also shaped these bodies for success within the social and cultural worlds that they frequently decried as broken and egoistical systems. Perhaps this should be expected, given that there was, at the end of the day, nothing more intimate or more powerful than gaining the bodily knowledge that came through the experience of "seeing" or feeling one's energetic body, or of commingling with other energetic selves. As metaphysicals cultivated natural bodies they shed not only the histories of their own specific selves, but likewise interest in exploring the lineage of bodily disciplines that shaped their new experiential possibilities.

Visible and Invisible Bodies

Discussing the body in metaphysical terms means, at the outset, coming to terms with two or more bodies, and the ways that most metaphysical body practices are intent in allowing metaphysicals to both sense these bodies and bring them into proper alignment with divine energies. The energetic body, or astral body (or subtle body), is "energetic," and as my respondents told me frequently, is a scientific reality, subject to the laws and rules of energy (as well as to some esoteric rules not yet proven by science) just as they understand the physical body to be always the same, subject to the same rules, proceeding with the same functions and capacities. As my respondents likewise expressed, the various esoteric practices that move and shape energy in the body are all at core engaging and training the same underlying reality, and are (in many respects) interchangeable. From within the world of contemporary spirituality, a person's choices to practice various bodily or ritual activities serially or multiply is not a sign of dabbling but, rather, an indication of their ability to identify the perennial and "scientific" realities that underpin everything from therapeutic touch to insight meditation.

Spiritual practitioners in the United States throughout the twentieth century have drawn liberally and imaginatively on South Asian languages of "chakras" to conceptualize and experience the energetic body. More so than other systems (for example, the "meridians" in Chinese religious traditions and the evocation of "qi," or energy), the "chakra system" and "prana" (breath, or vitality, or energy) gives shape to the energetic body and explains its relation to both the physical body and the energetic universe. Chakras were a familiar idiom through which metaphysicals talked in various contexts, not only about their energetic selves but likewise their physical health and their successes and failures at work and in relationships. Talk is not all there is, however, as ideas about the chakra body were represented in metaphysicals' clothing (and sometimes home décor) choices. (Turquoise, depicting the "communication" chakra at the throat, was particularly popular, as was lavender, which signifies wisdom.) Mystics give gifts with chakra significance, including flowers and other small tokens. Crystal handed out green stone amulets as party favors and told us they would "boost our heart chakras" if we wore them at the proper place around our necks. They sometimes commented darkly that people who were prone to wearing dark colors (such as the teenaged goths and neo-punks who were a constant fixture in Harvard Square) were unaware of the energetic imbalances amplified by their black attire.

More important, chakras were central components of many of the ritual and meditation sessions in various contexts in my fieldwork. Chakra meditations were possibly the most frequently employed rituals in Cambridge's metaphysical communities, with the exception of group chanting of "om." Through these rituals, metaphysicals learned about their astral bodies' shape and began to find ways to detect their meaning and health. Such was the case at the mystical discussion group, where Eric always led a chakra meditation. After lighting candles at the middle of our circle and turning off the lights, he instructed us to find a comfortable sitting position, to breathe deeply, and to close our eyes. Eric then began by directing our attention to a part of our body where a chakra resided. He frequently began with the chakra at the base of the spine and then moved up or down the chakra positions on the spinal column, always ending with the "crown chakra." Depending on the occasion, Eric suggested that we view our chakras as glass globes filled with light, blooming flowers, spinning tops, or glowing embers. We sat in a circle, some breathing deeply and noisily, others often on the verge of sleep. In a quiet tone Eric instructed us to "check in" with a chakra and observe it, eyes closed. He told us to take deep but natural breaths, and to notice how our breathing "charged" the chakra's color and intensity. Most printed chakra meditation instructions suggest meditating from the "lower" to the "higher" chakras, ending with the crown chakra; Eric, often more playful than doctrinaire, would often begin with the heart chakra, and then move down to the base before moving into the "higher" chakras, always ending with the crown chakra and linking us up to the energy sources that "flowed into us."

Through participating in these chakra visualizations, by chanting each chakra's "tone" in a yoga class, or participating in a Reiki healing session where the healer places his or her hands over specific chakra points, metaphysicals learn to sense and see the organization of the energetic body. Each chakra point is an energetic center that spins or vibrates; they present energetic evidence for spiritual (and by extension physical) well-being. The seven chakras are aligned along the spinal cord, each corresponding to a particular color as well as particular glands and organs in the physical body that it is supposed to control. The seven chakras have additional associations. For example, the chakra or energetic body is hierarchically arranged into lower, middle, and higher chakras that correspond to spiritual personality types. Together, the chakras articulate the invisible body that is tied directly to the universal, divine energy sources of the universe.

These practices teach metaphysicals not only *what* they might visualize but also *how* to visualize it. The meditating subject is relaxed, calm, focused on the interior, and breathing deeply but "normally." The perfectly controlled, balanced body allows the energetic body to become manifest, or so it seems. People learned to "see" and "sense" their invisible bodies through their physical bodies, as when David told his yoga students that it would be difficult but ultimately possible to feel their true form by paying attention. He described his teaching process to me as follows, *"I tell them, 'OK, now feel your feet.' [When] somebody glances down at their feet, I say, 'Don't use your eyes. Please be careful about how you use your eyes. Feel from inside.' And so they stretch. And I say, 'No, feel.' Or they move in stereotypical ways that are shaded by the past—the body has conditioned ways of moving. And I say, 'Now break that up, and put your head in a new place, where all the usual rules fall away. . . . It's very liberating, but at the time people complain about it, so I don't talk philosophy to them, I just say, 'Put your head back there, now feel it there. Feel the breath when it goes in and out. Now is that the same thing? So stay with what's new.' I'm a broken record. I'm like a deranged parent—'watch your breath watch your breath, feel the body'—I say the same kind of things over and over, but I try to be creative about it."*

David said that students are impatient when he starts talking about the "philosophy behind it," so he usually dispenses with that in his classes. But, as he also told me, it was possible to "feel" this body without knowing exactly how. The experience of the energetic body was knowledge of itself. At some level, it had to be experienced to be known. Thus metaphysicals and mystics in Cambridge understand that they come to know their energetic bodies through practice. These practices also reshape practitioners' experience with their physical bodies, as they are encouraged to treat them as containers or tools that can either block or facilitate proper energetic flow. In asking students to feel their bodies (but not with their hands), to observe their bodies (but not with their eyes), to register thoughts that "passed through" the mind (but not seize on any of them), teachers directed students to turn away from the ocular, sensate, and cognitive, and opened up ways to find another, more constant and powerful location of alignment.

What my respondents know about the chakras comes from a variety of sources, popularized books, and their own ongoing practices in various settings. When asked, most of my respondents would state that the term came from "the East" or "India." Few knew much about classical philosophies of chakras, and few seemed to care too much, given their view that chakras was only one of a number of ways to describe a more universal reality. This understanding, and much of what is contained in the popularized self-help and new age books about the chakras, can be traced to theosophist Charles Leadbeater's handsome volume, *The Chakras*. Leadbeater's book is the "virtual first word" in the American discourse.[6] The text moves back and forth between Leadbeater's own clairvoyant experiments and the "truths" he reads in Indian texts. He employs a perennial mode of reading Sanskrit, where the truths of the ancient texts are proved by his own experiences and experiments. Leadbeater presents a hopeful defense of his method, stating that he is merely exploring the scientific truths of the esoteric universe, which science will some day soon come to accept. "Students of medicine are now familiar with [the physical body's] bewildering complexities, and have at least a general idea of the way in which its amazingly intricate machine works naturally," he writes, suggesting that scientists will soon come to approach and understand astral matter with the same rigor.[7] Until that day comes, however, Leadbeater generously provides color plates and figures of the chakra system; their interrelations; the color, spin, and tone of each; and their position in relation to the physical body's various networks and systems. The book provides evidence of an astral body that is shaped by proliferating relations between various sources of energy, the physical body's organs, glands, nervous and respiratory systems; colors, "vibrations," and energies; stages or levels of esoteric astral "worlds" or "planes"; and on and on. It is, in short, a story of the esoteric universe written through the astral and physical body.[8]

Leadbeater's volume presumes that common people will not be interested in their energetic body, and that very few will gain the ability to clairvoyantly experience it. Its invisibility to all but the select few indeed seems to be part of its appeal. And while Leadbeater suggests that science will one day present irrefutable evidence of the auras and teach us even more about their laws and rules, until that point the ability to see the chakras will remain the gift of those who are spiritually progressed and aware enough to seek their knowledge. This tantalizing claim that only the most energetically and spiritually advanced selves could "see" the energetic bodies as they truly are surfaced from time to time in my respondents' discussions. But taking such a perspective ran counter to other aspects of metaphysical bodily practices, which claimed that studied attention would return any person to their "true" and aligned connection with their energetic sources, and thereby focused on the techniques rather than the gifts of seeing the invisible.

The democratization of metaphysical bodily techniques have been abetted by a rash of metaphysical "research" and writing that reinterprets the chakras and their experiential aspects with a focus on the techniques and practices through which one can observe one's chakras for oneself.[9] Mystical practitioners frequently mention to me that "scientists" have indeed "recognized" the body's electromagnetism, and pointed furthermore to a variety of technologies that they understood to provide evidence of the astral body. Kirlian photography, a type of photograph that creates a colored halo around the photograph's subject as proof of the energetic body's existence, was one such technological innovation. As Helen, the "auric photographer" I met at the Boston Whole Health Expo, explained, there was nothing supernatural about the auras that appeared in her photographs. An aura appeared, no matter who put their hand on the electric plates. Even plants had auras, she said, showing me photographs of flowers and leaves. When I asked her why different people had different colored auras, she said that some might be expressing their dominant chakra, or it might reveal a part of the astral body (or physical body) that was in need of balance or healing. (She added that while the photograph would reveal the aura immediately, it had taken her several years to learn how to diagnose physical and spiritual ailments from these photographs.)

Mystics most frequently used the chakra meditations and other practices to diagnose local problems and concerns rather than focus on their friends' negative or weak auric fields. For example, one evening Eric prompted Marcy to speak at the discussion group. She shook her head and apologized, "I'm sorry, I don't have an experience to share with you tonight." "That's OK," a few people murmured, but then Marcy gave a start and said, "I did have a dream last week. It was a dark dream and it disturbed me. I just remembered it. I was in some quicksand, and there was death there, present. But I pulled myself out of the sand I was in, and stepped back up onto the sidewalk. So, it was a terrifying dream even though it was eventually triumphant."

Usually, the person who told the story then offered an interpretation, but instead Marcy told us about what she was currently worried about. "A few of you know this already. I've been trying to make it as a yoga teacher, and I think this is what I am supposed to be doing. But I am tired of the chronic uncertainty. It's making me sick—affecting me physically. I came in here tonight with an incredibly stiff neck. And, when I am sick, I can't teach, and when I can't teach . . . " She trailed off before continuing, "So I am looking for guidance about what I should be doing. Is this what I should be doing? Maybe I should get a job that gives me some certainty. But should that be working 20 hours a week at Starbucks so I can get health benefits, or should I go back to advertising in corporate America? I know I'm very good at that, but it wasn't very satisfying."

Faye provided a pointed interpretation. "You said that your neck is hurting, and you know that your neck is your fifth chakra. That's the area of speaking and communicating. Maybe your body is telling you something about what is blocked right now."

"I hadn't thought of that, that's interesting—you know I've been thinking about getting into some writing again," Marcy said.

Faye continued, "Yes, if you have neck problems, you need some kind of energy release. If you don't have health insurance and you're an energy worker, maybe you can work out some kind of exchange— I've had an exchange with a chiropractor for the last fifteen years, and it has worked very well." Others offered their opinions as well, some focusing on interpreting her dream, but most turning back to the problem with the "fifth chakra."[10]

Tuning the Body

Doug frequently told others in his circles about his desires to use his spiritual experimentation and knowledge for the greater good. He was a great fan of Buckminster Fuller and other utopians, and saw no problem linking business and spirituality. Indeed, he believed that the time had almost come for the emergence of a new kind of businessperson, what he called a *"spiritual venture capitalist. I think that there is actually a lot of money to be made. If I could find enough people, I mean we could totally revolutionize the telecommunications industry!"*

I asked Doug to give me an example of the kind of thing he would like to develop. *"Take your cell phone,"* he said. *"It doesn't work when you go into a cave or a tunnel, or underwater—but it will work anywhere and everywhere with these other kinds of technologies. . . . In a sense there's a whole realm of interesting devices you could build that [link] nonphysical to physical. It's like a switch. And that's what we are, right now. We are the ultimate switch, because we are both not physical and physical at the same time. And there is this interface that somehow bridges the two together, and so it does work, we're living proof that the switch can exist like that. I don't know quite what the switch would be like, but we're kind of proof that it can be done. The basic idea is, you could build real interesting devices that bridge the gap and send information or whatever. You could use it as a mechanism for communicating with the spirits or people who have passed on."*

"Imagine ten years from now—I call this thing Spiritnet, OK? It's an idea I had. It's incredible, where you can literally e-mail your grandmother who has passed. You can literally—you can think of packets that go through this switch and go out there, and she has her computer or whatever out there, that can receive your e-mail and she can read your message. That is actually not hard, it is easier for them to pick up on what you're thinking—"

"You mean, it's harder to get it back?" I asked.

"Yeah. What is more interesting is that she then sends you a message, and it would all be encrypted and you would be the only one who would have the password so it couldn't be faked. You type in your little key to decrypt it, and you could read the message that your grandmother has for you."

One stumbling block in Doug's plan was that the "ultimate" link between the astral and the physical already existed. As he understood it and experienced it, the human body was the natural switch. I mused aloud: if people already had the technology in hand, why would they pay? Why would anyone pay for a machine when they could do it themselves? Doug laughed and answered, *"Here's the reason why. We live in a technology worshipping society. And we're all sort of worshipping it, and that is where all the economic activity and all the money and all the attention is. [So] what happens if the next big technology thing, the next advance in that particular technology, happens to be spiritually based? [What if] all of a sudden you have all these people who are using this spiritual thing, and they can't ignore it. Like if they are holding their cell phone in their hands and they are saying. 'Wait a minute this isn't working via radio waves, it's working via astral waves?'"*

Doug sounded remarkably like earlier American experimentalists when he claimed that science and technology were on the cusp of proving these energetic realities. These earlier men and women went to remarkable lengths to develop technologies that would allow contact between the dead and the living, or would prove the power of mental healing and mind over matter.[11] It is not surprising, given the robust embodied practices of metaphysical bodily desire, that twenty-first century spiritual practitioners would continue a fascination with technologies and disciplines for manipulating them, thereby advancing human experience.

Doug's discussions likewise strongly and clearly demonstrate how metaphysicals themselves think of their physical bodies as tools to discipline and shape into the "ultimate" switch. And while Doug was convinced that most Americans would rather worship technologies than learn to use their bodies, the mystics and practitioners I met in Cambridge (including Doug) recognized just how simple tuning the body actually was. A day did not go by during my fieldwork when I did not encounter a command to relax, to stretch and settle, to focus. Centering the self was the practice of settling an agitated mind and body. As a Reiki practitioner repeated, when we relaxed, *"dust settled,"* and divine energies flowed unimpeded.

Metaphysical optimism about every person's capacity to return to a natural, relaxed state was matched by claims that the road to relaxation was "simple." Charles, a forty-year-old "soul singer" and shaman who spent his day editing literary works translated from Old English, was adamant and excited about the body's potential to quickly return to its natural state. Charles leads soul-singing workshops in his house on the weekends, where he encourages people to make tones and melodies spontaneously. In doing so, he says, people recover forgotten natural abilities and their empowering possibilities. He begins by asking people to put their negative thoughts about their abilities aside. *"I have this little phrase that goes 'listen—breathe—and sing.' And it really is that simple, being completely in the moment. It's really letting your mind go, your thoughts, your fears, your ego, your—performance (you know this idea of performance, this idea of doing it right, any idea of doing it in a certain way). As long as there's trust in yourself, which can take people a while to gain, and to trust music or spirit or whatever it is that brings the Song into you, or that somehow, opens you up to it or makes you aware of the Song, . . . you can do it."*

Charles told me several times during our conversations that while he was trained in classical voice, he was not interested in teaching people to sing that way. Most people, he said, thought that learning to sing would take years and still result in "failure." Learning how to sing, he said, rather meant shedding those cultural notions, setting aside conventions such as musical notation and tonality. Singing meant mimicking what children do when they sing, doing all kinds of things with their voices that grownups *"learn not to do."* By the time children become adults, most have lost both their desire and their ability to sing: they have unlearned their natural way of singing and vocalizing, and learned the modern way. The spiritual consequences of this were, in Charles' view, quite stark. We have forgotten how to *"connect to the Song,"* he said, with an emphasis. *"To the Greeks music was spirit, you know with the muses. It was divine and from the gods. So to me it is very spiritual. To me [music] is spirit in its purest form. . . . It's ancient to humanity, and I think in Western culture it's something that's been forgotten. . . . Things have gotten fragmented, and in the arts, so much of it is about training. And what's neat is to discover that you don't have to have training, you don't have to be able to read music or know music theory in order to sing."*

Singing helped him to "get out of the way" of that spirit, and as a consequence he has been rewarded many times over. *"I never cease to be amazed at what my voice wants to do, or [where it] ends up taking me, the sounds it wants to make. The analogy or metaphor I often use now is, the voice is this territory. [For] most people, their voice is like the backyard of their home, and that's it. But there are vistas and mountains and valleys and meadows and woods and prairies that you have no idea are there. Until you let—your voice, being, body explore sound and song in this way. And I feel like I'm constantly being taken to new—if you're going to map it all, it would be like going to new places on the planet you've never seen before."*

The simplicity of the return to the natural body is most clearly and consistently articulated in the array of yoga studios and classes that take place daily. Cambridge's yoga teachers presented numerous variations on the themes of using yoga as a tool and means of reconnecting with the true self, of relaxing and aligning and discovering the true body, and of empowerment through calming the mind and nerves. I was frequently reminded, in the yoga classes I took and in interviews, that yoga meant "union." Yoga was not mere exercise or postures (asanas). It was a method of reorienting the mind and spirit through the body.[12] Yoga teachers repeatedly emphasized the simplicity of yoga. They claimed (as did soul singers, Reiki practitioners, and others) that they were doing no more than tuning people to their "natural" and true selves. David quipped, *"asana, the word that some people translate as 'position,' comes from the Sanskrit* as—*which means, you got it, 'ass.' Arse. He meant sitting on your ass."* He chuckled before getting more serious. *"When Patanjali says asanas should be steady and comfortable, he means sitting in meditation,"* he said, mobilizing the voice of the writer of the classical yoga aphorisms. *"[Patanjali] is not talking about doing dog pose or headstands or something like that. So right from the start, students are liberated by finding out what yoga really is about, what asana really means is sitting in awareness. The yoga of the classical meditation is sitting. Because then you have the right attitude. You don't mistake it for something else . . . in this particular enterprise, those are all completely wrong. Your success is just to sit. You're doing less rather than doing more."*[13]

Yoga was, however, also a discipline, one that needed to be followed with intention and devotion in order to reap its benefits. In other words, while the natural body was possible to attain, and relatively simple to approach, it took time and determination. David continued, *"Even doing less means that some work is required."* Perhaps because he knew that I played the piano, he drew on a musical example to make the connection. *"You see, for example, you don't have to be a musician to learn how* to play the piano. *If you sat down every day and learned where C was, and just started playing the C major scale, thumb index third finger, thumb index third finger fourth finger fifth finger, OK? If you did that every day, gradually over the course of a month or two, your neuromusculature would recognize that you are doing much more than you need to do. And that playing the scale is simpler and gradually, your hand, meaning your brain—you don't have a hand in isolation—your brain would begin to know the topography of C major. . . . And if you keep playing, and after a month or two, you'll be able to ripple it. And you don't have to have any native talent. . . . And you know what, that's the way asana is.*" No "native talent" was necessary to do yoga, but determination was. Alignment could be attained through repetition and determination. Christina, a teacher with a ten-plus year studio in Cambridge, said that yoga was merely about release from incorrect patterns, allowing for alignment that led to more prosperous, energetic lives. "*Everybody makes patterns mentally, emotionally, and in every way in our bodies. And the prescription is the same for changing any of them. Just repeat, reinforce. So when we want to change something emotionally we try to do it through awareness, and usually it's yoga that holds up the mirror to us and shows us how we need to change.*" Christina demanded that her students become disciplined in their practice, but offered the promise that true transformation was almost effortless and gentle, if it was practiced properly. "*I have found that yoga will transform you, you become aware of what you're doing through gentle movements, and it's transformation, mental, spiritual, and physical.*"

The necessity of focusing on and intending to relax was most apparent to me as I stretched and bent in various classes, listening to and following the involved and elaborate instructions that accompanied corpse pose (savasana). This pose entails lying prone on the floor and seems, on the face of it, to be the simplest possible thing to do. Yet savasana, which is the beginning and ending position of most yoga classes, is made up of several discrete steps. Joy and many other teachers followed the seven steps illuminated in B. K. S. Iyengar's *Light on Yoga* almost verbatim, instructing us to let our "eyeballs sink back into their sockets," and then a few moments later, to release our tongue from the top of the mouth and "let it gently find its home on the floor." Such instructions made it clear that lying on the floor did not mean that one was relaxed: one needed to follow several more steps to release tension and allow the breath or prana to circulate fully. Iyengar is quite clear on the process that he invites yoga students into, writing "by remaining motionless for some time and keeping the mind still while you are fully conscious, you *learn* to relax." Relaxation has a proper form: the eyes should be closed, the palms pointed up, the heels together, the toes apart. The breathing should be light, "with no jerky movements to disturb the spine or the body." The salutary effects of this asana are enormous, he soothes. It "destroys fatigue, and quiets the agitation of the mind," he notes, before adding, "Steady, smooth, fine and deep breathing without any jerky movements of the body soothes the nerves and calms the mind. The stresses of modern civilization are a strain on the nerves for which Savasana is the best antidote."[14]

Iyengar's seven steps for savasana seem sparse in comparison to Erich Schiffman's twenty-two, which take readers and practitioners through a more extensive "circuit" and thereby extend attention, or relaxation, to even more parts of the body. "Rest your awareness in the area of your hands: the palms, thumbs, fingers. . . . Forget about what they look like, what you *remember* they look like, and instead immerse your awareness in the way they actually feel to you now. Go into your hands and feel them. Gradually, you may begin to sense heat or warmth, then a pleasant, tingling, electricity-like sensation. Feel the energy in your hands."[15] The full elaboration of the type of attention that can be trained during savasana speaks volumes about what yoga (in its contemporary frame) demands in the name of relaxation. Joy read from Schiffman's book as well, often while we were lying prone in savasana. David's words likewise sounded this familiar refrain when he encouraged his students to feel rather than see their bodies.

The irony of working hard (and ever harder, as the transition from seven to twenty-two steps suggests) to do less was an integral part of yoga. And while the goal of "neuromuscular" realignment was held out as possible for all, in the process each person encountered just how difficult it was to "just" let go and relax. I had many chances to consider the implications of this as I struggled to pull my body into downward dog or the warrior pose. The naturalization of such unnatural poses, and the reinterpretation of unconsciously conducted activities "off the mat" as moments of agitation and stress offered hope that life could be reshaped. But "relaxation" would come only through the active transformation of regular walking, breathing, standing, and even sleep practices. Becoming relaxed would take a lot of work.

This was most apparent to me as I listened to how yoga teachers talk about sleep. Rather than observing sleep as a natural relaxant, yoga teachers emphasized the problem of incorrect sleep. In response to a student who admitted that she "carried her tensions" into her sleep, Joy told us to do the following. "This weekend, take one morning when you don't have anything to do. Allow yourself to waken naturally. Don't turn the alarm on the night before. Wake up whenever you wake up. As you wake, take a moment to check out your body." She gave us simple instructions. "Check—where is your tongue? Are your hands clenched? Does your back ache? What else doesn't feel right? Next, before you fully wake up pull up your dreams. What did you dream about? What excited you, what anxieties are you carrying over into sleep?" She continued, "Give yourself the chance to relax all those parts. Breathe intentionally through all of them: your neck, your arms, your feet. Start the day with awareness."[16]

Joy did not want her students to come to her classes as respite from a hectic schedule, although she recognized that this was frequently what students were doing. She encouraged us to do more than this, to see how yoga could transform our lives. Proper, ongoing attention to relaxation and bodily transformation would link yoga practitioners into divine energies and reveal yoga's true spiritual core. Marcy told me, "*It's a spiritual practice, when done right—meaning when you dedicate the time, with no distractions and being there in your body, in your breath, on the mat for an hour or 90 minutes, you are connecting with the spirit embodied within you through the breath. And through these connections and sensations, and the movement of energy in your body, you are also treating your body with reverence. You're strengthening your container. . . . My students come to me. They have fed back to me is that what they want is, it's the only time I get to relax all week, it's the only time I'm still all week, I feel so good and relaxed after, I feel peaceful, my body feels good.*"

How Asanas Came to the West: The Gospel of Relaxation

The relaxed and calm body that my respondents sought was also, of course, a powerful and strong one. The relaxed body allowed the energetic body to do its work, and thus began to attract more positive and empowering results in life than the agitated and worried body could accomplish. This, at least, was what my respondents told me. This relaxed, disciplined, natural body that metaphysicals imagine is thus, in addition, quite well attuned not only to living within but excelling within American society. While yoga teachers criticized the agitations that accompanied modern society, little within their discourse suggested that doing yoga would remove students from it. Indeed, yoga primed these bodies for a particular kind of success within modern culture. They are docile. They are not angry or unfocused. Metaphysical body practices shape bodies whose "success" is found in overcoming agitation and learning to succeed within the structures that engulf them.[17]

In order to understand how the worlds of prana, breathing, and asanas create "tuned" bodies that simultaneously critique American society and measure their success by its standards, it is helpful to look a bit more closely at the ways that relaxation and yoga have been linked in American yoga traditions. Yoga in the United States is simultaneously foreign and quite homegrown, a hybrid, transnational tradition that has been constantly renewed and reinvented in interchanges between various groups and nations. While my respondents imagine yoga as an authentic Indian body and meditation practice system recently translated into the American or Western context, its practice and history in the United States is somewhat more varied and complex.[18] Emerson and other nineteenth-century elites wrote about yoga, but it was not until the turn of the century that "raja yoga" became an object of interest and practice. One of its primary promulgators, Swami Vivekananda, traveled to the United States in 1893 to speak at the Worlds Parliament of Religion and spent the subsequent four years traveling in the States before returning to India. Among other adventures, he spent some time in the Brattle Street home of Sarah Bull, a Cambridge doyenne whose salon on philosophy and comparative religion was well attended by Cambridge's intellectual elite. It was here, apparently, where Vivekananda met William James.[19]

Vivekananda presented yoga and Vedanta philosophy to Americans in various public settings, including Sarah Bull's salon and in the New York Vedanta Society. Vivekananda was particularly well suited to serve as a translator (if not inventor) of yoga in a modern American context.[20] Vivekananda's descriptions drew heavily on popular Western descriptions of India (including those of New England's Transcendentalists) as a source of mystic truths that could aid in overcoming the ills of modern society. Vivekananda presented yoga as an ancient wisdom tradition that provided important tools and concepts for those suffering from nervous complaints, in so doing consolidating a variety of traditions into a single system that was specifically meant to appeal to Americans already familiar with a "spiritual framework that was 'non-exclusive,' 'scientific,' and seemingly universal."[21] In other words, Americans learned yoga from an Indian who was familiar with and likely in conversation with harmonial and metaphysical religious understandings about relaxation already popularly circulating in the United States. Vivekananda had multiple opportunities to learn about American "mind cure" and New Thought first hand, whether during his trip to Chicago, where New Thought and its various harmonial projects were in full swing in the 1890s; in New York, where Theosophical and

Spiritualist groups were dominant; and certainly in Cambridge, where Vivekananda met William James and others at Bull's salon.

It was at about the same time that William James encouraged his audiences to find respite from agitation through the powers of esoteric Protestant practices. In his 1899 address "The Gospel of Relaxation" James challenges his young listeners to grasp their innate powers by learning to relax, rather than fighting them and keeping them bottled up. Everyone, he said, must exhale and "unclamp." James was troubled by Americans' mental hygiene. Pent up, agitated, and on edge, young American men and women were like "bottled lightning." He advocated, in contrast, a posture that exuded "that blessed internal peace and confidence, that *acquiescientia in seipso,* as Spinoza used to call it, that wells up from every part of the body of a muscularly well-trained human being, and soaks the indwelling soul of him with satisfaction, is, quite apart from every consideration of its mechanical utility, an element of spiritual hygiene of supreme significance." James directs those who would wish to aspire to a more powerful life to cultivate good "spiritual hygiene," which involves comportment, relaxation, and breathing, but also a movement away from worry and "responsibility" to mere acceptance. "The transition from tenseness, self-responsibility, and worry to equanimity, receptivity, and peace, is the most wonderful of all those shiftings of inner equilibrium, those changes of the personal centre of energy . . . the chief wonder of it is that it so often comes about, not by doing, but by simply relaxing and throwing this burden down." The whole trick, of course, is to learn just how to relax through bodily methods, which can begin with paying attention to how one is sitting. "If you never wholly give yourself up to the chair you sit in, . . . [i]f you breath eighteen or nineteen instead of sixteen times a minute . . . what mental mood can you be in but one of inner panting and expectancy, and how can the future and its worries possibly forsake your mind?"[22]

James's sources for this lecture include Annie Payson Call and Ralph Waldo Trine, whose writings explicated various methods of "tuning" the bodies and mind to the infinite, or through the "power through repose." Annie Call devotes an entire chapter to the difficulty of sleep in *The Power of Repose,* an 1851 volume reprinted numerous times. She remarks at the absurdity of Americans who "do not abandon ourselves completely to gaining all that Nature would give us through sleep." Call's chapter presents a number of directives on sleep that resonate with yogic directions for savasana pose. "The head, instead of letting the pillow have its full weight, holds itself . . . the tongue cleaves to the roof of the mouth, the throat muscles are contracted, and the muscles of the face drawn up in one way or another." She tells her readers "first let go of the muscles—that will enable us more easily to drop disturbing thoughts; and as we refuse, without resistance, admittance of the thoughts, the freedom from care for the time will follow, and the rest gained will enable us to awaken with new life for cares to come. This, however, is a habit to be established and thoughtfully cultivated; it cannot be acquired at once."[23]

The similarities between William James's and Vivekananda's diagnoses and cures to what ailed tense, bottled up Americans suggests a fertile mixing and meeting of various Asian and American concepts. The relations and overlap traveled in both directions, suggesting to some that Vivekananda's representation of yoga and the "classical Pedantic tradition" have "far more to do with a psychology born in the context of esoteric Protestantism."[24] Not discounting the novel concepts introduced by these and other Indian teachers, interchanges among Vivekananda and American metaphysicals produced a particular hybrid expression where the provenance of certain ideas were never clearly marked. The yoga forms that develop in the United States can be viewed as a hybrid form of American desires for (and expressions of the power of) relaxation in an agitated world, translated through images of a mystical East and its ancient wisdom, reorganized and reshaped by Indian teachers with their own scholarly, religious, and political interests in establishing certain Indian religious forms as authoritative.[25]

Americans practiced yoga through the twentieth century, even though strict anti-immigration policies severely restricted travel by Asians to the United States and thereby the ability of Asian teachers to cultivate American ashrams or followings. In the interim, numerous European Americans, including scholars with close ties to metaphysical groups traveled and learned in India, returning with forms of yoga that they touted as more authentic and pure than those of their forebears.[26] It seems clear that in the early 1960s Americans interested in pursuing yoga were able to easily draw on both Indian and "American" lineages to describe yoga in America. For example, the best-selling *Yoga, Youth, and Reincarnation,* published in 1965, tells a story of American yoga through the story of Marcia Moore, a "Concord yogi" whom the author, journalist Jess Stearn, denotes as a direct descendent of "America's yogic tradition" carried through generations of Transcendentalists.[27] Stearn writes, "She came by [this lineage] honestly. . . . At seven she had been struck by mention of the word *reincarnation. . . .* At fourteen, she had read Paul Brunton's *A Search in Secret India. . . .* Growing up, she steeped herself in the transcendentalists. She lived in the libraries where their works were, and in the woods where they drew their inspiration. There were other influences . . . in the family were ministers and artists. Her grandfather James Moore was the biographer of America's leading mystic, Andrew Jackson Davis; and his widow Jane, in her seventies, traveled to Duke University to study psychic phenomena. Great-grandfather Newell, pastor of Cambridge's First Church for forty-nine years, knew the transcendentalists by their Christian names. This was her tradition."[28] Stearn recounts his search for youth through yogic practice: his journeys land him at Moore's bucolic farm. The pastoral scene of small-town New England overwhelms and marginalizes the accounts of Indian yogis whom Stearn interviews on the Upper East Side of Manhattan.

Stearn's story of American yoga "tradition" shaped through Moore's genealogical connections to Transcendentalism presents yoga as more homegrown than exotic. "Oriental ritual," he opines, has no place in the "hurly burly West." His ideas resound with a muscular metaphysical optimism that he tells us he learned from none other than Madame deVries, an early yoga innovator and wife of the "Omnipotent Oom." "The need for self-discipline was never greater. . . . Lawlessness and delinquency stem from lack of self-discipline. We are living in a world which has abandoned the old standards, and need self-discipline—control—more than ever. Since it is impossible to live by the old patterns when they have disappeared, the problem is to know yourself . . . and make the necessary adjustments."[29] Mrs. deVries heralds the new dawn of self-disciplinary techniques, and Moore stands in as the very portrait of self-discipline's American tradition and heritage. Yoga becomes fundamentally *American,* translated and sprung from its Indian origins.[30]

To drive home this particular image, Stearn visits the "nine remaining Shakers" in New Hampshire who happen to take yoga lessons from Marcia. "I couldn't help but wonder why Marcia was exposing me to these faded giants of Concord's golden age," he says. Marcia has a ready answer: "I just wanted you to know about our real yogis," noting that they have practiced "Karma Yoga—the devotion to duty and work—since they were children, and their meditations, rooted in spiritualism, made them yogic in their detachment." Stearn's encounter at this modern-day ashram draws him into contemplation of one of Thoreau's best known lines: "Why should we be in such desperate haste to succeed and in such desperate enterprises? If a Man does not keep pace with his companions, perhaps it is because he hears a different drummer. Let him step to the music which he hears, however measured or far away." Stearn closes in on something close to personal salvation in this text. Once a "volatile Westerner caught up in the nuclear age, seeking some respite from worry, boredom and frustration in martinis and promiscuity," he finds in Concord new pleasure in meditating about God, and thinking "of Him as being inherent in everything we saw, heard or felt . . . of being the wellspring of body, mind, and spirit."[31]

This story of an American yoga that was spurred and renewed through encounters between Asian practitioners and American and European imaginations, influenced strongly by the politics of immigration and colonization, emerges in Stearn's hand as a triumphal reclamation of ancient truths through American interventions. That few yoga practitioners or teachers in Cambridge are aware of the connections between their practices and traditions and "esoteric Protestantism" or show any interest in these strains of yoga history might hardly be surprising to us, especially given their claims to the scientific and natural properties of yoga practice. That said, yoga practitioners, among all practitioners in Cambridge, are most interested in their own teaching lineages, often invoking the names of their spiritual and practical teachers. Their ability to do so is quite different from Marcia Moore's: in 1965, the same year that Stearn's book claimed the reemergence of an American yoga, U.S. immigration policy shifted, permitting Asians to travel to and settle in the United States in larger numbers. This would have great consequence for yoga practice in America, reviving and renewing interest in Indian practice, ultimately submerging New Thought and Transcendentalist yogic narratives as Asian practitioners reshaped the face and presence of yoga in the United States.

The ground-shift is recorded in the first chapter of Harvey Cox's 1977 volume, *Turning East: The Promise and Peril of the New Orientalism,* which opens with an ethnographic montage of Cambridge transformed from a "prim university town" into "Benares-on-the-Charles." Cox reported that "forty or fifty different neo-Oriental religious movements" prosper in Boston and Cambridge, making the city "one of the four or five most thriving American centers of the neo-Oriental religious surge." Cox's interests lie well beyond the confines of Cambridge. Nonetheless he hints at its centrality, noting that earlier generations of Cantabrigians were deeply interested in investigating "orientalist ideas" (even if "there is no evidence that Emerson ever sat in a full lotus").[32] Cox observes that the post-1965 shift that brought Asian people and practices to bookish Cambridge reoriented American practitioners to the South Asian milieu. The consequences were (and remain) significant: new generations of American yoga teachers learned from Indians who lived in American cities, many of whom not only encouraged new teachers to develop strong relations with the schools and teacher lineages they represented, but also to spend time in India. The diminishing interest in homegrown American yoga of the kind espoused by Marcia Moore did not mean the diminishment of interest in yoga as relaxation, however, even as this emphasis began to share space with other interpretive practices and postures. Indeed, the American yoga described by Stern and articulated by early twentieth-century writers continues to reverberate in the instructions spoken to students on the mat, although it now is more strongly inflected by, and in conversation with, a new generation of travel between India and the United States.[33]

While Stearn's book evokes a moment when yoga practitioners in the United States often fashioned their practices with an understanding of Americans' ongoing twentieth-century interchanges with yogis, the post-1965 engagement with Asian religions and practices has made a new narrative possible. Yoga students and teachers alike herald the arrival of Asian religious teachers as authentic and knowledgeable practitioners from the 1970s on as avatars of true yoga, thus displacing earlier forms and expressions as less than authentic and glossing over the longer histories of exchange that shape yoga in both India and the United States. Ironically, these narratives often end up giving new life to turn-of-the-century notions of the power of repose and the gospel of relaxation by transforming them into gifts from the mystical East.

Other Bodies and the Problem of Edges

Wes regularly saw people's *"qi energy centers"* light up. *"When people talk about sadness, sadness shows up in their field, before they started talking. A lot of times, I can just anticipate what a person says. If you see red, they are talking in anger. If you see gray energy, you know it is sad. Love and happiness have certain qualities, a different coloration."* Wes noted that his ability to see an aura before he hears a word makes him more effective in social settings, and allows him to "turn" people's moods and energies in a positive direction. Wes called himself an energy intuitive. His abilities had come to him almost overnight, during a difficult period in California when he was out of work and living out of his car for two miserable months. His experience and encounter with an energetic source galvanized him to seek assistance in finding a job, and when he had saved enough gas money he drove cross-country to Massachusetts, where he remembered an old psychic friend lived. Twenty-odd years later he was still settled in Cambridge and active in the Theosophical Society, a regional dowser's society, and familiar face on the metaphysical arts circuit (he also collaborated with an MIT music professor).

Wes's connection to others' energy was constant, a fact that had often troubled him. He recalled the turning point he reached many years ago when he realized that he would have to learn to control it. *"I was hanging out with a friend at a coffee shop, and he was telling me about his divorce. I accidentally touched his palm and I got all this information about what his ex-wife was up to and I said to him—well again, it's not about tapping into other people's secrets."* Tapping into his friend's underlying mood and moreover receiving information about his personal life made him realize both how important it was to retain boundaries between self and other, yet also how difficult that would be as long as others misunderstood their energetic potential. Wes intuited that he was not unique, and that everyone could learn what he knew. He decided that he was supposed to teach others how to read energy as well. The abilities he had, he said, *"should be used for education."* He hoped that his classes would empower people to cultivate the abilities that he had, and that likewise they might learn to comprehend the power that others might have over them. He was highly critical of "healers" who did not teach people how to manipulate energy, and worried about the power imbalances that resulted. It seemed that Wes's genuine desires to teach others how to "use" energy and learn the techniques that he had been given was an attempt to level the spiritual playing field. As he said, if everyone could see invisible bodies, if there was education, then there would be no more hiding, no more falsehood, and no more secrets—and also no more discomfort with the problem of edges that these invisible bodies inevitably caused.

In comparison to the fleshy physical mass of the visible body, the invisible body's edges are unclear. While the astral body could detach from the physical during out-of-body experiences, trances, or lucid dreams, most people did not confront their energetic bodies as distinct from their physical bodies. Yet the edges between these bodies were not distinct: the astral leaked into the fleshy, influencing one's health, radiating out in the form of auras, and spilling into the physical. The fact that the astral body (and its energetic realities and truths) is not fully contained, and might be read by others, is a source of fascination and concern. At one level, the lack of clear edges and the ability to extend the astral or energetic body through time and space was a liberating possibility, one frequently articulated in guided visualizations and in the various commentaries that followed group chakra meditations.

At another, however, the porosity of the energetic self allowed for inter-mingling and mixing of selves, and for intimate penetrations that were beyond the possibilities of the flesh.

At the end of our first interview Wes said he could teach me how to "read" my own energy and offered to give a short demonstration. I agreed and turned off the tape recorder. He asked me to put my arm on his kitchen table, and he put his hand on my wrist and instructed me to do the same. He closed his eyes, took a light breath, and then asked out loud, "What did the energy feel like in Courtney's mother's womb?" He continued to sit quietly, and I squirmed in the awkward silence. He then opened his eyes and said, "See?" I nodded, not sure what else to do. I hadn't felt anything, and was not sure in fact whether it was he or I, or both of us, who was supposed to feel this. I wondered also about the significance of the womb, but mostly I felt quite uncom-fortable that Wes believed that he could in fact feel or sense something. Whatever it was he felt or didn't feel, he did not let on. Rather, he asked me to do the same for him, to ask what the energy felt like in Wes's mother's womb. Again I closed my eyes, wondering what I was sup-posed to feel. When I opened my eyes, he asked what I had felt. I an-swered honestly: "Nothing, nothing in particular." Wes did not seem particularly discouraged. Rather, he said, "You see, this is how I teach. I teach you how to do it for yourself—so that you don't need someone else to diagnose."

Despite my not having felt anything "energetic," and my strong sus-picion that the same was true for Wes, I was nonetheless surprised at how put off I was by Wes's claims that he had found a way into my energetic interior, or rather, that our energetic interiors were so read-ily available to touch and sense, and that all that we needed to do was ask. I took comfort that night in reading about prior Americans' fears of metaphysical practitioners' claims for "mental penetration of the self,"[34] but wondered how much more clearly these intrusions were felt when the claim was not entering another's mind but, rather, their en-ergetic and true body, that is, nothing less than an energetic *womb*.

I was occasionally caught short with just how unconcerned practi-tioners seemed to be, in fact, about the "penetrations of the self" that they enacted on each other (with permission) and that they reported after visualizations, trances, or even just in passing conversation. "Energy healers" and Reiki practitioners, shiatsu therapists, and oth-ers claimed that their only healing tool was the energetic forces that coursed through their own bodies when they worked. One day I asked Cathy if she was worried about getting "negative" energy from the people she worked with. Was negative energy contagious? It seemed that it might be, given what Wes told me about the ways that energy leaked out and infected others who were not aware. She told me otherwise: good energy always emanated outward. The flow of energy, she told me, created a "bubble" that protected her.

These protective bubbles were important to Cathy's and other healers' senses that they were able to maintain a positive energy boundary, pushing "good" energy outward while not mingling with the negative. Moreover, they did not balk at the idea that their energetic bodies' boundaries might be traversed by another's. Indeed, part of Cambridge metaphysicals' lack of discomfort was their expectation that energetic worlds were populated already by avatars, ghosts, ascended masters, noncorporeal spirit, and the like who could see and interact with them, and who in fact crowded and populated the world, unseen by us in our waking lives.[35] Marcy felt her angels "blowing love into her brain" during visualizations, and Cathy reported that she saw them when she conducted a Reiki session for her. Doug told us stories about the spirits of recently deceased people whom he encountered while out of body. Another self-styled clairvoyant doggedly persisted in telling me that there was an energetic body named "Steven" who hovered close to me, and tried to get me to divulge who the spirit might be. ("Not everyone has such a strong energetic source so close by all the time," he told me.) Eric loved the beings he met regularly in his dreams. *"They're real and they're really important, and I really love them. I have so much feeling for them."*

Testimony about encounters with other beings allowed metaphysicals to speak about the work that they did within and through their energetic bodies. These bodies had different relationships, different desires, different hopes and demands than their fleshy counterparts. It was within the energetic body that everything seemed possible and through which everything was illuminated, or at least so it seemed. One day when I was out for tea with Crystal, she told me about her former boyfriend, a fisherman. One night when he was at sea, she had a dream about him. He came to her in the dream and asked for her help. She did not think much of the dream when she woke in the morning, assuming merely that it was her own worries that had caused it. But the next night he appeared again, in a "different kind of dream." During the dream he took her to a beautiful place and showed her all kinds of things, "all the knowledge in the world, everything there was to know." After that, they had sex. Seeing me smile, she said, "Yes, sex in the dream. But not sex like you dream about. It was—how can I put it—cosmic sex, beautiful, sex. I mean it just blew my mind—there is, I mean, it was not like regular sex. It was . . . awesome." When they were finished Crystal's boyfriend told her that he was leaving her, and she said goodbye. She was "totally knocked out" by the experience.

The following morning the news reached Crystal that her boyfriend's fishing vessel had been lost at sea, and everyone aboard was presumed dead. The boat had come upon a storm and weathered it for two days before capsizing. Crystal immediately realized her boyfriend had been in contact with her, first through his energetic self, and perhaps the second time as a spirit that connected with her energetic self. The experience left her stunned. She fell into a deep depression for many months, at times unable to get out of bed. She hoped that he might come again in another dream and she longed for his touch, but his last "goodbye" had had such a ring of finality that she knew that he would not. And while the "merging" that had taken place during her last encounter with him was beautiful, she admitted that it did not make up for the fact that she missed his physical touch.

The sense of longing that accompanies encounters with spirits is part and parcel of ghostly communication. Ghosts are sociologically interesting as stories about haunting, unresolved things, longing over pasts, and missed opportunities that take shadow form.[36] Encounters like Crystal's certainly reflect such longing. Yet within the realms where people live in and through subtle bodies, encounters with spirits and ghosts articulate not just longing, but also expectations for the future time where astral bodies will be conjoined and fused in more powerful and essential ways than what is felt in the present. Metaphysicals thus spoke of cultivating the parts of their subtle selves that linked to the source of all that was good and powerful, and enfolded them in a stable, unchanging universal love that erased all distinctions between selves and others. Yet at the same time, the promise of cosmic sex, of learning from other spirits and astral bodies held out the additional hope that progress toward this source would not result in the erasure of the self but merely an expansion. In this respect, mystics in Cambridge play out "the practice of making the invisible visible, of concretizing the order of the universe, the nature of human life and its destiny, and the various dimensions and possibilities of human interiority itself."[37]

The logic of a divine energy that is not merely invisible but ultimately immanent and stable, universal and all powerful, suggests that the intimacy that astral and physical bodies share is ultimately the intimacy of self-knowledge. Each subtle body is a shard of a universal whole. This is a liberating feeling for some: it presents opportunity to imagine a universal connectedness and also to feel it and encounter it through the blurred boundaries that energetic selves engage. But these also harbor a variety of concerns, infrequently spoken, about what it means to live energetically. If the subtle body is the real one, and its energies are both beyond the limits of the physical self and available for all those who are adept to see and even manipulate, then the question of the limits and edges of the self become newly problematic, and the promise of a new self slips quickly not into the promise of new body but an absence of its definition altogether. If there are no limits to the self, and every encounter drives one back to the realization of one's "connectedness" with all others, then the self disappears.

Conclusion

The practices that shape metaphysical bodies present paths to full engagement and absorption into divine energies and networks and simultaneously call attention to the dangers that accompany those promises. The allure of being embraced by an ever-loving channel of power and the expansion of the self's power in a world of otherwise unthinking, mindless, unaware "zombies" (as Doug put it) also makes it clear that getting ahead is not about acting against the invisible forces but rather coming to feel and sense them, and to acquiesce to their overwhelming and loving power. The concept that the self is made in its relations with others and is formed in relation to emanations of light lead to the mystical view of union and engulfment of the self, and likewise to the problem of edges that are both yearned for and, at times, quite frightening.

The ambivalence contained within the promise of realizing one's energetic body and becoming engulfed resonated within the stories that Mike told me. Mike had experienced several near-death experiences and was a regular on the speaker's circuit in the Boston area; his primary message was that God was love and that death was nothing to fear. Mike was planning on getting married soon to his girlfriend of many years. She had stayed with him through thick and thin, including his severe illness and chronic fatigue, he told me, speaking with such gentleness that I could sense quite clearly how central their relationship was in his life. Yet she had categorically refused to go with him to his speaking engagements. At first, he said, her refusal angered him. The experiences were central to his life as well, and to the trajectory he was on. As he gave more speeches, however, his anger abated.

He had originally been so caught up in the energies released when he spoke that he had thought that was all there was. But as time went on, he more and more looked forward to returning to their home and to his girlfriend's presence and touch. That life together was about *"burping and peeing and eating and normal grounded life experiences . . . not about that awesome light that I just momentarily grasped."* Even as metaphysicals worked to cultivate disciplines that marked them as spiritually advanced adepts, as relaxed and empowered beings able to tap into the source of all and move beyond the body, these practices often also worked to turn spiritual people back toward their flesh, and to a renewed understanding and perhaps stronger embrace of its fleeting pleasures.

FOUR

Karmic Laundry: Imagining and Embodying Spiritual History

A familiar bustle of suburban domestic activity greeted me as Cathy opened her front door. Christmas carols played on the stereo, and teenage boys jostled in the hall pulling on coats and hauling sleds behind them. I looked into the living room on my right and waved hello to Sally, who was sitting in the living room, paging through a photo album and talking to Cathy's daughter. Cathy motioned for me to follow her to the kitchen, and I did, a box of warm chocolate chip cookies in my hands. Sally and I were the first to arrive for an "ornament making party" and cookie swap. Cathy had invited most of the other regular attendees of the Mystical Experiences Discussion Group as well. Cathy put me to work arranging cookies on plates as she put out English china cups and kissed her husband and daughter goodbye. "They're going to see *Harry Potter—*again," Cathy remarked as the door closed behind them. Relative quiet descended as Cathy peered out the front window once more to see if any of the others had arrived. "Eric is always late," she stated to no one in particular as she ushered Sally and me to the card table in the corner of the living room, where she showed us how to wrap thin golden wire around fragile glass globes and thread on the tiny beads as we did.

The beading required some concentration, so I listened quietly as Cathy and Sally chatted, comparing notes about whether they were seeing any results from the new "anti-aging" treatments that their friend Travis, "a biochemist," developed in his basement laboratory. Soon they turned to talk about the three single women who had started attending the group that fall. Cathy had been excited, when we talked on the phone midweek, that this would be my chance to meet them, but Crystal had another engagement and couldn't come. "That's too bad, I like her," Sally said, adding that she hoped that Marcy wouldn't come in that case. "She has a lot of negative energy—at least she did in the group the last time." And Cathy told us that Annette wouldn't be coming either, since she was sick with the flu. "I think we should go sing carols to her and take her some cookies later, what do you think?" Cathy queried. Sally nodded and replied, "I guess you feel like you need to take care of her."

"Yeah, I do," said Cathy. "I told her to come over earlier this week, and to bring her laundry. I owe her a *lot* of karmic laundry." They both laughed and I looked up, confused.

Sally caught my eye. "Hasn't Cathy told you? She thinks Annette was Max's wife."

"Really?" I asked. "Max," I knew, was the man whom Cathy believed she had been in her most previous past life. As I started to ask how she knew about Annette's identity, the doorbell rang and Cathy stood up to invite Marcy, Doug, Eric, and his wife into the house, calling back to us, "Yeah, I figure she did a lot of laundry for me in the last one, and so it's time that I do some for her."

The rest of the afternoon at Cathy's house passed without any further mention of karmic laundry or Max. Although I knew that everyone in the group had heard about Cathy's past lives, I had reasons to suspect that Max was a somewhat contentious subject, and I didn't know who else knew about this new revelation concerning Annette. The laughter, craft project, Christmas music, and gossip did little to distract me from my growing curiosity about how Cathy learned that Annette was her wife in her past life, and what Annette might think about it.

In some respects Cathy's revelation that she was connected to Annette through a past life did not surprise me in the least. Past lives came with the territory of mysticism in Cambridge, an accepted part of the landscape for most, even though few could pinpoint the specifics of their past lives to the degree that Cathy could. Many of the mystics I met knew something about their past lives, gleaning or recognizing past life knowledge through a range of experiences. The commonality of talk about past lives pointed to their usefulness within the worlds of mystical connection that spiritual practitioners built in Cambridge. More than mere beliefs that provided philosophical answers to what happens to the soul after death,[1] past lives mapped layers of story and history onto the present in ways that enlivened, deepened, and ultimately complicated current social relationships. Metaphysicals build and navigate tenuous but real social worlds through remembering, sensing, and experiencing past lives.

Despite the regularity of past life discourse and practices and the seeming constancy of belief in the possibility or reality of reincarnation among Cambridge mystics, Cathy's offhanded remark that she had identified Annette, a young single woman just arrived in Cambridge, as her wife in her most previous past life challenged my expectations about how past lives worked. Indeed, for most mystics, past lives worked, and were made real, without attention to a past life's details. It was generally enough to know that one had many lives, and that (as we will see) these lives had been lived among a group of familiar souls. Cathy's elaborate story and narrative of her past life as a German Nobel Prize–winning scientist, in contrast, was filled with details and complex memories. As she implicated Annette in her story, I became more aware of the possibilities and the limitations through which history, memory, and tradition work among mystics as they build and live within tenuous social worlds.

Studying Past Lives: History, Memory, "the Past"

Past life experiences are ubiquitous parts of the worlds that Cambridge's mystics inhabit and, for this reason alone, require some attention. Given that these experiences are additionally important resources through which mystics imagine and understand their place in time, past lives become even more important sites of inquiry. For mystics, past lives are not merely philosophical ideas and issues for imaginative conjecture. They are lived out, embedded within memory and in social relations. As such, we can draw on these expressions to understand in part how such practices of remembering situate mystical and metaphysical selves in relation to multiple times, and with what consequence.

Becoming a Nobel Prize–winning physicist, a mystical saint of the fifteenth century, or even a servant girl in Atlantis takes work. To imagine, remember, and place oneself in relation to such a past life presents metaphysicals with a number of questions, some quite vexing, about their commitments to family in this life. Metaphysical past life memories also can present alternative and transgressive interpretations of life's purpose. Thus, while there is a strong temptation to explain away past lives as merely therapeutic metaphor (at best), investigating past lives allows us to think more clearly and in a more sustained way about what kinds of pasts, and what kinds of memories, matter for metaphysical practitioners, and to likewise think further about the consequences such pasts have for our understanding of the distinctions between fantasy, history, memory, and myth.

It is perhaps a truism that religious groups narrate their own histories, often living within socially formed, changing narratives that transform both the orthodox religious stories of their traditions and the secular historical narratives into which they are frequently thought to be enfolded. The narrative practices of metaphysical practitioners are no exception, and in fact frequently stretch and expand common understandings of universal, homogeneous, and global history.[2] While we are familiar with the manner in which some religious communities articulate the coexistence of multiple times and spaces (God's time and human time, for example), this does not in itself unsettle the claim that there are two different types of history, where ritual or mythic time is distinct from secular time and its historical unfolding. Thus, where religious narratives and histories are undoubtedly social facts for the communities that live within them, they are nonetheless mythic or figurative worlds when viewed from this other position.[3] Yet growing interest in the variety of practices of memory and history focus attention not only on the ways that myths and fictitious histories become real, but also raise questions about this distinction altogether. When joined to practices of memory, history becomes a process and set of practices and structures (hence, "historicity").[4] Historicity in this sense focuses attention on the authoritative social practices through which individuals and groups live in time, and in which stories and experiences of the past ultimately shape their lived worlds and understandings of it.[5]

This work unsettles the distinctions between religious and secular histories, suggesting, as Michael Lambek offers, that instead of "making unilateral and binary distinctions between "mythical" and the "real," we can delineate the play between them. Bringing their interplay into focus raises further questions. Not only might such recognition of temporal play suggest that our histories might require consideration of the agency of mythical agents,[6] it likewise makes it difficult to argue that new religious groups lack authority because they lack a "real" history.[7] As questions about history become more situated in the practical concerns of analyzing "to what extent and how" the social past is "implicated in what the individual does and is," this sticky question of the imagined, real, the fantastic and the mythical finds no clear resolution.[8]

Nonetheless, the past lives of Cambridge's mystics are an entry point into these unresolved issues, as they open up potentially fruitful ways of engaging and understanding metaphysical practice. In particular, the unsettling of these issues call new attention to the ways that mystics participate in a number of different practices that shape and inflect their position within *several* distinct pasts. These include their own biological family pasts, the recovered or felt pasts of other lives, the pasts that their narrative genres evoke, and mystical times that disrupt efforts to make history.

We begin with Cathy's investigation of her most previous life as Max, a Nobel Prize–winning scientist. Cathy's stories and experience are deeply textured, and I focus primarily on her experiences here. Like many other metaphysicals, Cathy distinguishes past life experiences from other experiences. While dreams, encounters with spirits, and out-of-body experiences provide her with useful information, a past life experience is distinct in that it presents an opportunity to link her experiential knowledge with something (or someone) historically factual. As Cathy's story suggests nonetheless, the facts of a past life are not easily come by, and the process of aligning the biography of a historical figure with one's experiences of being that person raises a number of questions for Cathy about how and whether the past can be resolved in a single narrative, told by a single person. Cathy's emphasis on "proof," the emphasis on "soulmates," and ideas of the soul's progress through multiple lives suggest a connection between contemporary past life belief and nineteenth-century views of the self, history, and morality. I turn to consider the (forgotten and remembered) past life of past lives in America, where the concepts took shape within Spiritualist, Theosophical, and New Thought literature, giving shape to a peculiarly American set of beliefs about reincarnation. These are encoded in a set of practices and moral evaluations that continue to be reproduced within contemporary past life explorations. We could say, in short, that Cathy's own exploration is itself an experience that places her in the presence of forgotten and remembered practices.

As fascinating as these issues were to me, the past life experiencers I met in Cambridge have little knowledge of such metaphysical pasts. Indeed, the stories of the kind I learned about reincarnationists-of-the-past were never as compelling to Cambridge's mystics as the ones they invoked within their own past life experiences. Their disinterest in the history of past lives in America in mind, I turn in the latter part of this chapter to address how the mystical pasts of past lives become meaningful through various narratives, and through local demands that metaphysicals place on each other to acknowledge past life relations. For contemporary metaphysicals are able to make demands on others through the idioms and memories of past lives, and in so doing link themselves with others in ways that reach well beyond the randomness of friendship in the all-too ephemeral present. Past lives shape commitments to others through histories that are visible only to those who experience them. They also reveal their commitments to metaphysical pasts as they use the idioms and practices of earlier ages to shape these commitments.

Becoming Max

Cathy strode onto the stage wearing an aquamarine dress on a humid September evening and looked out at the eighty people who had assembled for the Mystical Arts and Talent Show. We listened, transfixed, as she told us how she had changed from a "regular Christian church lady" to a believer in past lives, and how she had in fact become convinced that her past life had been as a well-known Nobel Prize–winning biochemist, Max M—. I called Cathy the next day to ask her if she would be willing to sit for an interview. She was delighted that I called, and said in fact that she had been expecting me: Eric had "told her all about" me. We set up a time to meet, and on a rainy October morning I visited her house for the first time. She talked for two hours about her spiritual journey, and it was only as I packed up that I realized that I hadn't heard anything about Max. Cathy laughed and told me to come back the following week to "hear the rest."

When I returned and settled again into Cathy's wide living room sofa again, I expected that Cathy would begin where she had left off in her spiritual biography, but instead she reviewed the years we had already covered. Once more she told me about how she became interested in practicing Reiki, and about one of her clients, an older Jewish woman with cancer. The first time Cathy told me the vignette it led to a story about an out-of-body experience during which she had met Jesus. This time, however, her Reiki story was but a mere introduction to her journey of exploring the reality of past lives.[9] It all began, Cathy said, when during her client's Reiki treatment she saw her client as a young girl at a train station. Narrating using the present tense, Cathy said: *"I see her, waving out her train window. I can see her mother, in my mind's eye, it's like I'm there on the platform and seeing everything that's happening. And then I realize that I'm also seeing things from the point of view of a man, and he's trying to get his family out. He's saying, 'We must get the children out!'—and I'm thinking, this is English with a German accent. You know, it's like, why am I hearing this in English with a German accent? It doesn't make any sense. But I know that he's a professor, I can see them with—basically with a luggage dolly, with their bags. It's not all their worldly goods. It's just some suitcases there, trying to get on a train undetected. I can tell it's a life or death situation for them, and they're trying to save their lives by getting out of Berlin. I know it is Berlin. And then later on, I see them, in my mind's eye, trying to get to a warehouse at night under cover of darkness. And if they get to the warehouse they'll be OK. I don't, didn't know where that was but it was like—a port, a warehouse in a port. Berlin's not a port, but—but it makes sense later. And I'm like, 'Who is this?' And the name Max M—was just in my mind. It's like, somebody told me that's what it was. And I wrote it down."*

Cathy told me that she paid close attention to the voices and names that she learned while conducting Reiki treatments because she often received information about (or for) her clients in this manner. In addition, names were specifics that she could verify and use to validate the knowledge she received, an aspect of her practice that helped her clients. Cathy told her client, *"'I got this name Max M—, does this mean anything to you?' And she says, 'Nope.' And I say, 'Do you think it could have been someone that your parents knew, because I felt it was different from your story.' And she said 'Nope, never heard of him.' And then I said something about 'When you were getting on the train in Berlin.' And she said, 'We* didn't *go through Berlin—that would be a very stupid place to evacuate the Kindertransport!'"*

Cathy found it odd that her Reiki client didn't remember Max, but she wrote down the name in her client's files. *"Now it's September or October of 2000. And I've read all of the Brian Weiss books—"* Cathy started to say, but then smiled and stopped.

"No, I'm sorry, I have to insert another—February 2000. Don't worry—it has to do with reincarnation! I've read the Brian Weiss books and I say, well, until I experience it, it's not going to be real for me." For the next fifteen minutes, Cathy told me how in February of that year she paid a visit to a hypnotherapist in Boston who practiced past life regression therapy. In a series of vivid sessions Cathy regressed to her life as "Floriana," a

sixteenth-century healer who lived in Switzerland.* In that life, the parish priest had banished her from the town and accused Floriana of killing his mother; Cathy also learned from this experience that the priest is now reincarnated as her son. While Cathy was intrigued, she soon became impatient with the therapist, whom (Cathy explained) was less interested in proving the existence of Floriana than in using the story

* Cathy's interpolated story about Floriana is as follows: "So I find a local therapist who has— who is a "real" therapist, who has her EdD from BU, and to me that's a valid degree. So she's not a new age kook, she's a real therapist who happens to do past life regression therapy. And . . . at the beginning of the second session she's like, what do you want to find out about. You need to have a focus to your session. I said well, two things. I want to find out why I'm obsessed with this idea that I have to be a healer . . . and, two, . . . why do I have such a contentious relationship with my son. And she walks me through the process—you're in a hall, and you're going to see light on a door, you're going to go through the door and you're going to be there. And I go through the door, and she says 'Where are you?' and I said, 'I'm on the floor of your office on a mat, and I can hear the garbage trucks coming down the street.' And part of my consciousness is saying 'Ha ha ha! Not real! See, you knew it wasn't real.'

Now I had done hypnosis in grad school, so I believe in hypnosis, and I know there's a part of your mind that kind of narrated. So the narrator is saying, 'Ha ha ha! Not real!' . . . So she redid the induction with me, and by then the garbage truck was gone, and I opened the door and I'm in this smelly hut. . . . And I can see herbs hanging from the ceiling, and she says look down at yourself, and I can see white hair—I'm a woman—I have white hair down to my shoulders, I'm wearing brown coarse linen or wool, and a robe, just a shapeless robe. I have bare feet. The hut I'm in stinks of animal shit. And I say to myself, 'It really smells in here. I'm having an olfactory hallucination.' I tell her it smells really bad, and she says 'What does it smell like?' and I couldn't come up with the word I wanted—I wanted to say shit, and I'm saying to myself, I can't say that in front of her—I can't say shit under hypnosis! So I said, 'It smells like waste.' . . . She said, what are you doing there, and I said 'Oh! I'm this herbalist, I make teas and stuff for the local townspeople. I'm all alone in this hut.' . . . I knew it was the 1600s, somewhere, the seventeenth century. Just knew all this stuff. And it was like I was looking through a very dark glass at this scene. Some of it was movie quality and some of it was just like a slide show. It wasn't like things were happening, I was just getting a knowingness of what was going on. And she said 'What does this have to do with your life now?' And I said this is why I volunteer at the hospice so all the cranky old ladies don't have to die by themselves.' And I was like "Bing!" this big light went on in my brain, because I specialize in the cranky old ladies at the hospice where I volunteer.

And so she then asks, 'Why are you all alone?' And I say, 'I've been banished to this hut in the woods . . . the priest tells me I'm not doing it right. I'm not worshiping correctly, my beliefs are not in line with the Catholic church, and also he thinks'—I said, 'The priest is my son and he thinks—he thinks I killed his mother.' And she says, well wait a minute, 'if you killed his mother how can he be—and you're still alive—how can he be your son?' And I said. 'Oh no no no no!—he's not my son in that life time, he's my son in this lifetime.'

He was Father F—, this bald, tonsured priest, and he was telling me that I killed his mother, I poisoned his mother, and I kept saying, 'But I gave her tea. I knew she was going to die anyway, what I did didn't kill her, I just made her more comfortable at the end.' And she said, 'So tell him, you didn't kill her.' So I'm laying on this mat, on the floor of her office, and I can hear people out in the waiting room, I'm aware that I'm here. And I'm also in this hut, and I'm screaming at the priest, 'I didn't kill her, I didn't kill her!' And nobody was listening to me—it was like nobody was believing me. I had to go live alone in this little hut. That was my punishment."

Cathy felt as if a "giant weight had been lifted off my chest," itself validation of what it meant, and that it was true. "I was like wow, I can just let that go now, and it doesn't have to be in my energy anymore. . . . I was able to give up a lot of the need for controlling him because one thing I understood was that he was an authority figure over me at that time, and now I'm an authority figure over him, and part of my job is to teach him what it is like to be a benign, unconditionally loving authority figure. That is part of my responsibility to get him to understand what it is like to be on the receiving end of a benign, unconditionally loving authority figure. Not a punitive, controlling authority figure."

to heal Cathy's relationship with her son. Not content with working out current family issues through what might well be metaphor and imagination, Cathy sought stronger evidence for the reality of past lives. Beyond this, however, she would need to know more about a past life that she could independently verify, and she was (she imagined) unlikely to find evidence of Floriana, an illiterate Swiss healer from the sixteenth century.

More and more curious about past lives and spirit guides, Cathy began to practice self-hypnosis, and in the process learned more about Max. There *"was a wife and at least one child, [and] he was a professor. And I said a professor of what, and what I got was a professor of semiotics. Now I had never heard—I had heard of semiotics but I didn't know what it meant so I had to look it up."* At this point Cathy started looking for Max in earnest, thinking that there was a *"connection"* between them. It was at about the same time that she started to attend the Mystical Experiences Discussion Group, and she talked with group members about Max several times. Cathy told me that several members suggested that Max might be likely a spirit guide who, like a ghost or spirit, was assisting Cathy in her earthly mission. Cathy was open to this possibility, she said, especially after she started receiving medical diagnoses for her Reiki clients (including unfamiliar Latin terms) during hypnosis. Such interventions seemed more in line with what others described relating contact from *"the other world,"* rather than recovering a memory of her own.[10]

At around this time Cathy received a call that a place had opened up for her at the Omega Institute's oversubscribed weeklong workshop on past life regression, led by Brian Weiss. She took this unexpected opening (there had been seventy-five on the waiting list) as a sign, and eagerly paid the hefty registration fee and endured a week of vegetarian food at the Rhinebeck, New York, holistic center in order to attend daily sessions with Weiss, one of the leaders of past life regression therapy in the United States. Every afternoon, Cathy retreated to her dorm room with her roommate to "practice" regressing. When Cathy asked for "more information" about Max, she was returned to the train station where she had first heard Max's name. Cathy laughed, saying that while on the platform she was *"talking in a German accent in English. And I kept thinking 'Oh Cathy, this is so bizarre.' . . . The observer part of me is going 'Cathy, this is so hokey, you do not have to speak in a fake German accent!' So I immediately switched back into regular English. And my roommate asked what's happening. I said, 'We have to get the children out.' And I started to get—my chest started to tighten and I couldn't breathe, and it was very frightening. She backed away. . . . She didn't have the confidence to have me process the negative emotions."*

While the train platform scene was familiar, the experience this time was stronger and more specific. The German accent was fake, but it was nonetheless Cathy who was using it. Cathy in addition felt Max's anxiety in her own body. Cathy then moved to the *"next significant experience"* and Cathy *"saw this warehouse, we were trying to get this warehouse in the dark. And it seemed like it was in a seaport, but I wasn't quite sure. But it wasn't Berlin. But again, I didn't get a clear idea of who this guy was, I just knew that he was a professor."*

Cathy told me that even after this regression she was not sure if she was Max. Increasingly she felt she needed to know whether Max was a real, historical person. To verify his existence became an all-consuming concern. In guided meditations she would ask her guides *"'is my energy—is the energy that's in Cathy the same energy that's in Max?' The answer I got was yes. . . . So I'm tapping into this other dimension. But I still don't have proof."*

Cathy wanted proof for several reasons. She wanted to know whether she was remembering events in another person's life that she had some part of, energetically speaking. She did not want it to be merely an imaginative recalling or a subconsciously recombined dream. She was not content to work with her hypnotherapist through an imaginative talking cure. Not content with mere metaphor, Cathy wished to learn about what she understood to be layers of causality and intersecting fields of relations ("karma") that she thought would uniquely be able to make sense of this life's limits and give shape to future lives. She worked from the Internet to research Max, and read what she could find in the public library about midcentury German intellectuals and Berlin university linguistics programs. She even tried her hand at automatic typing.

These searches yielded little, yet all the while Cathy continued to receive more "information" about Max from meditation sessions. It was not until she returned one evening from an uneventful night at the Mystical Experiences Discussion Group meeting that she glanced through a printed-out page of search engine "hits" for Max and noticed for the first time a *"variant spelling"* of Max's last name, one that she had not used before. She rushed to her computer and received over six hundred "hits" for *"Albert 'Max' M—,"* a German Jewish scientist and physician who had made a hurried escape to the United States with his wife and children at the onset of the Second World War. Several Web sites described the family's journey over land to Paris, and then from Marseilles to the States. Cathy now had independent evidence of Max's existence.

Cathy summed up this part of the story saying *"that was a huge epiphany, it was like: You got this intuitively. It's a real person. They existed. I'm still not sure [if] it's [me] or not, but, there were just too many parallels. . . ."*

Making Evidence of and for Past Lives

While Cathy's story becomes real through (generically influenced) expressions of evidence, the demands that scientific proof place on Cathy are not easily met, even by these careful narrations. Indeed, the unrelenting emphasis on the scientific reality of past lives tends to unravel and call into question the experiential proof of feeling Max's emotions and seeing through his eyes. Even at the moment of Cathy's epiphany, when she discovers that Max was a real person, she is *"still not sure [if] it's [me] or not."*

Rather than continuing to seek for what she considered "objective proof," Cathy shifts her approach at this point to reflect in a number of ways on more interesting questions, namely what her past life meant for her present one. Before investigating the dialogue that commences between Cathy's selves and the roles that Annette and others come to play, it is worth asking not only how this proof is generically shaped, but whether we can learn anything further from her emphasis on engaging the "scientific bases" of past life experiences.

Creating the conditions under which Cathy first experiences and then discovers Max develops through a skillful assembling of elements within a particular temporal pattern wherein Cathy can first experience and then learn about Max, similar to those described in chapter 2. Validity unfolds temporally. While finding the historical Max is necessary to the narrative, it cannot happen before Cathy has intuitively experienced him. This creates a strong narrative tension: Cathy's desire to discover Max needs to be checked and held at bay. In Cathy's narrative several missteps and cloudy information (misspelling his last name; believing that he is a semiotician; considering alternatives for Max's identity, including that he is an "angel guide")[11] extend narrative time and provide a reasonable account of how Cathy's desires to unearth more "proof" are checked until the appropriate moment.

This tension surrounding intuition and proof is central in many contemporary books and accounts of past life regression.[12] It is a central theme in Brian Weiss's *Many Lives, Many Masters* and the best-selling popular literature on past lives to which Cathy refers. Weiss's books provide an important template through which readers can learn to experience and evaluate past lives. And, as Cathy's own ruminations about her experiences suggest, these stories of past lives in some respects become true by conforming to a recognizable literary genre.

Weiss's books are the most frequently mentioned in a surprisingly large field of popular books on past life regression, reincarnation, and "soul mates."[13] His 1988 *Many Lives, Many Masters* begins with the story of Weiss himself, an "Ivy-league trained" psychiatrist, and his treatment of Catherine, who suffered from obsessive-compulsive disorder and abnormal fears of choking and drowning. Weiss decides to use hypnosis to treat Catherine, with the expectation that this tool will lead to the recovery of the childhood trauma from which her fears and psychoses arise. Under hypnosis Catherine remembers and relives being drowned and being buried alive: to Weiss's surprise, however, these experiences happened in prior lifetimes. Thus begins Weiss's journeys to understanding what he calls the nature of reincarnation.

Like Cathy, Weiss takes great care to explain to his readers why past lives are not mere figments of his patient's imagination or repressed memories projected into a fictive past. His explanations begin with a recitation of his academic credentials and Ivy League pedigree, and his professional commitments to skepticism. He gives his professional opinion that Catherine is not trying to fool him (she is a good Catholic, a Christian with no reason to believe in or make up fantastical tales). Once Weiss ascertains that neither he nor his patient have any reason to make these things up, Weiss turns to note the "scientific literature" on past lives, and likewise presents findings in the "historical record" of past civilizations' beliefs in past lives. Drawing on his dusty textbook from his "undergraduate course in comparative religion at Columbia University," Weiss notes that "the early church fathers had accepted the concept of reincarnation. The early Gnostics—Clement of Alexandria, Origen, Saint Jerome, and many others—believed that they had lived before and would again."[14] It so appears that at the same time that Catherine recovers her pasts through hypnotic apprehensions, so Weiss also "recovers" a history of reincarnation belief through similar processes, "apprehending" clear evidence and traces of prior peoples' understandings in various (Western esoteric) texts. The submerged and forgotten past life of past lives is thus recovered, albeit in a way that suggests additional links and relations.

Weiss's initial interest in convincing his readers that past lives are real gives way quickly to fascination with the messages that Catherine channels from the "Masters." Weiss meets the Masters in the spaces or times between Catherine's lives, where spirits talk to the dead and counsel them on their future life choices. Intrigued and enthralled by the various lectures that he receives from the Masters, and the knowledge that "they" have of his own secrets, Weiss continues to place Catherine under hypnosis well after her phobias are cured through regressions in therapy (like Cathy, Catherine is "cured" of her phobias by merely reliving "real" past life traumas). Eventually Weiss becomes concerned that he is using Catherine for his own investigative ends and begins to talk directly to the Masters.

Several aspects of Weiss's narrative suggests relations to early and mid-twentieth-century American reincarnation theory: the focus on mystical, Gnostic Christianity; his concerns with the interstitial moments between lives; the value put on conversations with nonhumans; and, above all, the emphasis on scientific "proof" are common themes and tropes in each. Weiss's history of past lives overlooks the most proximate American examples (except for the scientist Ian Stevenson). The stories of past lives elaborated and recounted in midcentury bestsellers (including Morey Bernstein's *The Search for Bridey Murphy* and hagiographies of the trance healer Edgar Cayce, including Thomas Sugrue's *There Is a River* and Gina Cerminara's *Many Mansions*) offer a probable reason for this lacuna.[15] These books, along with Weiss's, emphasize that major proponents of "past lives" come to their knowledge from experience alone. Thus Sugrue elaborates how Edgar Cayce (the noted spiritual trance healer) began to receive information about his clients' past lives in order to help heal his clients, long before he had even heard the term "reincarnation."[16]

Cerminara relates Cayce's struggles over whether to consider material he was receiving in his trances "valid." It is through the intervention of a friend who happens to be a Theosophist that Cayce "learns that early Christians knew about reincarnation" but that such stories were written out of biblical accounts. After many "discussions, probings, and exploratory excursions into books on history, science and comparative religions" and after "confirming" trance information by reading external sources, Cayce comes to accept not only that good Christians can also believe in reincarnation, but that it is a "scientific" and universal truth that governs all religious tradition.[17]

The 1950's best-seller *The Search for Bridey Murphy* follows a similar pattern, with discoveries gleaned in hypnosis and other experiential moments are followed by external validation. Bernstein, who describes himself as merely interested in hypnosis, accidentally "regresses" a young midwestern housewife named Ruth Simmons. Simmons returns to one of her most recent past lives (the eponymous Bridey Murphy) under hypnosis and recounts numerous details of her life and her surroundings. Most of the book is a faithful transcription of Simmon's/Murphy's descriptions of nineteenth-century Ireland, and also reports on Simmon's/Murphy's between-lives stint as a "ghost." Bernstein is more interested in whether he can prove the existence of Bridey Murphy independently than he is in the meanings that these various states of the soul might have for Simmons or himself.[18] With an advance from Doubleday publishers, he dispatches investigators to Ireland, who learn indeed that many of the names, dates, and places that are recounted in the story are "real."

The genre's persistent emphases on the "reality" of reincarnation, the law of karma, and what a person might learn by investigating one's past lives or the period between lives draws attention to the robust tropes and understandings of reincarnation that shape early twenty-first century past life practices. My respondents would say that the similarities between the experiences of people who have no prior knowledge or interest in past lives lend proof to the argument that these are stable, enduring phenomena. Yet claims for the "universal" and perennial qualities also suggest that they are shaped within the metaphysical milieu, which, we have seen, does have a history and a set of practices that sever it from its own pasts. With this in mind, we can investigate how earlier metaphysical arguments about reincarnation give shape to contemporary practice, and ponder how these stories and practices lend themselves to shaping visions of the past that resist standard historical narration. While contemporary writers rarely refer to these more proximate American pasts, preferring to draw on Gnostics or other ancients, their ideas are revived and reproduced in both the ideology of reincarnation and in the practical views of what past lives mean and how they can be experienced and understood.

American Reincarnations

Texts like Brian Weiss's or even Morey Bernstein's follow the forms and generic properties of metaphysical narratives about reincarnation that emerged in a new way in the late nineteenth-century debates between New Thought writers, some Spiritualists and Theosophists.[19]

Metaphysicals began to argue about the possibilities of "regeneration," the transmigration of souls, past lives, and reincarnation at a time when the heavens were burgeoning with ghosts, astral beings, angels, spirit guides, and ascended Masters. The evident impetus for metaphysical interest in reincarnation was the growing popular attention to Asian philosophical and religious texts, carried forward by interpreters as diverse as Emerson and Helena Petrova Blavatsky, Swami Vivekananda, and Yogi Paramhansa. Reincarnation beliefs took shape within a field already rich both with metaphysical possibilities and with internecine conflicts over their relative merits,[20] and within a cultural climate that was suspicious of (if not horrified by) Indian notions of karma and reincarnation, which most viewed as a "repulsive . . . unnatural" and "loathsome" abomination.[21]

To counter these criticisms, proponents emphasized that reincarnation was not the sole purview of Asian philosophies or cultures, but rather was discernable in all esoteric religions. It was, in other words, one of many universal truths carried forward within true religion. Proponents taught those who would listen to trust their own experiences so that they could detect the traces of past lives, and likewise drew upon esoteric reading practices to discern the presence of reincarnation theories within various religious texts. Reincarnationists honed metaphysical reading strategies that allowed them to distinguish the truths of scriptures using esoteric keys that unlocked the true meaning of text. These strategies at times consciously dismissed interpretations that were mired in the "material" or in "history." Esoteric Christian writers Edward Maitland and Anna Kingsford cautioned that the truths of scripture would remain inaccessible to those who remained rooted in the "phenomenal and objective." In contrast, for "those initiated, the mind is no longer concerned with history; the phenomenal becomes recognized as the illusory—a shadow projected by the Real, having no substance in itself."[22]

The reincarnation that these writers promoted and encountered in reading and experiencing was "peculiarly modern, conforming to the latest findings of modern science and even prefiguring Darwin's theory of evolution."[23] In many ways, reincarnation was an easy fit within American Spiritualists' and Theosophical understandings that souls moved toward perfection and unity with the divine by advancing through numerous, progressive astral planes (or "heavens"). The karmic demands of rebirth were the grist that perfected and refined souls, opined New Thought author Charles B. Newcomb: "The mills of the gods grind so slowly that the grist of to-day may have been put into the hopper in some incarnation far remote; but doubtless by the man's own hands, for it is only our own grist that comes to us through the mill of life."[24]

Progressive reincarnation was easily distinguishable furthermore from "abominable" Indian versions. Reincarnation that advanced souls ineluctably toward union with the divine was constantly distinguished from the debased philosophies and examples that came from India. In particular, metaphysicals recoiled from the idea that humans could reincarnate in the future as animals. In contrast, they argued that no matter where in the line of evolutionary soul development a soul started, it could not "regress" back into animal form once it had been coupled to a human body. The "true meaning of the doctrine, the human ego can no more retrograde by reincarnating in brute form than, according to the Darwinian theory, man can degenerate into a monkey, or a monkey into a mosquito" said Paul Tyner. French Spiritualist Allen Kardec agreed, stating men cannot descend to a lower point from which they have risen. "As regards his *social position,* yes; but not as regards his degree of progress as a spirit." Kingsford and Maitland similarly project evolutionary Darwinism into the astral realm as they note, "man also has a divine spirit; and so long as he is man—that is truly human—he cannot redescend into the body of an animal or any creature in the sphere beneath him, since that would be an indignity."[25]

Ultimately, these universal truths and metaphysical comparisons encouraged readers to discover the truths of reincarnation within their "own" tradition. Writing under the pen name Yogi Ramacharaka, for example, New Thought writer William Walker Atkinson counseled American Christians to recover this lost, universal wisdom for Christianity. As the Yogi Ramacharaka explained, readers did not need to look to India for the truths of reincarnation and human liberation. Rather, these are fully evident in the Christian texts that Ramacharaka/ Atkinson encourages Americans seekers to accept. One does not need to look to the "East" to find truth, the shape-shifting Atkinson states. Rather, the true "mystic Christ" "believed in, and taught the doctrine of Reincarnation [along with] many other Occult Truths, the traces of which appear constantly in the Christian Teachings." The traces of the true gospel can still be found in the text, the yogi explains to his readers, and beginning with an understanding of the laws of karma makes this possible. The Virgin Birth, he explains, refers not to Mary's chaste body but to Jesus's uniquely nonreincarnated spirit. "His Spirit had not traveled the weary upward path of Reincarnation and repeated Rebirth, but was Virgin Spirit fresh from SPIRIT. . . . The Virgin Spirit was incarnated in His body, and there he began the life of Man."[26] Given the growing, widespread interest among metaphysical proponents to prove the truths of religions through scientific means and investigation it is no surprise that reincarnation's proponents claimed that these newly developing techniques would prove the fact of these "universal laws." Echoing numerous others writing in the first decades of the twentieth century, Yogi Ramacharaka claimed triumphantly that emerging theological and scientific methods, namely the "Higher Criticism," the "Criticism of Science," would "prove the truths of [mystical Christianity's] fundamental principles"[27] Maitland and Kingsford likewise note that such views are evident in the Bible: "had it been accurately translated, the doctrine that all creatures whatsoever represent incarnations, though in different conditions, of one and the same universal soul, would not now need to be re-declared . . . For the doctrine of a universal soul is the doctrine of love, in that it implies the recognition of the larger self. . . . Humanity as the one universal creation of which all living things are but different steps."[28] Using the same practices and procedures, metaphysicals recovered both the universal, hidden truths of reincarnation and likewise their own hidden past lives.

In the metaphysical worlds of nineteenth-century New England, arguments against reincarnation far outweighed the claims in their favor. The stakes to prove their existence were quite high. Some, including Blavatsky, refused to rise to the challenge, arguing that while karma and reincarnation were "universal laws," they nevertheless could not be adduced or proven through the body or its individual memories. Past lives are lost to everyone who is reincarnated in physical form, and available only to those who have advanced past bodily reincarnation altogether. While individuals are embodied, she wrote, "ego will be furnished with a *new* body, a *new* brain, and a *new* memory. Therefore it would be as absurd to expect this memory to remember that which it has never recorded as it would be idle to examine under a microscope a shirt never worn by a murderer, and seek on it for the stains of blood which are to be found only on the clothes he wore."[29]

Despite the enormous attention that psychical researchers paid to a variety of paranormal activities, including psychic abilities, mediumship, and hauntings, few had any interest in investigating past lives. The American Society for Psychical Research remained resolutely disinterested in reincarnation well into the twentieth century, owing most likely to the Society's emphasis on testing Spiritualists' claims of life after death communication and reincarnation's connection with Theosophy (which the Society had "exposed" as fraudulent in 1885). The Society's Annals and Proceedings mention reincarnation only in passing in its first few decades, and these references tend to be derogatory and dismissive.[30] This did not keep reincarnation's proponents from working to prove that it existed, however. They encouraged readers and believers to trust their instincts and their sense of déjà vu. People find that they have "the vague remembrance of their past; the result of progress previously made by the soul, but of which it has no present consciousness." Remarking on the sometimes surprising displays of individual skill, Kardec asked, "From what else could those intuitions be derived? The body changes, but the spirit does not change, although he changes his garment."[31] In all of these practices, the body and its memories became prime sites of recovering pasts. Strange attractions or "recognitions" became more and more a focus of attention, in particular the strange attractions or sense of familiarity that strangers might sense.

The mutual attractions of strangers in fact became an important way that reincarnationists understood past lives to be manifest in the present. Refashioning the Spiritualist notion of "soul mates," where each soul had a complementary spiritual and physical companion in both life and death, reincarnationists described soul mates as "life to life" companions that sought each other out, time and again, in order to fulfill their progressive destiny together.[32] Kardec explains that "chance" encounters were nothing less than the ineluctable result of souls searching out their true mates. "[T]he attraction resulting from the ties of a former existence is often the cause of the most intimate unions of a subsequent existence. . . . It often happens that two persons are drawn together by circumstances which appear to be merely fortuitous, but which are really due to the attractions exercised . . . by two spirits who are unconsciously seeking each other amidst the crowds by whom they are surrounded."[33] Finding one's soul mate not only proved the reality of past lives, but it also rendered one's own mystical path as an unfolding intersubjective and social project. These ideas strongly suggested that one's true obligations were to one's soul mates, and likewise suggested that those demands and obligations were so strong that they would overcome all obstacles. "True Love is stronger than a thousand deaths. For though one die a thousand times, a single Love may yet perpetuate itself past every death from birth to birth, growing and culminating in intensity and thought."[34]

While most early reincarnation writers embedded their claims for past lives' realities within sensations of intimacies and the pull of "unseen intelligences drawn to us by congenial thought,"[35] others sought out more specific experiences with past lives. In self-administered trances and meditations, some could reach into deeply submerged memories of past lives (and even submerged memories of the afterlife) and reencounter (indeed, in some cases, "relive") pasts with specific times, dates, and personae. Not everyone was able to do this, however:

indeed, some argued that only more highly progressed spiritual souls were able to recollect their pasts with any specificity.[36] Those who could remember their pasts without the aid of the technologies of hypnosis and regression therapy (which would take shape in the mid-twentieth century and beyond) could claim a higher status by virtue of their ability to recall. Charles Fillmore, like other New Thought leaders, wedded reincarnation with perfection, stating "those who failed to manifest the Christ Consciousness and regenerate their physical bodies would return in new bodies for more spiritual work." Fillmore, the founder (with his wife Myrtle) of the Unity Church, furthermore claimed that he was the reincarnation of the Apostle Paul, and opined that Paul's fate had been to be reincarnated: despite all of his worldly accomplishments in building the church, he had nonetheless "left hundreds of admissions of his disobedience, weakness, ambition and double-mindedness. . . . [H]e was a good man, and sincere, but he had his faults. He was possessed of a towering ambition."[37] Fillmore's claims to learn the details of Paul's failings during various meditation sessions caused unease for many Unity followers. But such claims also represented the apotheosis of a particular strain of perfection theology, where worldly success, perhaps especially the work of building a religious institution that dismissed many of the spiritual truths that Unity promoted, represented something less than perfection.

Fillmore's turn-of-the-century claims to recall specific past lives also ultimately would present the opportunity for the elevation of the modest lives of modern-day bookkeepers, laborers, and housewives to new mystical heights. Fillmore's visions suggested that knowing details about past lives might allow people to better comprehend their purpose in this one,[38] a claim that also emerged as trance channeler and healer Edgar Cayce channeled information about his clients' past lives in order to heal their psychological and relationship problems.[39] Cayce's visions often located important past lives in Atlantis or the far reaches of time; in comparison with Fillmore's visions, Cayce's were often short on specific details that might place them in the historical record.[40] Nonetheless, Cayce's messages strongly suggested that knowing the details of karmic connections would result in more fruitful lives in the present and also suggested that it was not only the spiritually advanced who had to gain from interrogations of past lives. Nonetheless, for Cayce as for Fillmore, recovering those pasts depended on trances, meditations, and "perceptions" rather than on what American metaphysicals consider to be "scientific" techniques.

What would be necessary to make this transformation, however, were new techniques that enabled all people to access their pasts. As the twentieth century unfolded, new technologies of regression brought the possibility of investigating one's past lives to a wider range of people. As hypnosis became used as a psychological tool for curing psychological neuroses in the years after World War I, psychical researchers and amateurs began to discover that hypnosis could regress individuals past birth and into previous lives. Hypnosis became a viable strategy of recovering past lives, and these recovered memories could then be explored and verified through historical investigation. Memories recovered under hypnosis presented rich details that simultaneously healed individuals of neuroses and obsessions and verified the realities of remembered pasts, insofar as memories could be linked to a historical record. Hypnotic technologies presented new ways to uncover and experience pasts that earlier proponents had argued were lost forever, thus playing a role in democratizing past life knowledge. Now everyone, and not only the most spiritually advanced, could revisit their pasts. All the same, hypnosis brought with it the concern that it preyed on the preternaturally weak minded, and that it merely brought to life a subconscious, not a past consciousness. Newly emergent practices of learning about past lives sought to answer and fend off some of these concerns and criticisms; these practices of verifying past lives actively reinforced the sui generis aspects of past life knowledge and effectively buried the proximate histories of past life investigators in favor of apprehended and experienced pasts. Thus, while we see that these practices continue to be reproduced within the varied ways that metaphysicals apprehend their past lives, they are not part of the discourse or part of the story that they tell. Indeed, metaphysicals continue to root meaning in mystical links and connections that demonstrate their participation in various narratives of the past and its force on the present.

Living Past Lives

Cambridge's mystics live out the various kinds of past life experience, reproducing their tropes and practices in daily relationships. Past lives do more than engage their participants in creative philosophizing. They are important *social* products through which their participants shape current relationships and understand their place in the world. Determining or discussing a past life does not merely extend a person's history back in time. It additionally adds another layer of mystical connection and history to a person's genealogical history, mixing up and complicating ideas of familial duty and attraction.

Most past life stories that I encountered were brief and arose in regular, daily conversations between Cambridge's metaphysicals. Brief references to shared past lives were not told to establish clear links to one's own historical past, but rather to solidify the connections between two or more mystics. In other words, discourse about past lives evoked connections (and marked moral claims) to others' lives. These claims were "experiential," often "felt" or "sensed" rather than discovered under hypnosis or other concentrated techniques. Mystics evoked past life "connections" and "recognitions" to explain or to reinforce friendships and to confirm life choices as part of a broad cosmic plan, or to make sense of a range of feelings and longings (romantic and otherwise) and even revulsions that were socially or morally problematic. Like other religious narratives that construct a shared past, past lives genres linked disparate individuals within powerful and real (yet at some level unseen) friendships, family ties and romantic alliances, disrupting some moral ties and creating others anew through encountering and imagining unknown pasts.

Connecting in the Cosmic Order: Friendships and Acquaintances

Cathy had been sorely disappointed that I had missed meeting Annette, Crystal, and Marcy when they started attending the Mystical Experiences Discussion Group. As she told me, and each of the newcomers later also related, they had all appeared at the group on the same night: each of them had read about it in the free local magazine *Spirit of Change* and each of them had moved to the Cambridge area within the previous few months. None of them knew anyone in the group, and they found it quite auspicious that their search for a spiritual community had led them to the group on the same evening. Each of them took this chance meeting as a clear sign that they were meant to attend the group regularly, and that they were meant to be friends. Others in the group, including Cathy, also found this to be likely. "Something drew them all to Cambridge, and to the group," Cathy remarked to me later. Crystal, an energy healer, and Marcy, a yoga instructor, were both about the same age and found further common ground in their attempts to make a living doing spiritual work. They spent much time together and, as Marcy relayed to the mystical experiences group in December, determined that this was not the first life that they had spent together as close friends.

As it turned out, Crystal was not at the group that night, but she had described the same revelation over a pot of tea in a Central Square coffeehouse earlier in the week. As Crystal told me, she had invited Marcy over for an energetic healing session (similar to Reiki) to work on Marcy's back, and she had received a *"sensation"* during treatment. What kind of sensation? I asked. *"It was not just a sensation but a deep knowing,"* she told me. She "knew" that she had been Marcy's friend in numerous previous lives. She didn't have a clear sense of what any of the lives had entailed. What was more important was the "lives long" commitments that they had with each other. Crystal continued, saying that when the session finished, she asked Marcy tentatively if she had "felt anything," and Marcy said yes. *"Since that we've been hanging out and doing lots of things together, and it is just, it's just like—when I am with her, I get this feeling of coming home."* Like Crystal, Marcy sensed the reality of her past lives with Crystal and received glimpses "like snapshots" of other lives.

In contrast to Cathy's increasingly close reading of Max's "biography," the details of Crystal's and Marcy's past lives were rather vague. The existence of their past lives was confirmed in their individual bodily experiences and in their mutual recognition of their connection. The stories or histories of the past lives that they lived together did not advance beyond simple "snapshots" that Marcy accessed during meditation on the treatment table, and Crystal's "deep knowing." Vagueness in this respect allows soul mates to refrain from wading into the murky territory of "past life regression" therapy, which focuses intense interest on the struggles and (frequent) violence of past lives. In addition to keeping at bay the recollection of past lives like the one that Cathy encountered (where she realized her current son had banished her in a previous life to a life of misery), the vagueness of Marcy's and Crystal's "sensations" and "snapshots" allowed them to work together to build commitments through past lives that are hard to contradict with facts. As we will see in Annette and Cathy's case, pinpointing actual past relationships within documented historical relationships destabilizes mystical connections and requires mystics to move beyond the practical elements of past life connections to ponder with more precision what past life memories are for.

Crystal and Marcy were not drawn into such questions, however, during my fieldwork: in the months that followed their revelations, their mutual recognition of past lives allowed each woman to call on the other for emotional support in ways that far surpassed the normal bounds of a budding, months-old friendship. The language of homecoming, echoed by many, evokes both a hope and desire for a comfortable relationship with strangers. At the time of my field research, neither woman was in a committed relationship (Crystal was recently divorced), and both had pulled up extensive roots elsewhere when they moved to Cambridge. Finding an "old" friend confirmed for them that their decisions to come to Cambridge were in tune with the order of things, even if neither understood completely what that order was or what their place in it would be. These experiences and shared stories also provided cultural resources that allowed the women to actually make these relationships real. Recognizing a shared past life, or agreeing to another's "sense" of such a past life, meant likewise to accept the duty and rights that attended to it. Their "sense" of lives-long care for each other enjoined each to continue to care for the other as well.

Karmic responsibilities are specific and interpersonal: the lives and souls that continue from life to life are, much like those described by early twentieth-century New Thought writers, recognizable selves who "learn" and "remember" from life to life to life, progressing ever toward union with God. Mystics who experience their position with a broader, expansive sense of time and space do so nonetheless in the company of familiar souls. These cosmic families figure prominently in American reincarnation literature and in lived religious experience.

Mystical Families

By January, it was dawning on regular attendees of the Mystical Experiences Discussion Group that perhaps their connections to each other on the whole surpassed their mundane and superficial interests in talking about their own unique experiences. There was much in the literature that mystics read to suggest that this would be possible. Several of the channeled entities that Doug, Eric, and Cathy consulted and read as part of their channeling classes suggested possible connections; the "Michael group" in particular had put forth the idea of "soul clusters" stating that individual selves are nothing but "fragments" of larger soul clusters that advance and evolve together, often interacting together to work out specific issues of the soul cluster in human relations.[41] A central aspect of American reincarnation practice is the sense that souls can recognize familiar souls from one's past life. For many, this vision that souls can recognize each other led to the concomitant view that we are in fact likely to recognize souls from the past because we are linked to those souls for all time: personal evolution is linked to the evolution also of our familiars. These familiars take on the character of a "true" mystical family that exists in tension with the biological families and relationships in which mystics find themselves. American reincarnation stories rarely, if ever, suggest that mystical families reincarnate within the same historical or ancestral family lines.

The tensions of lives-long attractions are not only matters of contemporary fascination. Indeed, the writings of Kardec, Cayce (via his hagiographers), and various channeled entities at times seem fixated with the troubling possibility that reincarnation experiences weaken family commitments. Against those who claim that past lives destroy filial commitments and devotion to ancestors, Kardec says rather that "[they extend] those ties, but [they do] not destroy them; on the contrary, the conviction that the relationships of the present life are based upon anterior affections renders the ties between members of the same family less precarious. It makes the duties of fraternity even more imperative, because in your neighbor or in your servant, may be incarnated some spirit who has formerly been united to you by the closest ties of consanguinity."[42] The tension that mystics in Cambridge engage when they think about and discuss their links to a mystical family is not dissimilar: the members of the mystical experiences group did not use these ideas of the cosmic union of soul clusters to reject their physical families as unworthy of their commitments. Rather, cosmic connections placed family ties in conversation with ideals of family and connection, allowing them to imagine their current family relationships (and their problems and intimacies) as either necessary lessons and burdens, or as rewards for past life struggles through difficult times. Mystical and biological families thus are rarely distinct, even though the vision of a constantly evolving, perfectible mystical family is almost always viewed as less problematic and thus the source of desires for true intimacy and comfort so rarely found in more mundane relationships.

In short, the recognition that one belongs to a mystical family that reincarnates together, life after life, with each soul taking on particular, necessary roles in order to advance the entire group toward evolution or (potentially) union with God provides almost endless resources with which to imagine and evaluate family relationships. Difficult relationships, bad decisions about spouses or intimacies, intractable personality conflicts between family members, distrust and infidelity all become inflected with karmic meaning. Each becomes an opportunity to work out karmic issues and to better understand the nature of one's true allegiances. Yet, unlike many other religious narrative frameworks that require individuals to measure current family relations in this life against a clear set of ideals exemplified by a divine family, the mystic family experienced imperfectly from life to life provides a powerful but quite different space to therapeutically question and reorient relationships as important steps toward redemption of the whole.[43]

Many of my respondents discussed their families in these terms. Marcy, who had a troubled relationship with her father and her married sister, often spoke of the things that she was supposed to "learn" and the appropriate way to practice "loving kindness" that would help repair these relations in the next life, if not this one. Annette, who married and divorced in her early twenties, frequently talked to me about the intense, lives-long connection she had with her former husband. As she understood it, their mutual attraction had been strong throughout many lives, as had their conflicts and incompatibilities. Rather than deciding to stick through a marriage that was emotionally and (more importantly) spiritually draining, she hoped that making a conscious decision in this life to reject the baser attractions to her husband, and by following her "higher path," she might make spiritual progress. These stories and understandings were likely made possible in part by the developing ritualization of the mystical family of the regular experience group attendees, displayed most clearly to me during a dinner party that Cathy hosted for the spring equinox, a week before Easter.

Cathy's husband was out of town on business, and she had once again dispatched her son to a friend's house for a sleepover. Cathy's daughter peeped in and out of the living room with a friend she had invited. After making a figurine of "Hera" for the ritual after dinner (I had drawn this card from the goddess stack) and talking with Eric's wife about her recent art exhibit, I walked out to the kitchen where Cathy and Marcy were deep in conversation. Cathy put me to work carving a lamb roast while she pulled a strawberry trifle out of the refrigerator and called Doug and Eric to pour water and wine. When I remarked on the seasonal theme, Cathy said, *"Oh yes, I've made Easter dinner one week early—I won't get to do this next week, since we're taking our family trip to Sedona."* Cathy had laid her dining room with her best china and linens, and as we gathered, Cathy replaced one family with another, announcing, "Annette and I have been working on the seating arrangement." Annette sat at the head of the table at the far end of the dining room in Cathy's husband's normal chair, and Cathy sat at the end closest to the kitchen. Around them, they had arranged Eric and his wife at Cathy's right, Doug next to me, and Marcy and Crystal flanking Annette. Cathy's daughter also sat at the table with her friend. As we started to eat, laughter and occasional dark looks shot across the table. Things said and unsaid gave voice to the complicated relationships that the individuals around the table would entertain, at least for a time, as both unavoidable and demanding. The dark looks, however, also evoked a number of intimacies between these gathered that arguably moved well beyond simple friendships and familial ties. Past life idioms also held out the possibility, if not the "fact," of lives-long passions and intimate unions between two souls.

Desire

More than any other idea, "soul mates" captured the imagination and desires of spiritual men and women. The idea of soul mates articulated in New Thought and other early twentieth-century literature cultivated ideals of romantic intimacy that have developed into a robust literature of its own. Although soul mates are clearly not a new idea, they appear now to be a perennially popular one. Dozens of best-selling books on soul mates offer a range of advice from the most conservative to the most libertine, counseling the lovelorn how to identify soul mates and what to do if she or he is stuck in a relation with someone who is not. Most offer the possibility that one's life will be fulfilled spiritually, emotionally, and physically, and most likewise suggest that only a few unique souls will be able to satisfy desires for such fulfillment. Not surprisingly, many mystics in Cambridge—whether married, partnered, or single—hoped that in this life or the next they would connect with the person who would complete them and with whom they could conquer all human obstacles through true passion and connection. Not content with good looks or even a physical connection, they wanted (as Vivica, a thirty-five-year-old yoga instructor, put it) *"the person who will connect with every part of me, not just my brain or my body."* The idea that there was one person (or soul) in the world with whom one would uniquely and perfectly connect (especially when coupled with the expectation that close soul fragments often reincarnated in close proximity) heightened optimism about their romantic futures—if not in this life, then in the one to come.

The thrilling possibility of meeting the one beloved soul in the universe who would fully complete one's own life is not without its hazards, insofar as it offers divine sanction for pursuing what might otherwise be considered an illicit attraction. In the language of soul mates, refusing to acknowledge a connection to a spiritual twin is a moral failing, perhaps more grave than leaving a non-karmically connected partner. Reincarnation literature thus often combines the promise of perfect intimacy with warnings about pursuing it headlong. Edgar Cayce's redactor notes, for example, that while "social norms" such as marriage and fidelity are "less sacrosanct than many people might think," one does not have perfect license to abandon commitments. Rather, individuals "must learn to accept [marriage's] difficulties and frustrations in a sacrificial spirit, realizing that our lesser self is on trial so that our great Self may be born."[44]

The very idea of an erotic, intellectual, and spiritual soul mate searching for fulfillment gave shape and voice to mystics' desires and worries for their relationships, allowing many to place themselves in stories where they could work out their own disappointments and hopes, while also introducing a sense of palpable danger in one's relations with other metaphysicals. Cathy had a loving, respectful, and respectable marriage, but she was also certain that she had spent "many lives" with Eric. And Eric and Cathy were very good friends and companions in mystical circuits in Boston. They took channeling classes together, e-mailed frequently, shared books and Web sites, and for a time met for dinner once a month. Cathy had noted numerous parallel interests and interesting commonalities in their biographies. Noting these connections was thrilling to Cathy but also caused her constant worry. If Eric was her soul mate in many lives, then how to explain their relation in this one? This question dogged Cathy throughout my fieldwork, and she brought it up with me, with others, and also with Eric himself.

In the month before I left Cambridge, Cathy met me for pasta at a local diner and told me with relief that she had come to a resolution on the matter. She now realized that they had lived many lives together, not as lovers but as friends or siblings. She realized this, she told me, only after she acknowledged and ritually "released" her unhealthy interest in soul mates at Annette's birthday party. The party, held a few weeks earlier, had been part festive girl's party and part mystical ritual. We had started the afternoon with cake, tea sandwiches, massages, and a lot of talk about channeling and soul mates. The central ritual took place as Cathy stoked the fire in her hearth (lit on an unseasonably warm day) and told us it was time to throw symbols of things that "held us back" into the flames. Marcy threw in a dollar bill, hoping to overcome her obsessive worries about financial health, and I threw in an unsuccessful unpublished article. A few others took their turns, and then with a sigh Cathy tossed in a well-thumbed book on soul mates. Annette, fresh from her divorce and looking for her true love, likewise sighed as she threw in her glossy wedding portraits. Cathy gave her a hug as they silently watched the book and photos burn.

Soul connections lived simultaneously through multiple lives and places enlivened the "real" worlds of Cambridge's mystics. Resolutely crossing and contaminating the boundary between the mystical and the real, both mystical relationships and physical-biological relationships made claims on the other. The genres of past lives were important gauges of, and resources through which, mystics built and solidified social connections, and at other times disrupted them. Living past lives within social worlds, however, at some point required a suspension of the kinds of endeavors to "prove" past lives that Cathy learned to pursue through reading books on past lives. Cathy's elaborate stories about Max and her ability to link them to historical facts were important touchstones for those mystics who relied on mere "sensations" and déjà vu experiences. Yet her claims also raised a variety of questions and conflicts among her friends, as became clear when Cathy revealed that Annette had been Max's wife.

Max's Wife

When Cathy announced at the Christmas party that Annette was her wife, I realized that I would have to revisit what I thought about Max. Focused (as I believed Cathy to be) on proving the experiences to be true, I had paid much less attention to what she had told me at the end of our second interview about her concern with figuring out the meaning of her current life by learning more about Max. Reading one life for another, while generative, nonetheless ultimately required ever more stories. Far from settling things, in other words, Max's story had suggested various meanings, some of which Cathy could not have herself anticipated. As Annette arrived in Cambridge, the two women were caught in these unsettled and unsettling narratives.[45]

Cathy and I were first to arrive in the chapel parlor on that cold January evening: we slowly unpeeled our coats in the cold room, Cathy telling me about her trip to New Hampshire where she had heard Kryon, a channeled entity. Eric arrived a few minutes later, looking tired but smiling. Cathy asked out of the blue, "Do you have watermelon tourmaline in your collection?" "Oh yes," he answered. Both Eric and I expected another question from Cathy, but at that moment her attention was fully diverted by Annette's arrival. A pretty young woman with dark hair pulled back in a ponytail, Annette was much younger than I expected. She took off her coat and settled into the couch next to Cathy who put a protective hand on her shoulder. "How are you feeling—sick again? Oh dear, can I get you some tea?"

"I'm just not used to the cold—" Annette protested, as Cathy stood up to fuss with the temperamental teapot housed in the corner of the room. Thinking of karmic laundry and making note that Cathy had not asked Eric if he wanted a cup of tea, I barely registered Eric's question to Annette, "Where are you from?" Before Annette could answer, Cathy called out from the other side of the room, "She is from Arizona, and then Los Angeles, places where it stays hot."

Annette added, "I've been cold before, skiing and all that, but I have never lived in it, and that's all." We continued to talk about the weather until Cathy settled back down at her seat and pulled a book out of her bag. She folded back the cover so I couldn't see what it was, and she handed it to Annette, interrupting her ongoing conversation with Eric.

"How do you feel about this picture?" Cathy asked Annette.

Annette squirmed a bit. The intimacy of Cathy's address, her interruption, her body leaning into Annette's, seemed to make us all uncomfortable, and Eric got up out of his chair as Annette answered. "Gee, I don't know."

"You know who it is, don't you," Cathy prompted, still smiling.

"It's the son, isn't it?" Annette answers more quickly.

"Yes—at first I thought it was Matthias, the other one. Here, you take a look at it, there are other pictures of the family in here."

Annette continued to page through the book and then stopped at another page, saying, "There she is."

"Funny, I remember that she had blue eyes, but she obviously doesn't," Cathy added, nodding at a picture that I couldn't see. "You can take a look at it, keep it if you want for a few days."

Annette took the book. Cathy and Annette never identified "the wife" by name, I realized (I never learned her name in fact).

Cathy had told me during our initial interview that she had come upon a recent photograph of Max's children in a German newspaper. They had returned to Germany to help dedicate a hospital wing named in Max's honor. When she first saw them, Cathy said, *"I just got all tingly when I saw them, just, from head to toe, like, 'Yeah, these are yours.'"*

"And, I thought wouldn't it be cool to write to them," she continued *"But what if you got a letter from somebody saying, you know—'I'm your dead father.'"* Cathy and I had both laughed at the time. Despite the laughter, Cathy decided to write to the oldest son, a retired professor, to ask whether his father (she) had believed in God and to clarify the "truth" of some of the differences between her memories and what was recorded in the things she had read. To her surprise, she received a reply. It included information about where Cathy could buy the family

memoirs, which she read and which revealed, among other things, that Max had not died while raking leaves.

The memoir provided scant details about Max's religious proclivities, but did report extensively on his marriage, which had been difficult, marked by his wife's struggles with depression. Cathy told me, *"the marriage—I guess the wife had some mental illness problems. She had postpartum depression and was hospitalized. She apparently was a physics and math genius, and took on the role of being the wife of the famous professor. And I kind of thought well, you know, I'm sort of resonating with that, with her—it's like I'm balancing out and now I'm getting that perspective on life. Because I consider myself in a support position to my husband's job."* For some time, Cathy read her current life through Max's. At first, Cathy said, she found explanations for why she had always longed to visit several European cities, including London. They were all places where Max had worked or had collaborators. She also now understood her career-destroying choices to work with the "older, senior, Jewish professors" in graduate school who provided her with little career guidance. It now made sense to her that she was acting on desires to connect with her (or Max's) scientific peers. While these decisions had been deleterious to her, she now understood that her current life was in some ways the coda to Max's, where she worked out some of his unfinished business. Her current status as a housewife and mother was a choice that her soul had made. From within the logic of progressive reincarnation, this choice was a step forward along a spiritual path. Cathy became convinced of this as she continued to enter into Max's memories and relive his emotions and experiences under hypnosis,[46] and their stories became more intertwined, as her shifting narrative voice makes clear. Asked by her hypnotherapist to go to "Max's last day," Cathy obliged and told me, *"I was holding this rake, and it was one of those old bamboo rakes. And I'm thinking, 'Oh my God!' And I'm saying this out loud, 'This rake is one of those bamboo ones!' I was totally astounded that it wasn't the kind of rake I use now. And there was this dog in the yard, yipping. And I wondered if they had a dog. And then I could feel everything going black and you know,* [changing perspective] *he's like drifting out of his body.*

"And the therapist brought me through [to the other side] to, you know, 'Who's—is anybody there, who do you see?' And [changing perspective again] *I thought, 'Oh they all look so healthy, Mama and Papa are there, and they're not all emaciated skeletons, they look wonderful.'* [changing perspective once more] *And I'm wondering if he lost his parents in the Holocaust. I'm not sure when they died. Everybody looked so young and healthy, was my reaction."*

Cathy's narration through two "I's" raises questions about where Max ends and Cathy begins, or put another way, about the ways that the events of the deep past continue to shape metaphysical, energetic bodies and shape them from one life to the next.[47] These moments wherein Cathy's voice is transformed or blurred into Max's or where she feels his heart pounding cloud the distinction between the two selves and make it possible to see the energetic body continuing in time. One's physical existence is transformed into what it was before. Becoming Max allows Cathy to engage the world in highly imaginative if oblique ways, and to find meaning in the world through reading another's life through her own.

Past life stories do not replace but rather add narrative resources to daily lives. Past-life stories have the added advantage of shifting the ground so that a second or third narrative or biography is not fictional but rather interlinked memory, continuous in some way with the present.[48] Max's history, encountered in books, memoirs, and other material was external to Cathy's regressed "experiences" of Max, and took on increasing importance as supplementary material through which Cathy read and interpreted her current life's meaning.

Some material, however, was not present in the memoirs and could be accessed only through meditation and hypnosis. In one such session she asked what the purpose of Max's life had been. *"What came to me was something kind of mundane, it wasn't very, particularly spiritual. It was, 'It's OK to run away to save yourself.' I think Max felt very guilty about leaving behind colleagues, students, and you know people of his culture, to die in Germany. I think that really weighed very heavily on him. But what he learned was that it was OK to save yourself."* She then asked what it was that Cathy's life had to do with Max's—what was the link? She said she still didn't know, but she thought perhaps it was *"unfinished business. There's got to be something that he wanted to do that he didn't get to do, or some growth that his soul needs to go through that didn't get addressed in that lifetime. What I feel is for me now is integrating science with faith, because it's my impression that many lifetimes before were spent in spiritual communities. And he had a very scientific and non-outwardly nonspiritual life."*

Cathy's vision of her life's purpose developed through an interpretation of Max's life, found in history and in her "memories." It took on yet another dimension when Annette appeared. Cathy's decision to do Annette's laundry (and her multiple attempts to pay back a lifetime's worth of care) wrote Annette into the story of Max's and his wife's life, and in so doing positioned Annette doubly (in this life and the past) as the acquiescent and complicit player in the drama of Cathy/Max's lives.

Not long after I met Annette I proposed that we meet for coffee, and she eagerly accepted. A few lattes in Harvard Square later, Annette came to my house for a taped interview. More so than any of the people who regularly attended the group, Annette's life and her "spiritual journey" were marked by "seeking" and moving from one idea and project to the next. Annette acknowledged this and laughed about it, saying that her life was *"still in formation. . . . It's a bunch of loose threads that I hope are coming together."* Given that Annette was at the cusp of her "Saturnine return," an astrological turning point that occurs every seven years (as Philippa, an astrologer, later explained to me), she was not too concerned about the major shifts going on in her life, including her divorce from her college sweetheart, her cross-country move, and her decision to leave her profession and career behind her. These changes notwithstanding, she was guided by several spiritual beings and a strong internal spiritual intuition. She also regularly consulted a spiritual mentor who lived in the Midwest.

Annette arrived in Cambridge at the onset of the coldest part of the year, without work, contacts, or a clear sense of the cost of living in the area. Cambridge quickly presented itself as more of a challenge than she had initially hoped or expected. One day I asked Annette why, of all the places she could have gone, she had chosen the cold Northeast. She laughed and shrugged. She didn't really know, she said. Her spirit guides and her inner intuition had suggested Cambridge or Portland: she figured that she had something to learn or someone to meet, and of the two cities she had chosen the one that was farther from her ex-husband. Without any further prompting, Annette then offered, *"Cathy thinks that [I came because] she was asking for the wife to come. She thinks that she sent out this energy, and this was why I came to Cambridge. That probably has something to do with it, but it doesn't have everything to do with it. I think I was drawn to be with the souls of friends and for whatever reason a lot of them are here."*

With that opening, I asked Annette what she thought about Max. *"What is your take on it? I haven't heard you say."* Annette smiled. In response she reported an experience that she had had when Cathy had put her under hypnosis.

"[Cathy] actually did a past life regression, and I didn't have all of the background [on Max] that she did. . . . And I experienced her depression. And it's like, I don't want that." Annette laughed nervously. *"I am not ready for that! I have already experienced enough now, that when I—when she regressed me back to that, I was overwhelmed. It was such a dark space. Oh—it was awful. But I could totally see, I could totally see in my mind's*

eye the house that she grew up in on the college campus—I don't know if it was hers or Max's. I got her feelings, her surroundings. And she was, what I experienced was that she was a very stoic person. And very repressed. And it really shook me, because, it came up to the present." Annette cleared her throat and continued in a more light tone. *"So yeah, I don't want to do that again. That was a lot to process. You know maybe for whatever reason we carry some of our past life stuff with us, and maybe it's all good in the sense that I need to release that, or something. And I am going through a lot of processes right now that—again, I don't ever think that anything that happens in my life is bad. But I do feel, I feel like there are better ways, the highest path is what we seek. But there is always a lesser way of doing something to learn from it."*

Annette had experienced being Max's wife. She had felt her *"feelings—her surroundings."* She believed that it was true and accepted that she had indeed been Max's wife. While Annette could see her own past in her "mind's eye," what she felt was her depression. That depressed person was not worth encountering again. Indeed, Annette wanted to keep this life in the past, and became quite adamant that mystics must live in the present and "in the body." Doug, an experienced out-of-body traveler, was extremely critical of those who tried to live in the past, just as he was of those who wished to live only on the astral plane. Doug reflected that past lives were burdens, best forgotten. The most *"valuable thing is not really remembering where you came from. Because if you remember every little detail of your past lives, it's a lot of baggage to carry. And if you look at it, you can look at someone at the end of their life or toward the end of their life, they are carrying around a lot of baggage themselves, and they have these various limiting beliefs. . . . If you hang onto them, you can only go so far, you can only go to a certain point. So, it is good to wipe the slate clean and say, OK, let's leave that behind and start over. That makes sense to me, that we should forget previous lifetimes. At least on a conscious daily basis we don't really remember them, because they would interfere too much with what we're trying to work on."*

"So we have enough stuff to deal with in the now?" I interjected, thinking of Annette's complaints about Max's wife. Doug nodded his head in assent. *"You're not giving your current life enough respect to actually, um, carry forward what you're working on now. It makes sense that we don't completely know all of our past lives. It's probably OK if we get little vignettes and little pictures of some things, patterns and things like that, that might keep repeating themselves, because if that's what is happening, you're repeating some pattern it is good to eventually get over it. To say, I need to fix it or figure this out so I can move on. And this can happen even on a smaller scale,*

even within one lifetime, when you might be repeating a pattern again and again, that might not be benefiting you. So you eventually acknowledge it and see what it is and then you can kind of resolve it, and say this is not serving you, I don't need this, that's helpful."

Annette likewise pushed back against Cathy's insistence that she had something to learn from her past life. She did not dispute Cathy's interpretation, nor did she deny the powerful means of self-knowledge that hypnosis could present. But Annette was much more comfortable remaining in the vague déjà vu realms of mystical soul connection. I was caught up short when Annette asked me one evening, had it occurred to me that we might have once been sisters? Fumbling, for a moment, recognizing the dangers of saying either yes or no, I said that I didn't really know, what did she think? She nodded, smiling. *"There is something in your eyes that I recognize I know you from some other time."* I laughed lightly and was relieved when Crystal interrupted from across the room, asking if I would join them the following Wednesday when they would be channeling Annette's entity. I declined, uncertain about whether I was sad or happy that I had another commitment.

Past lives place metaphysicals in multiple histories. These simultaneously imagined, redeemed, forgotten, and resonant pasts become real through their absence; their "discoveries" and their experiential powers bring to our attention the possible pleasures and terrors of living in conflicting temporalities. Past lives do less to settle the limits of the self in time and space than to raise questions for metaphysicals about the depth and length of meaningful social commitments. These practices and genres mark them as rooted in numerous histories and social worlds. Socially enacted past lives shape relationships, allowing apparently disconnected individuals to creatively and powerfully build meaningful commitments to others, and also to fruitfully (if not always easily) reconsider their responsibilities to a host of others. "Past lives" shape and at times unsettle ongoing commitments, even as they signal desires for (and hopes in) a "time" when all passions and commitments will be perfected. In participating in these stories, mystics give voice to both familiar and surprisingly new evaluations of the social and historical worlds in which they live. Mystical practice not only rewrites local worlds and relations. It also engages and critiques the authorities, experiences, and narratives used by others to lay claim to the past and future. These claims are the subject of the next chapter.

FIVE

"Zooming Around": Mystical Lands and Cosmopolitanisms

Metaphysical practitioners' past lives provide a window into the understandings of the past that help to shape their identities and perspectives. In this chapter I extend those observations to elaborate on the ways that the Cambridge mystics participate in various geographic and spiritual imaginaries. The sometimes surprising manner in which my respondents place themselves in time *and* place articulate different answers to old questions about how spiritual practitioners draw upon, borrow, and appropriate others' cultures and traditions; these borrowings, reinterpretations, and universalizing discourses propel them within a broader context. Hence, we can understand their role as shaping a mystical cosmopolitanism. Their practices help to fashion and bolster visions of cultural absence and desire, suggesting that modern contemporary spiritual practitioners are in need of traditions (and moreover, authentic traditions) that are absent from both modern times and modern landscapes.

Parsing Religious Identity: Chronotopic Appropriations

Perhaps the most common criticism of new agers is their penchant for appropriating various practices and ideas from all manner of religious traditions. Contemporary Americans latch onto a seemingly unending number of imagined primitive, ancient, or foreign cultures where they locate true religion, authentic practice, and unending wisdom. My interests here are not to reassert well-known critiques that point out the dangers of the spiritual marketplace. Rather, I investigate the practices that articulate a place for mystics within the world; a place that allows them to participate in what seems like predatory cultural borrowings in good conscience. While criticisms of spiritual appropriation ring true in many respects, the recent focus on contemporary spirituality's connection to consumerism (in the "spiritual marketplace") as the engine of appropriation gets us only so far toward understanding the logic of spiritual borrowing.

The spiritual practitioners of Cambridge, Massachusetts, are well versed in many of the standard sociological and popular critiques of "new age" interests in indiscriminately laying claim to others' religious practices and traditions. Indeed, they draw on these critiques themselves and actively distinguish their own authentically developed participation in some religious traditions from those of perceived spiritual dabblers.[1] In other words, Cambridge's mystics share an awareness of the dangers and embarrassments that such appropriations connote. They likewise believe that inappropriate uses of others' traditions is a barrier to spiritual growth. But at the same time, of course, they actively engage practices wherein they discover esoteric theological understandings in others' texts and traditions, and reproduce strategies that establish these understandings as sources of deep and universal human (or spiritual) wisdom that are deeply their own.

The chronotopic worlds they imagine and in which the world's religious practices are open to them (when properly pursued) press us to move beyond the facile critique of contemporary American spiritual forms as mediated through the "spiritual marketplace" and toward a stronger investigation of the cultural and spatial logics that render mystics' self-understandings immune from the battery of criticisms associated with cultural appropriation and religious consumerism. To do so, we need to gain some understanding of how spiritual practitioners position themselves in the world, and how in so doing they struggle with modern and postmodern questions about the boundaries and uses of culture and peoplehood, the autonomy of individuals and their identities, and other concerns.

Julia's experience is illustrative of some of these practices. A 60-something activist, Julia has spent most of her life working for non-profit organizations and participating in a number of progressive political projects. She was proud to live simply and often close to the margins of poverty. When I met her she was living with a friend in an apartment just over the Cambridge-Somerville border. It was a ramshackle place, filled with cast-off furniture and thousands of books. Before we sat down Julia showed me some of her photo albums dating from the 1970s that documented her involvement in various groups and successful street theater and political action protests, including a massive protest that blocked the Massachusetts Turnpike from running through Cambridge. There were many other albums, Julia said, but she was eager to tell me about the spiritual roots of her activism, and so as the interview began Julia couched her commitment to belly dance in a story that responded to possible concerns that she was living vicariously.

"After I got back from the South—I mean I loved dancing to black music but I knew it wasn't mine. It was more like, I was borrowing someone else's culture. I was grateful but it wasn't mine. And I was looking for, sort of, what was my culture? And, I was looking, looking, looking. And I never sort of found it. And I liked . . . for example I loved women who were wearing Indian saris, but that wasn't mine either, I knew it wasn't right. And I kept looking for what is mine. And again, talking about that sense of something from beyond, not this present time but something—ancestral. I don't think I knew the concept of past lives then, but [I was looking for] something that went historically back. And—in 1967, or 1968, one of my roommates invited me to a party with some Arabic people that she knew. And they were playing Arabic music and—it was mostly guys. And they would get down on their knees and they would dance on their knees like this. And then a woman who was actually a white woman, was a belly dancer, and she came—she was wearing a dress, she wasn't wearing a costume. But I just said, this is it! This is the culture. I just sensed it. There was something about the music, and the sound of the music and the rhythms, and even the way they were moving. I said this is, this is it."

Julia's identification with belly dance was immediate, experiential, and "vibrational." This embodied association allowed her to learn belly dance and, as a consequence, to find a home within this practice and within a (largely imagined) Arabic culture. As our interview continued, Julia told me how that evening's experience propelled her to move to New York for a short period to take dancing lessons from an older woman with national origins somewhere in the Middle East (Julia did not specify). She then returned to Cambridge to teach the form to other women. While Julia noted that most of the women whom she taught did not have the same vibrational relation to belly dance, she believed that the form also connected women to a universally accessible, divinely feminine energy. Belly dance released and realized that energy. Julia thus claimed the form as her authentic right through an elaborate set of energetic, experiential, and theological visions in which she was embedded in spiritual geographies, and which shaped her (at least in her own view) as an authentic interpreter of the form.

Becoming a carrier of religious practice, as Julia believes that she is, positions her in practices that depend upon and reproduce understandings of spiritual and sacred landscape that counter and challenge the mundane borders and boundaries of different religious traditions and cultures. In interrogating metaphysical and mystical practices of building spiritual worlds, several things become apparent. First, we begin to hear again the "traditions" that inform contemporary spirituality, in particular Theosophical, Spiritualist, and New Thought engagements with geography within both historical and energetic-metaphysical registers. Second, we can observe how the varieties of sacred geographies that layer onto the worlds that mystics live within make issues of appropriation and identity quite different than what we would expect. Furthermore, we can interrogate how these geographies reinforce (and perhaps in some ways help establish) North American metaphysicals as people without authentic cultures of their own. With this in mind, we can also investigate, as I do at the end of this chapter, how the practices of metaphysical geographic imagination shape and refract mystic cosmopolitanisms.

Our sense of agency and identity is bound (as we know) within broad understandings of the limits of space and time, thus as Bakhtin argues in his long essay on the chronotope, "the image of man is always intrinsically chronotopic."[2] As phenomenologists have long demonstrated, furthermore, we live in multiple "worlds" and chronotopes, placing ourselves in different relations to time and space, sometimes in ways that challenge or subvert the claims of materialist history and geography and the political and national boundaries that seem so clean and clear.[3] While spiritual practitioners in Cambridge do not collectively work to challenge political claims to various territories, they participate within and thereby forge spiritual geographies that allow them to articulate different kinds of claims and presence in the world.

Remembering a past life also means remembering past places, and such memories (or felt vibrations or other spiritual-geographical connections) mold the understandings that individuals have about their place in the world. To follow Bakhtin again, memory shapes what kinds of people metaphysicals understand themselves to be. Cambridge's metaphysicals are thus like other religious people, given that religious projects are molded and constructed in relation to various processes of imagining sacred places and lands. These, in turn and in so doing, shape their sense of peoplehood, identity, and relation to the divine. We might likewise identify Cambridge's metaphysicals' chronotopes as "off-modern" in the sense that they locate them within histories and places that both depend upon "modern scientific" understandings of identity and space, and also challenge dominant and taken-for-granted understandings of peoplehood built via natal affiliations of race, nation, or ethnicity. The spiritualization of geography and the selves embedded within these spaces are developed within practices, particularly those of recovered memory, spiritual experimentation, and astral exploration.

Metaphysicals layer spiritual geographies, encountered via "vibrational" energies and other practices into their own narratives. These processes of self making seem similar to how Bakhtin suggests various novelistic and "real" worlds are interanimated, for just as "the real world enters the work and its world as part of the process of its creation, as well as part of its subsequent life, in a continual renewing . . . they are indissolubly tied up with each other and find themselves in continual mutual interaction; uninterrupted exchange goes on between them."[4] Different spaces and times do not collapse into one another; in other words, mystics do not live in purely spiritual geographies, eschewing the politics and claims of "material" reality. Nonetheless, spiritual geographies are powerful shapers of practitioners' place in the modern world. The various imagined and mundane geographies, interanimated in mystics' various stories of their selves, shape mystics' and metaphysicals' possibilities, hiding and exposing different trajectories of being. By paying attention to these chronotopes, we can begin to see how mystical practitioners both draw on others' religious traditions and practices and simultaneously distinguish themselves as their authentic users and interpreters.

Searching for a Homeland: Metaphysical Nostalgia?

Metaphysical and spiritual practitioners in Cambridge agree that it is wrong, both morally and spiritually, to draw on the spiritual practices of others. They hold low views of people whom they perceive to be dilettantes, and their arguments often turn on the perception that such people are bound to fail in their approaches, given that they were not open to finding the resources and the things within their own souls that would open them to self-betterment. In short, spiritual practitioners explain that individuals could encounter religious practices that, though belonging to others, precisely, are nonetheless theirs. The experience of discovering these practices, in short, embeds them within their true spiritual home. Yet in doing so, contemporary spiritual practices also give rise to chronotopes of homelessness, and to homes that they often could not inhabit. Numerous practices locate individuals and groups within various spiritual geographies and shape chronotopes that, in placing spiritual authenticity and identity in unreachable places, reinforce the feeling and position of homeless seekers.[5]

Hans, a shamanic drummer and banker, met me for coffee in the early evening, still wearing his business suit. He cut a dashing figure in his pinstripes and cuff links and spoke with a light German accent. Hans had been "journeying" and "practicing" shamanism for over a decade, having first encountered it before moving to the United States for work. He nonetheless called himself a "beginner" and admitted that he would likely never master journeying, at least not until his old age. He told me that one of the central concerns for the Cambridge journeying group was the issue of how a person learns properly to be a shamanic journeyer. *"Something that I think that everyone faces is [the question] how do you become a journeyer? It is a really big issue. No one seems to have any good answers. How do you learn how to do this—what's the process? . . . That's a big question."*

The "questions" that most troubled Hans were whether in fact one could "really" learn to journey without living within a "shamanic culture." As he saw it, there were two unequal paths: *"Either you have access to indigenous people and have the time to be educated by a shaman, and if you really want to do it, you need several years. Or, you do it the easy way, you take a seminar."* Hans was in the latter category and recognized that his *"level of knowledge, of education"* was nothing like what it was among "shamanic peoples." What Hans had learned was a kind of shamanism that came refracted through seminars at an international school for shamanic studies. He had attended quite a few of these seminars, where, he told me, the leaders *"boil down quite a number of indigenous shamanic ways into core shamanism"* that does not have *"any local element or way of thinking."* Hans explained that according to the center's programs, learning core shamanism gave people a strong grounding in the nuts and bolts and techniques. After that, the center encouraged people to *"apply whatever [culture] you feel connected to, like the Native American, or the Celtic. Celtic is most popular around here. Or, the Nepalese or Tibetan. So, there are all kinds of styles, but you can actually apply that later on. . . . It's almost the coloring, the embellishment."*

It was not clear to me whether Hans really approved of these practices or thought it was possible to boil down various shamanic traditions into a "core" tradition. So I asked Hans if he favored one.

"Um, I would say something between the Germanic, Celtic, or Siberian. Personally I'm very interested in Native American ways and cultures, and all that. But more from an historical or anthropological point of view. Especially since I didn't want to come over here and you know, take over—really, they . . . and, I think, at some point it's pretty much every person finds out about his or her own group and involves that type. But some do not. Some really use some other people's cultures." Hans disapproved of using "other people's cultures" and told me that he appreciated Native American ways and cultures, but not in order to use them, but rather to "appreciate" them. Coming to the United States from Germany, he believed, would provide the opportunity to meet "real" living shamanic cultures and practitioners, but these were not his own. Instead, as he said, he favored *"Germanic"* shamanism, or *"Celtic or Siberian."* As it turns out, these latter two were added on because Hans believed that it was not possible to access Germanic shamanism.

He continued: "[The] *hard thing is that the Germans—the prehistoric Germans, which include everything from Scandinavia down to Austria, the Alps are the border—there are no indigenous representatives anymore. With the Native Americans you can go to Lakota or Hopi or whatever you're attracted to. And you can actually go to those people. With the Germanic, it is much harder because there isn't any person you can go to there and ask, what is the actual teaching? It got lost."* This loss was even further sealed, Hans told me, by the Nazi misuses and misrepresentation of folk traditions: *"[The Nazis] took that spirituality and culture for their own and totally mixed it up and perverted it for their own advantage. So, that has kept many people from investigating it, because they didn't want to go over to the Nazi corner."*

Hans's sense of his irrecoverable loss of a prehistoric Germanic knowledge gave shape to his frustrations in encountering living Native Americans, whom he found disappointingly uninterested in shamanic journeying (or, at least, in journeying with Hans's group). Toward the end of our conversation I asked Hans about the composition of the drumming circle he met with, and he noted with some disappointment that the group was "all white." He added that he thought this was a serious problem. I asked what, if anything, his circle had thought about doing to correct that. Hans then noted that his group had just *"recently changed our mission. We consider ourselves a multicultural drumming circle, and what we mean by that is that we want to attract people from other than white ethnicities. Occasionally we have two Latinos, who were educated here. Nobody indigenous. We don't have any African Americans, no Native Americans, which is a bummer."*

"So, do you think it would be a good thing to have Native Americans?" I asked.

"It would definitely, especially Native Americans, just because I feel like they are still alive . . . being here, well they should be here. But the [Native Americans] I have encountered, I find it's not that easy to communicate with them. . . . It might be, well maybe I've encountered the wrong people, so I don't want to say all Native Americans are not willing to connect with us at that level, but we don't have any Indian people, no Asian people either. I don't know why. It might be something that they don't have interest in."

Hans's understanding of authentic shamanism was somewhat ironic. His participation within shamanism did not bring him to a home, but rather reinforced and developed an understanding of his own loss. His "own" indigenous spiritual roots were lost for good: every shamanic journey that he took, drawing on others' shamanic traditions, was marked by a loss and, by extension, by a sense that his own identity was incomplete (and incompletable). This understanding, shaped clearly by the understanding that shamanic cultures can be carried only within native and indigenous cultures also contributed to his interactions with the few Native Americans he met in the Boston area. The spiritual imaginaries that Hans participated within drew clear distinctions between indigenous cultures of shamanism, which "continued" an unchanging ancient knowledge, and "modern" cultures like Hans's own, which were marked primarily by the absence of such knowledge. The perceived inability to recover his own true identity seemed to lessen the discomfort of drawing on others'.[6]

Hans was clearly working through his own questions about the ethics of poaching or appropriating others' traditions, which had been set in motion by his understandings about cultural authenticity and about his own inability to participate in any. Hans was an immigrant to the United States, married to an American, and the father of children who were dual citizens. He was extremely well traveled, politically liberal and skeptical, an omnivorous reader of books, versed in both art and music. All of these aspects of his life reinforced the trouble he felt about the inauthenticity of his own shamanic practice. Those aspects of his life, coupled with his practice, did not make way for a "return" but rather continued to underscore the impossibility of finding a home. This irony set uneasily with Hans, who paid large sums of money to attend courses conveying that shamanism was based on a "core set" of shamanic practices on which various cultural differences were but variations on a theme. Culture could not be mere embellishment on the core, Hans noted, but all the same, immersing himself in a cultural tradition of shamanism that was not "his" would also mark him as an imposter. Far from being disinterested or disengaged with issues surrounding appropriation, these topics were at the center of Hans's practice. Shamanism in its practice and technique was vested in explorations and unfulfilled understandings of authenticity. Hans viewed himself as a member of an unrooted society and never as a living remnant of an indigenous culture. His engagement with Native Americans and his shamanic practices continued to reinforce his narrative of rupture.

Hans's sense developed within his spiritual practice. The project of shamanic journeying placed him and other practitioners within spiritual cartographies that valued imaginary spaces and pasts, intact culture, and indigenous knowledge that was in very consequential ways not open to or accessible to Hans. This chronotope of loss was reinforced, if not created, by journeying itself: Hans and others participate and live in a world that is shaped by spiritual lines and boundaries. It distinguishes indigenous and modern cultures by way of their connections to a primordial past, and furthermore organizes individuals as members of ethnic or national groupings that are either rooted or free floating. Hans's project was thus deeply nostalgic, albeit built on nostalgia for an imagined territory and past that he engaged through his understanding of unappropriable others. These nostalgic imaginaries create "experiences of losses that never took place" and, as such, invert "the temporal logic of fantasy . . . and create much deeper wants."[7] In many ways, Hans's appropriations take shape within a form of nostalgia that is "retrogressive," one that engages "mourning for the impossibility of mythical return, for the loss of an enchanted world with clear borders and value."[8] Shamanic journeyers like Hans draw upon others' shamanic cultures with an acute realization that these are not their own. Imbibing others' traditions embeds the imbiber within self-critique. Absent a religious culture of his own, or one that presents the possibilities for shamanic journeying at least, Hans has no choice but to appropriate others' cultures and to learn what he can about their practices through *"anthropological, historical"* engagements.

Hans's spiritual geography marked the territory in which he lived day to day as empty and secular. In contrast, many metaphysicals in Cambridge participated in spiritual chronotopes that gestured to a possibility of connecting with one's true spiritual homeland. For example, the spiritual communities Julia connected to "vibrationally" articulated a different sensibility and set of answers to the possibility of claiming and realizing others' religious cultures. As Julia's story suggests, "heritage" and "nation," while useful categories, have little to do with family descent: one's true spiritual heritage was rather discerned through mystical senses and tools, and mapped a quite different type of spiritual world.

Vibrational Cartographies

Julia grew up in a large and intense Jewish family in Brooklyn. Trotsky was her father's patron saint, Martha Graham her mother's. Julia's religious education consisted of her mother's statement, "God is a nice man who lives in the sky." Unlike the rest of her "atheistic" family, however, Julia was drawn to "religion." She read through the mythology section of the library before she reached her teens, and it was from those volumes, Julia said, that she formed her first understanding of the relationships among all of the varying religions in the world. One day as a child she told her mother that she believed that all religions were on separate paths, but that the paths were on the same mountain, and at the top sat a supreme god toward which they were all traveling. Julia's mother stopped what she was doing when she heard her daughter's theory and told her, *"Oh, no no no. The Jewish god is the best one!"* As Julia tells the story, she was surprised by her mother's sectarian reaction, especially because she thought her mother was secular. *"After that I kept my own counsel,"* Julia remarked.

Julia graduated from college and enrolled in a PhD program in philosophy. The summer after her first year in graduate school she joined in the Freedom Summer movement to register black southerners to vote. When the summer ended she decided to abandon school work and took a position in the Atlanta offices of the Student Nonviolent Coordinating Committee, where she stayed for two years. In Atlanta she was part of a *"holy community. . . . There was a deep core of spirituality in the movement, tied very much to the Christian faith,"* but one that was nonsectarian and that allowed people to come together to *"question so- ciety and all sorts of things—social class assumptions, education assump- tions. . . . And oh, I loved the music! We always would have parties, and we would dance. I was very happy in many ways, being there."*

Julia recounted that in the beginning of 1966 *"Black Power came in, and black people said, 'We don't want you telling us what to do, go back to your own communities and organize.' And it made a lot of sense. But all of a sudden the people who had been very nice to us stopped talking to us. So we had to leave. But we agreed—you know if we really believed in what we said we believed in, we had to leave."* Julia returned to Massachusetts, stung by the sense that her time in Georgia had been something of an illu- sion; her friends there now demanded that she find her own people and organize a holy community that was more organic to her own cul- ture. But Julia had come to the South estranged from the Jewish-atheist worlds of her parents, which she found simultaneously too parochial and too secular, and there was no "return" to that culture, where she could not imagine finding a holy community to join.

In its place, and as a critique, Julia found her home through the vi- brations of belly dance. "Arabic" dance connected her to an ancestral home. While belly dance may have marked a resonance with her own mother's life as a dancer, Julia did not highlight any maternal link. In- stead, she stressed over and over the "vibrational" connections that she felt with Arabic people and cultures. As she explained, everyone has a "vibration," which she could sometimes feel; these vibrations, fur- thermore, were linked in some unarticulated way to race or culture, and were rooted in the "soul" or in some aspect of the astral body. She first became aware of her ability to sense others' vibrations when she was in college. One day, traveling on a subway from Brooklyn into Manhattan, she *"noticed that the subway felt different. And I looked around and I thought 'Oh, it's because only the Protestant people are riding on the subway, because all the Jewish people are in synagogue. And it feels different.' We didn't know the word 'vibrations' yet, or 'energy,' but that's what I felt. There's something cooler about it, but I could feel it, that there was something different about it. So I knew that I had some kind of sensitivity. And it was an amazing way to find it out. . . . I was feeling the vibrations and the thing was, I understood this, and it wasn't some kind of prejudicial thing. By that time I had, I was—in college I majored in sociology and philosophy, and the philosophy of science. So I knew about different cultures, and the different ways that people were raised, and it was just obvious to me that people from different cultural backgrounds would have different electro-chemical makeup, and different electro-vibrational makeups. And especially if they were urban and modern, versus tribal. So I think, it's not surprising that different religious, or cultural-ethnic backgrounds have different vibrations."*

Not only could Julia feel different vibrations, these were organized along cultural, religious, national lines. While Julia did not further elaborate the types of vibrational distinction, they were recognizable, just as the music, rhythm, and form of the "Arabic" music were. Julia was, according to her own story, one of the first women in the Boston area to learn to belly dance; she started dancing professionally in Boston and Cambridge night clubs. *"So here I am, in my little skimpy costume, with my makeup, I'm writhing around on the floor in this nightclub in Cambridge, and all these women march in with their short hair and their army boots and their karate uniforms, and they march in and they say, what are you doing down there? You're a traitor to the revolution!"* Julia was very sympathetic to the feminist movement (which she identified as growing out of civil rights) and yet also found belly dance to be an important form for her self-realization. *"So then I had to find out what was belly dancing really all about. Because all I knew was it was some kind of dance from the Middle East, and it clearly was a sensual dance, but there had to be more than the women who would dance for the sultan in harems and stuff like that. And the fact—like I said I was so compelled to do it when I saw it, it was something deeper. So I began doing research."* Julia located articles by a woman with a *"PhD in political science from Columbia, who spoke eight languages,"* and who had disguised herself in order to travel to the Middle East and study *"belly dancing in its original form, where it's about childbirth."* It was through this research that Julia learned that belly dance was actually about women's power, and that *"that's why you roll your belly because you're imitating labor, the contractions of labor, and that's why you get down on the ground, because you're giving birth."*[9]

For a decade thereafter, Julia taught hundreds of women in Cambridge how to *"tap into the feminine divine."* Her desire to teach was spurred on by a sense that she was teaching her own tradition and practice to others who could benefit from it. Her ownership in this practice was felt doubly, linking women's natural and divine feminine powers with her own particular vibrational tugs. These distinct but overlapping energetic chronotopes shaped her practice's authenticity and power.[10]

Julia's story calls attention to the ways that spiritual autobiographies in Cambridge literally vibrate with racial and national imagery. Metaphysicals frequently embedded their own biographies in a variety of conceptions about the links and distinctions between various national and racial energetic vibrations. For example, Wes, a good friend of Julia's, told me that everyone he met had a certain vibration and that these types were organized by national origin. *"Every nationality has certain styles,"* he said, *"so when you are actually teaching people how to become more versatile [with their energy] you have to be careful not to remove what they value."* Wes told me, *"if you're Polish you'll have a tendency to generate a very argumentative and stubborn energy very quickly. But Polish [people] are also very quiet, they can sometimes go into the most incredible quiet. I thought I was good at meditating because I was skilled, because I practiced, but it's because I'm Polish."* Wes reflected that teaching energy techniques often meant waking people up to their national predispositions to energetic vibrations.

Wes, like Julia, presumed that these vibrations were ingrained in the *astral* self, the true self that was (unlike the physical body) moving forward in progressive lifetimes, yet at the same time were linked to a person's biological origins, or perhaps "culture." Wes rarely stopped to figure out the details of this confused system, nor did he or anyone else stop to reflect on the fact that Americans carried with them the vibrational tones of past nationalities. Americans, it appeared, had (have) no vibrational tone of their (our) own, raising a host of questions. At the end of the day, however, Wes and Julia were less worried about the confusing theoretical, geographical, or theological import of their ideas than assessing their practical effects. In their view, fighting against one's own vibrational "type" led to health problems and other ills. The only way to excel in life was to come to terms with one's energetic type, no matter how it seemed to fit or diverge from one's physical body.

The notion that a body's vibrations are the central clue to locating a person in physical and astral geography is hardly a new idea; it has had a thick history within various Spiritualist, Theosophical, and metaphysical conceptions of the self and the nation. Indeed, while many progressive metaphysicals of the nineteenth century challenged the "realities" of physiognomic races, they frequently replaced biological race with spiritualized forms, sedimenting them in even more intractable, multiple-leveled hierarchies where individuals and nations were ordered and reordered according to their vibrational qualities.[11] The geography of the astral world mattered, and everyone had a place within it. A spate of turn-of-the-century writing made this clear, reporting on the orderly organization of the heavens, the tiers of the astral planes that distinguished various levels of spiritual intelligence, all of which mapped onto the physical world and its nations and races with some not-so-surprising regularity. As Charles Leadbeater reports in *The Astral Plane: Its Scenery, Inhabitants, and Phenomena,* "The poetic idea of death as a universal leveler is a mere absurdity born of ignorance, for, as a matter of fact, in the vast majority of cases the loss of the physical body makes no difference whatever in the character or intellect of the person."[12]

The continued appeal of various spiritualized hierarchies within metaphysical geographies can be considered an extension of the familiar and much discussed distinctions among "world religions" that took shape in the same cultural and historical crucible.[13] Insofar as these ideas continue to operate in the practices of spiritual identity, however, it counters simple stories of American spirituality that conjure up rootless consumers or the transformation of religious traditions via the engine of commodification. Listening to Julia and others who find and acknowledge their "true" roots and homes via spiritual vibrational practice instead point to practices wherein spirituality presents paths to homelands and to unity through engaging other cultures. It is thus we see that the spiritual realms, much like the earth itself, are tiered, sectored, and open for travel by those who can spiritually attune themselves to their "true" culture and homeland.[14]

Otherwheres and Astral Realms: Exploration and Encounter

Much as "past lives" (discussed in the previous chapter) present resources for people to simultaneously participate in multiple pasts and families, so these spiritual cartographies alter racial and genealogical identities and filiations by mapping them onto various mystical past places that are more "real" than the types of geographic connections recognized in everyday life. In so doing, these cartographies posit selves where race and family, national identity, and the like are representations of a soul's current position within an unfolding and progressive movement toward divinity. The "lands" to which these identities refer are not visible to the naked eye but are nonetheless overlaid on individuals' and groups' identities within our own terra firma. Such theories construct a person's true identity as being fulfilled through developments in progressive lives and present a contrast to the nostalgic self that Hans and other shamanic practitioners articulated.

Astral geographies are oriented both toward an ever progressive future but also toward the present. Astral worlds are more real than material worlds and, according to some, mark the places where "reality" takes place; they thus shape our encounters and actions in ma-terial realms. Nothing made this clearer than the evening I spent at the Theosophical Society, listening to Philippa's astrology talk on Vul-can, an esoteric planet that lies between Mercury and the sun. I met Philippa in May 2003 during a concentrated period of talking with a number of people who taught classes of various kinds at the Theosophi-cal Society. Philippa told me that she holds a master's degree in esoteric psychology (a field based on the writings of Alice Bailey), and that she supplements her knowledge of Theosophical texts with explorations in "Buddhism and Native American religions." Philippa made a living teaching courses on conscious living and conducting astrological con-sultations. Along with a group of friends and family, she had just pur-chased a small farm north of Boston and was planning to move there and open an esoteric retreat and conference center. Until she moved, she planned to hold her classes primarily at the Theosophical Society. I asked Philippa to explain esoteric astrology, and she suggested that I attend some of her lectures and offered to waive the $20 astral chart fee when she learned that I had never had my "chart done."

The warm spring air was heavy with lilacs on the evening of Philip-pa's lecture, and the windows of the Theosophical Society were open to let in the fresh air. From the darkened path I could hear people talk-ing inside the building; twenty-five men and women were in the main room when I entered, many of them sitting in small groups. Three young men and women stood with Philippa at the front, and it took a few minutes to get her attention to ask for my chart. She rummaged through a stack of papers and folders to find it, continuing all the while to talk with a young man with a ponytail (it appeared that he was her main student in conscious living). The chart, a circle with spokes, was completely foreign to me. The hand-drawn circle had no key to the signs and symbols, which included Roman numerals and what I took (correctly) to be astrological symbols. I took a seat toward the back, next to a middle-aged woman dressed in a black pant suit and her hus-band, clad in jeans and a polo shirt. I stole a glance at their charts, which had been annotated in several colored pens. They smiled and said hello, and asked if I was new. I said I was, and quickly added that I was a novice in the world of astrology, hoping that this admission might prompt them to translate my chart if it became necessary.

Philippa clapped her hands to get everyone's attention. She stood in the front of the group, a whiteboard propped up to the side of her makeshift lectern set up in the middle of the main room. The topic for the evening was Vulcan and its place within esoteric astrological forecasting and psychology. "Now, what is Vulcan?" Philippa asked rhetorically before answering her own question: "Vulcan is an esoteric planet. What do I mean by that? I mean that Vulcan is not formed, as a gas, a liquid, or as matter like this," she said, rapping the table next to her with her knuckles. "It is formed out of *etheric* matter. And it is located close to the sun, between the sun and Mercury. Modern science also knows about this planet, Vulcan—because they notice that there is a wobble in Mercury's orbit.[15] They sometimes see something a bit strange in the corona of the sun. So, since science is always looking for something that you can see with your eyes, it will probably be a while before anyone can 'see' Vulcan!" The group laughed at Philippa's critique of scientists' insistence on material evidence, and Philippa laughed along with them.

"No matter what the scientists say, it is there, it is made of etheric matter. It is made of things—like gamma rays and other things of that nature, which are not gas, not liquid, and not hard matter like this table," she said, knocking on it again. Having established the scientific reality of this etheric planet, Philippa drew a link to esoteric astrology. "One of the things that we focus on in this *science* is the relationship between the myths and the planets. The reason we focus on *myths,* and tonight we're going to touch on Vulcan and some aspects of the Venus myth, is because myths are the collective memories, and ideas—the full round ideas, of how things work." Philippa continued the lecture, slipping back and forth between declarations of the "scientific" facts of etheric and astral realms, and the scientific bases of astrology and the "memories" encoded in myths. I struggled to keep up as Philippa launched into the stories of both Venus and Vulcan, detoured into a set of commentaries on Pluto, the overuse of Prozac and Ritalin, the Buddha's upcoming birthday, and finally back to the esoteric charts themselves. Philippa asked me several times to read the position of several planets on my chart, and the woman sitting next to me quickly took over, answering Philippa's questions for me.

The invocation of an "actual" astral planet was one clear place where the realities of the "astral planes" intersected with the mundane, material world. Esoteric planets (it appeared that there were others within Bailey's astrological system), like "real" planets, exercise their pull and force on individuals' lives and on world history. Much like the stories of "lost" terrestrial lands of Lemuria or Atlantis that are also part of the metaphysical imagination of our worlds, these "discovered" planets are part of human history and human trajectories. Unlike "past lives," which tend to be encountered through specific, internal interrogations, these esoteric "lands" are not embedded fully in the subjective, but rather have realities for groups: they are a type of territory in which all souls are organized and in which all souls, even those of us who do not "believe," also live.

Astral realms are thus not merely metaphors but also spaces that are coexistent with ours, and thus both populated and open to exploration and experimentation by the spiritually alert. Doug, the out-of-body experiencer, told me that when he was as young as five he would leave his body and walk through his house. He remembers *"wandering around at night, like—throughout the house. And, I would meet my dog, he was a loyal dog, I had my pet dog, this was my astral dog. And also I met my parents and we would talk, out of body. But they wouldn't remember it."*

"Oh yeah?" I asked.

"Yeah, whenever I had OBEs and I would meet other people out of body, I would have a conversation. And they didn't—I would even tell them, ask them, 'you know what you're doing right now?' but—they're sort of like zombies. They are not really aware of what is going on. They're not very conscious. You know, you can kind of talk to them, and if you ask them afterwards, 'Do you know what happened? Do you remember what you were doing?' They say they don't remember anything. But if you had two people who were very focused, you could have OBEs and actually remember them and I suspect you could actually corroborate each other's experiences." Doug believed that all people's souls move around in the astral plane, but that only a few are aware of what they say or do there. They are "zombies," the living-dead, yet people who might awaken to their astral selves, but who would probably find the truth of this sphere more convincing after they had died. Doug intimated that this was the reason he had become more interested in talking with the spirits of truly dead people, as well as the spirits who had not been "in body" for a long time, if ever. For example, he recalled during high school that he had failed to study for a physics exam, and in an exhausted state decided that he would try to elicit the help of Albert Einstein to teach him physics while he slept. *"And it totally happened, it was great. I'm sitting down, Albert Einstein is up at the board and he is showing me all this stuff here, and I remembered all of it, right? For this exam that I knew nothing on, and I would have failed, right? So [during the experience] I'm learning all these different things about physics that are applicable to this exam, from Albert Einstein. Or, at least that was my perception. Maybe it was Albert Einstein, maybe it wasn't. As far as I'm concerned it was Albert Einstein. So, I wake up the next day and I'm like, OK, it all makes sense to me now. I go in and get the highest grade in the class. I get 98 percent."*

169

Many of Doug's metaphysical friends appeared to agree that his stories were marked by a certain naïveté. Few thought that he had "actually" encountered Einstein in the astral plane, for example, but they were nonetheless willing to go along with his stories rather than challenge his "reality." And of course, Doug was clearly less interested in whether it was Einstein at the chalkboard than in the information he received for his exam. In other words, the visuals of astral beings were less important to him than what they communicated "telepathically." Whenever Doug traveled in the astral realm, he entered a world where *"communication is absolutely perfect. There is no room for error, you don't have to be very careful about what it is you're articulating because communication is absolutely perfect. It's your* intention—*it's your sort of perfect thought form that is being communicated, not the words. So you can have someone who speaks French as their natural language and someone who speaks Russian, and they'll have a perfectly beautiful conversation and understand each other entirely well. Because it's not the language that they're communicating, they're actually kind of expressing telepathically the essence of what they intended to say."*

Doug's and others' casual attitudes about the relationship between their perceptions and the phenomena that they see in the astral realm both build upon and bend the visions of the astral planes embedded in books like Charles Leadbeater's *The Astral Plane*, which literally map out hierarchies and spaces for various groupings of souls, national or racial "vibrational" energies, and progressively reincarnated beings. Leadbeater encouraged enlightened readers to explore the astral realm, the next "highest" plane of existence or energy that those of us still in physical form can visit. This next plane of reality "can be visited and observed by persons who have qualified themselves for the work, exactly as a foreign country may be visited and observed."[16] Much like the physical world, the astral world closest to our own is populated with ghosts, the zombie-like souls of humans who are unaware of their presence in these etheric realms, and also the spirits of beings who have never been cast in physical bodies (entirely "astral" beings might occasionally dip their toes into our lower plane, and sometimes communicate with those of us who return to a waking life). The purpose of visiting such a world is not, as Doug might argue, to ace a physics test but rather to realize that "we are all the while in the midst of a great world full of active life, of which most of us are nevertheless entirely unconscious." These crowded worlds of the next "astral" plane contain untranslatable, unspeakable knowledge. The difficulty for the astral traveler is not in comprehending what takes place there, given the "telepathically" clear communication that takes place there. Rather, the difficulty is in translating such experiences into language at all. Leadbeater states that the explorer who wishes to describe the species in previously unknown tropical forests faces an easy task compared to the psychic investigator who confronts "first . . . the difficulty of correctly translating [what he has observed in] that plane to this the recollection of what he has seen, and secondly . . . the utter inadequacy of ordinary language to express much of what he has to report."[17]

The worlds that Doug and other astral explorers encounter are nonphysical yet present; they are worlds without language and without visual representation. Yet they are nonetheless real places, overlapping with physical spaces that we live within and that extend vertically or hierarchically or on some other coordinates. Doug's understanding of the astral world is directly and indirectly linked to writings like Leadbeater's, the content of which has spilled into numerous esoteric texts, lectures, and discussions. Leadbeater's travelogue and descriptions frequently appear without attribution in contemporary new age writing, and have even been wholly lifted and reframed in a slim text by Swami Panchadasi titled *Astral Worlds: Its Scenes, Dwellers, and Phenomena.* The Swami Panchadasi, one of William Walker Atkinson's several pen names, draws liberally from Leadbeater's volume, excising all of the technical Sanskrit terms along the way. The Swami's version of the guide to the astral worlds likewise does away with many of Leadbeater's warnings that only the theosophically adept can mount an exploration of this kind, instead encouraging every reader who might pick up the volume to "use this manual as a key to unlock many mysteries not as a book to while away an idle hour. . . . Be an earnest, thoughtful, occultist, ever unfolding and evolving as you progress along The Path! Look Forward, not Backward! Look Upward, not Downward!"[18]

It was Panchadasi's book that Kurt Leland encountered on his grandfather's bookshelf and that, Leland writes, helped spur his interest in out-of-body exploration, which he writes about in several books and teaches in classes attended by a small cadre of astral explorers, including Doug and Eric. Leland's *Otherwhere* is no mere pastiche of observations culled from other books. Leland instructs explorers how to travel to the astral realms and takes up the question of translation and description that troubles the transition from "otherwhere" to physical reality. Addressing Panchadasi's (or Leadbeater's) problem of untranslatability, Leland argues that the visions and experiences that take place in the astral are deeply keyed into each individual's position and perceptions. As a consequence, he tell his readers that he is not describing actual physical things (or actual Einsteins) but rather the types of spirit functions that exist in the otherworld, and that travelers of various different cultures and dispositions might encounter differently. Traveling to the astral world is required in order to understand the knowledge that it contains, he states. "I believe each of us can answer the eternal questions for ourselves, through personal experience instead of hearsay. Shamans and medicine people have been doing so for centuries through visits to nonphysical reality. Because we live in completely different circumstances, the ancient shamans' answers may not be of much use to us. But perhaps we could follow their example and come up with relevant answers of our own."[19] Drawing on a range of various texts from Dante's *Divine Comedy* to *The Tibetan Book of the Dead*, to "research papers" by parapsychologist Robert Monroe, Leland notes the similarities between various "sets of images" reported by numerous individuals through time that "describe the same experiences."[20] The reports that anyone makes from such places are ultimately the work of one's subjectivity, creativity, and imagination.[21]

Leland's vision of the "otherwhere" is quite distinct from that of Wes, Hans, or Julia. His vision that an understanding of what goes on in astral planes is available to people in the flesh only through visuals, translations, and their own perceptions allows him to criticize the view of those who would see human projections (and their presumed cultural "blinders") as astral "realities." Leland's encouragement to others to participate in creative translations of untranslatable experiences in untranslatable places certainly challenges the verities in older astral guidebooks, including the replication of human hierarchies (racial or national) into the heavens. Yet Leland's book continues the expression wherein the physical world is nothing but a manifestation of someplace else, both here and not here, and that learning the truth requires a journey to another place, and special tools or skills to navigate that world.

Cambridge and "Stonehenge USA": Vortices and Absent Centers

Spiritual geography works on and through bodies who can experience a spiritual homeland as possibly lost and unrecoverable, or "vibrationally" present, or as inhabitable through out-of-body or other mystical practices. A common theme in these various practices is that of loss or of absence, where attention is drawn away from the mundane and the local, and where local geographies signify absence of religious or spiritual significance, or appear as shadowy counterparts of more energetic landscapes.

As my considerations about Cambridge as a spiritual landscape took sharper focus, I became even more aware of how my respondents' spiritual practices turned their attention away from the places where they lived day to day. This is not to say that my respondents were not actively engaged in institution building, civic activities, and community events, but rather that they did not perceive of, or do much in their joint or specific actions, to envision or articulate Cambridge as a place of significance. I was excited when Annette announced to me and a few others that she had moved to Cambridge because she felt drawn to the region for reasons she did not understand but wanted to know more about. Annette had moved from the Southwest after a two-year stay at Esalen, the storied home of the human potential movement and spiritual retreat in California. I kept expecting that one day in her sojourns she would encounter Walden Pond or Concord, Transcendentalism, or any other "connection" to the region's metaphysical history. That is, I kept waiting to hear a story about what would make her trip to the East Coast about the place itself. But as we saw in the previous chapter, Annette quickly came to think that Cambridge's draw was about the people she encountered, rather than the place itself.

Annette remained topographically committed to landscapes that were objectively absent from Cambridge, including the panoramic and dark nighttime skies and the warmth of the desert. The strength of her personal and spiritual associations with those places made her attempts to "find" nature in Cambridge always dissatisfying. Annette and I frequently walked along that same nature path between the Alewife train station and Arlington, the town next to Cambridge. Although still in the city, it was quiet and a refuge for songbirds and water fowl. I tried to talk with Annette a few times about the path, and each time she quickly started a litany of everything she found missing. The birds seemed commonplace and boring to her, and while the signage at its entrance suggested that there were a variety of four-legged animals living in the area, she had never seen any. Annette was intent on seeing a red fox, her "animal familiar" according to her channeled spirit guide. Every walk became a disappointment, the animal's absence reinforced both nature's and spirituality's absence from Cambridge. In this reading of Cambridge's natural landscape, Annette began to build a story about her move to Cambridge as a temporary step on her journey: her move to Cambridge was about people who would help her grow and not, as she had originally suggested, about finding a place to settle down.

Annette shared a taken-for-granted assumption with my other respondents that "nature" and the earth's "energies" existed somewhere else, outside of Cambridge. Their sense that they apprehended a local landscape that was not mystically aligned was further reinforced by both far-flung travel stories and visits to regional "power spots." Such spots are of interest to many new age practitioners, and many of my respondents had made a point of visiting such places if they were nearby. No trip to the Southwest was complete without visiting the pink rocks of Sedona, Arizona, or Glastonbury Tor while in England. Some told me that they had made specific trips to powerful places, or to Morocco, India, or other distant places, to participate in rituals or because of a feeling of being drawn there.[22] Faye described traveling to Mayan ruins as sparking a strong sense of a homecoming. She did not know if this was because she was picking up on her prior life as a Mayan, or because the Mayans had chosen to build on top of a powerful energy field. Regardless, Faye's "homecoming," like so many others I heard reported, always took place elsewhere. Cambridge had no evident vibrational pull; no one talked about feeling physically, geographically, and spiritually at home in Cambridge. It was not on the spiritual landscape in the ways that these other places were, and the town's energetic aridity was constantly reinforced by metaphysicals' journeys, travels, and reports on them when they returned. Even local pilgrimages to regional power spots such as Stonehenge USA in Salem, New Hampshire, a two-hour drive north of Cambridge, could work to reinforce the view that important spiritual landscapes existed elsewhere.

Stonehenge USA is a relatively recent designation for a formation of rocks that resembles (on a miniature scale) the famous English site of that name. Mika, the mask maker and ritual specialist who organizes solstice rituals at the site, told me that it was probably built several thousand years ago by ancient European settlers. Faye told me that the builders were "probably Celts," adding that she favored this theory because Celts developed dowsing technologies that they used to locate places for their ritual and astronomical sites. According to Faye, the site had been "forgotten" and "buried" until quite recently. It was opened to the public when the land was bought by a private group and converted into a park. It was at that point, Faye and Mika told me, that scientists and archaeologists became interested in the site and determined that it was not the work of Native Americans, but rather of European settlers. (It was not without some sense of irony that I listened to the ways that this Stonehenge story allows modern Cantabrigians of European descent to claim an ancient American power spot without having to wrestle with indigenous people who might lay claim to it.)

Driving two hours north of the city to visit a "natural" power spot identified by "ancient" and forgotten people presented yet another opportunity to mark Cambridge as a secular space devoid of any particular importance. The recent and recoverable past of metaphysical religions' flourishing in Cambridge or Boston, including the various traces of Cambridge's spiritual pasts that were most fascinating to me, held no thrall. To drive this point home, Faye and Wes began offering spiritual walking tours soon after I moved away from Cambridge. Excited to hear this, I e-mailed Wes about his plans and about the route. He told me that the tours wound along the banks of the Charles River, where they had used dowsing techniques to detect strong energies surrounding "very old trees."

Cambridge is not naturally missing a spiritual landscape any more than Stonehenge USA is naturally a power spot: metaphysicals' practices and movements shape both spaces and their meanings, in relation to each other. The work of sacralizing some landscapes involves the secularization of others. As such, we can see that the developing sacred geographies often works to render a place like Cambridge comparatively uninteresting, displacing attention from the kinds of work and cultivation of social and physical realities that spiritual practitioners continue to do. The effort to locate divine powers and resources elsewhere makes it difficult to observe the work that they do in their own towns, homes, and local communities, whether that work is to retrace or expand social networks, establish or maintain local groups or businesses where people interact, share texts or engage in experiential investigations. These potential sites of power and effect are rarely if ever noted. To the shopworn question of how contemporary spirituality shapes a response to feelings of alienation that attend to modernity, we must necessarily ask how contemporary spirituality itself articulates social alienation in the center of its projects.

Zooming Around: Mystic Cosmopolitanism

The empty spaces of Cambridge in the social and religious imaginaries of contemporary spiritual practitioners contribute to "cosmopolitan imaginaries" that often fail "to recognize the social conditions of [their] discourse, presenting it as a freedom from social belonging rather than a special sort of belonging, a view from nowhere or everywhere rather than from particular social spaces." Being without culture and place is an expression of privilege, and while it ritually articulates neutrality or the attainment of a universal objective position, it nonetheless remains a kind of belonging. It emerges in particular cultural positions and is the result of labor that makes commitments to others contingent.[23]

The social and religious practices of Cambridge's contemporary spiritual practitioners demonstrate at least one way that cosmopolitan imaginaries take shape and root. This social imaginary is not merely imagined or thought but embedded in chronotopically inflected practices that allow them to take up places in the world that are at a distance from *every* place. It is this kind of imaginary that shaped the activities of the two dozen people who gathered at the Swedenborgian Chapel's parlor in February 2003, on the eve of what many worried would be the beginning of a long and drawn-out war in Iraq. Uncertainty was in the air; earlier in the day thousands of high school students from Cambridge, Belmont, Arlington, and Somerville had walked out of school to protest the impending intervention. I heard them from my office window, shouting and banging drums as they walked on Massachusetts Avenue, turning onto Main Street toward the Longfellow Bridge, where they stopped and sat, blocking traffic for a brief period. Cathy sent out an e-mail to alert us all to watch the evening news; her son had joined in the protest, and she was clearly proud of his decision to be an "activist who stood for love and justice."

Iraq was on almost everyone's mind, and a few people noted the relation while we stood around talking and drinking tea as Eric and Marcy searched for extra chairs. We started late, and I wondered how it would be possible for everyone to share and still be finished with the meeting on time. Eric seemed to be worrying the same thing. His usual laconic style was replaced by a brief, rushed description of the group and a very perfunctory "chakra meditation" before ceding the floor to Cathy's guided visualization. Cathy's soft voice immediately changed the pace of the preceding. She breathed deeply, and then said in a soft voice: "Take a few more deep breaths to feel yourself connected to that chakra, the crown, the white light that is coming down, and connecting you to it. Now imagine that this white light is coming down over your body, you are pulling it down over your crown, your head, your eyes, your neck and down over your body, until you are bathed in this white light, this source of love, universal love."

We sat in silence, eyes closed, as Cathy continued, "Now with your mind's eye turn your attention to the crescent moon that is shining brightly in the western sky. It is often used, the crescent moon, as a symbol for Islam." After a few moments of silence, Cathy then directed, "Now, we are going to connect our energies together, and send them to the Middle East. In a moment, we are going to move our energies toward the center of the circle, and we are going to use our energies together to send a beam of light and love to the Middle East. Now imagine, you are moving your energy, the light that is around you, to the middle, and it is mingling and intermingling with all of the others' together. And now, we are going to send that light up, into the night sky, and across the world, and it is going to shine down on Iraq, and we are going to send our love to the people of Iraq, to the people who live there, and we are going to acknowledge their love, their existence, their beauty, and we will ask them to acknowledge ours. Now just rest for a moment, feeling that love sent there, bathing that country with this universal light."

We sat in silence for a few more minutes, and then Cathy's voice broke in again. "And now, if you feel comfortable, we are going to take this light, and we are going to direct it to someone who is in power, and who is taking part in what is going on in world events, it could be someone in this country, someone in some other part of the world whose heart is filled with hate and anger. And we are going to take this light, and we are going to connect our light and love to their heart chakras. Take a moment to do that. Don't be afraid, you are safe, enveloped in the white light, and no one can harm you."

After a few more minutes, Cathy "brought us back" first to the group light beam, and then back into our individual bodies, and finally asked us to open our eyes. Everyone opened their eyes, and a few people stretched. Eric looked around, and told the people around the circle that the tradition was to "go around the circle and say what we got from the meditation." Over the next half hour people in the room elaborated on what they had seen and felt as they traveled out of their bodies to other places in the world, with people often speaking out of turn and shaping a conversation that was quite unlike the normal, serial expressions that Eric preferred, with the result that there was more of a building momentum, and conversation, than what typically occurred, despite the fact that half of the people in the room were newcomers. Crystal was the first one to speak and began with enthusiasm. "I just felt so much euphoria in this room, especially when all of our energies were pulling together in the middle, it was like—*wow* look what we can do together. And I was just—feeling that energy and being a part of it, and all that love. So thanks, Cathy and Eric." She seemed to be finished but then turned to address Cathy directly. "Oh—and I wanted to say, that when you invited us to send our love to someone who was full of hate? I was really glad that you said, 'Don't have any fear, don't be scared,' because I was feeling a bit concerned. Thanks for reminding me that I was bathed in light. Then I could do it."

Paula interrupted, "Yes—that was really great. When we are asked to imagine a person, I thought of George W. Bush. I always think of him as a child, like a little boy, immature and childish. So, when Cathy said to send him love, I thought of him as a baby and sent my love to him as a child. But also, when you said that we should send our love to the people of Iraq, it was really vivid. I felt like I was zooming in. I actually saw a mother and a child together, and she was holding the child in front of what looked like their house. At least, I think it was. It was so vivid though, I wonder—I really felt a really strong connection to her, and them. To the real people who are there. And I thought, this is what it is about, sending our love and our power to them, because it is the mothers and children in Iraq, they're the ones who have the power."

When it came to my turn I followed the pattern of thanking Eric and Cathy for a "relaxing" meditation and mentioned that I thought Cathy's reference to the crescent moon was quite nice, as I had been enjoying the moon on my walk to the chapel. "Can you still see it out there?" Cathy asked, turning to look out the window. She turned back and addressed Crystal's opening comment. "You know, the reason I said 'don't be afraid' is because when I was doing the visualization, the person who leapt to mind immediately was Saddam Hussein. And, when I connected to his heart I felt a real prick, like a sharp needle. It hurt. And so, that's why I said 'don't be afraid' because I was afraid, and I needed to remember that I was in the light in order to go into his heart."

Annette jumped in, saying, "I thought about Saddam Hussein too, but just like Paula, I thought of him as a baby, as a child, about sending love to him as a child. That was easier, than sending love to him as a grownup man. I remembered that he was a child once, that we were all children once. That was a much easier way to send love to him."

Changing the subject somewhat, Annette continued, "You know that visualization, it really connected with me. I've been thinking about being an agent of peace in my life. I've had the feeling that that's what I'm supposed to be, so the fact that, that you made it clear that I'm not just to be peaceful in my own life, but also giving peace to the clients and people I see at my job, and my coworkers, and also in the world, that we can work together to make peace, that is really powerful.

So now I see why I've been going around being a person of peace these last few days."

Annette shifted the subject from the impending war to her work life, and on this cue, and as if arising from a slumber, Steven and John, two middle-aged men, shook off their lethargy and sat up straight. Steve asked Eric, "We don't have to talk about world events, do we?" Several people gave a resounding "no," and Steve told us all that he was a newcomer to the group and a friend of John's. "John recommended that I come, because I have a really high anxiety, stressful job. And I haven't been sleeping well, and I have been trying to meditate and read on my own. But it's not really easy to do that on your own." I noticed several people nodding as he continued. "So, anyways I told John about it, and he told me that we should come tonight, that it's helped him a lot, and well—that was the most peaceful I've felt in a long time. I don't know when I've felt like that before, I think I maybe fell asleep, I was so relaxed, and if I did I apologize. So, that's what I have to say, it's not about world events, I wasn't really paying attention to that part."

John was always the least loquacious person in the group, and staring shyly at the floor with his hands cupped in his lap, he added only, "Yeah—it's like Steve said, it's really a good thing to do the meditations. I always go into a deep trance with the chakras. So, I want to commend you, Eric, for the work you do." Eric took the praise with a smile and for a change did not tell us the story about how he does the visualization on the train on his way to work. Like the others in the room, he wanted to tell Cathy that the "visualization was really powerful. I felt, really, this powerful pull into the vortex of our energy together. It was just so much energy—and I felt myself moving over the world, and I saw the globe glowing as our light went out around the world."

It was only at the very end of the evening that Kevin, another newcomer, spoke up. Picking up a different strain, he said when "we were turning our energy there, I felt—I got the feeling that there was already lots of light and energy there. That there was enough, that they didn't need any more of ours there. The people there also have lots of light, in the Middle East, in Iraq. And I also had the distinct impression that there is a sage in the Middle East, someone who is of that tradition, in the Middle East, or in Iraq, who feels the same way we do, who has the same feelings and is working for peace, and that was good to have that feeling that that person is there."

Everyone who was gathered nodded and thought that they too hoped that there was a "sage" who would bring peace to the Middle East, missing Kevin's quiet attempt to rebuke the logic embedded in these visions. While the mystics gathered in the space of the chapel were hoping for peace and justice, and Cathy's visualization led us through familiar tropes of critique of American foreign policy and war-mongering, the entire ritual reproduced a spiritualized imperialism, where those in the United States could travel quickly and effortlessly to other parts of the world, and lift up both spiritual and "real" women and children from the lock of spiritual and political tyranny, enter into others' hearts, and then return untouched to the familiar. The worst that one could suffer was a "prick" of an evil heart, but even this terror could be overcome by a protective shield of mystical light. Eric's (and the rest's) ability to "zoom around" the world, to observe the globe from outside, was not an unfamiliar practice for metaphysicals. Nor, for that matter, was the notion that "love" and "light" represented a strong spiritual Esperanto that allowed mystics to not only encounter but enter into the true hearts of others. These hearts, at least in their pure, childlike, and uncorrupted versions, showed themselves to be all the same, and familiar to the equally good-hearted individuals gathered in the Swedenborgian parlor.

In several recent articles on "cosmopolitan virtues," sociologist Bryan S. Turner posits the importance of the virtues of "ironic distance," but adds that "irony may only be possible once one has already had an emotional commitment to a place. . . . Perhaps irony without patriotism may be too cool and thin to provide for identification with place and with politics." He notes, thus, "cosmopolitanism does not mean that one does not have a country or a homeland, but one has to have a certain reflexive distance from that homeland."[24] While Turner's call for a reflective and ironic distance sounds worthwhile as a pursuit, the possibility that he raises depends on particular religious and secular constructs of alignment with a nation. It arguably holds no place for the highly cosmopolitan postnationalist visions that metaphysicals hope for and (in visionary projects like the one just described) participate within.

Metaphysicals in Cambridge raise the question of whether their "zooming around" represents not a postnational project but rather the recovery of a particular kind of *American* cosmopolitanism, one that drinks deeply from transcendental wells, where the American and the universal are culturally tied in powerful ways to evocations of universal energy, of the astral connective tissue that carries through time and space. Mystical visualization presents an opportunity to think about the ways that "cosmopolitan virtues" are resonant with the chronotopes elaborated within the various projects of nineteenth-

and twentieth-century mystics and metaphysicals, and that are fused at present with particular concerns and legacies that mark "American" people as those without culture, without past, and thus perhaps without society. This theme is hardly new: in the nineteenth century "nostalgia was perceived as a European disease," and nations including the United States that "came of age late and wished to distinguish themselves from aging Europe developed their identity on an anti-nostalgic premise; for better or worse they claimed to have managed to escape the burdens of historical time." Hence early Americans "perceived themselves as 'Nature's Nation,' something that lives in the present and has no need for the past" leading to the nationalization of progress and the "American dream."[25]

While such broad cultural sketches of the metaphysical projection of an always-unfolding national culture that never quite finds its home might sound strange to some, the spiritual imperialisms developing through these imaginative uses of space are nonetheless present in many metaphysical communities. They are discussed, ritualized, and embodied, and yet in the process their politics obscured through claims to metaphysical and mystical connections that are pure, open, and *empty*. America emerges as mysticism, and as a mysticism that is not yet realized.[26]

But question of whether we are ready for "America as mysticism" is perhaps put to us too late, if Cambridge's mystics are any measure. Their spiritual imaginaries and the landscapes that they traverse show that America already figures as mysticism, yet one that in the very characterization of its futures as borderless and filled with love and light participates within contemporary American projects of expansion. As these stories illuminate, we are never free from the past. Rather than give ourselves over to the radical present of American mysticism and its secular dreams of an open, borderless, cosmopolitan future, we ought to redouble our efforts to tracing the ways that these practices and their imagined places and times continue to propel us toward such dreams, where we zoom around, freed from our pasts and thus our sins.

Conclusion

Spirituality emerges over and over in our collective imaginations as free floating and individualistic. Spirituality appears to be a condition of modern life: it has no past, no organization, no clear shape. Studying spirituality thus appears akin to shoveling fog. As I have argued, however, we can no longer conscientiously reassert these positions, or the problematic logics that continue to reinforce them. Instead, we must approach spirituality and "the spiritual" in America as deeply entangled in various religious and secular histories, social structures, and cultural practices. When we begin with the observation that spirituality in the United States is shaped through and within religious discourses and practices that are produced within numerous institutional fields including the religious and the secular, we move far from the description of spirituality as a perennial product of disconnected individuals. It is, rather, a set of historically embedded, reproduced and changing ideas that have been regularly ignored. This "neglect" is not due to their esoteric or subterranean nature but rather because of the predominant theoretical logics of secularization that implicitly and explicitly deflect sociological attention from the continued circulation of religious meanings, yearnings, and imaginations in spaces understood to be secular.

My argument in this volume has been not only that spirituality is lived in concrete and complex ways in contemporary American life, but furthermore that spirituality is produced in multiple social institutions, including many that we regularly do not consider religious. Locating the production of spirituality in so-called secular institutions unsettles the logics of institutional differentiation that continue to lie at the heart of our theories of secularization and, thereby, our projects of analyzing religion.[1] This calls us to investigate the multiple spaces (including secular ones) where religious sensitivities and selves are robustly explored and cultivated. Locating spiritual practice in this way does not contribute to an argument that secularization is a ruse, a myth, or a colossal misunderstanding, any more than it contributes to an argument that American institutions are actually "resacralizing." Rather, it makes clear that the binaries of religious and secular institutional differentiation are inadequate to our analysis of religious life in America, even as they have been generative for a variety of religious and spiritual dispositions and subjectivities.[2] Consider, for example, how Cambridge's spiritual practitioners find medicine, the arts, psychology, and other institutions to be valuable sites of exploration precisely because of their apparent secularity. With this in mind, the future path lies in cultivating analytical approaches that recognize the processes of secularization as historically embedded, complex and unfinalized traditions.[3]

The spiritual practices and discourses that I highlight in this volume all have long histories. We can see how they are developed and repurposed within a variety of settings, and how they are transformed in the process. Thus we can also see that the historical tendrils of spiritual practices and their social impact is quite different from American congregational religion. Nonetheless, the fact that the spiritual selves that take shape through these practices are organized differently and learned in different kinds of social interactions does not make them any less social or less religious. Nor, for that matter, does it make spiritual practice's political and social consequences any less important to address. With this in mind, we can see more clearly now how problematic the commonplace distinction between spiritual "conditions" and religious "traditions" have been. This distinction has resulted in multiple lost opportunities to explore or expand our vision of how spiritual practices (and even spiritual "traditions") engage with various parts of American social and political life, shaping Americans' understandings of what it means to be a citizen of a single nation or to move within a global society. As we have seen throughout this volume, spiritual practices organize specific concepts of a mystical American collective by combining old and new racial, national, and cosmopolitan trajectories. Spiritual discourses and practices provide metaphysicals with the political worlds they inhabit, as well as the bodies that are necessary to experience them.

————

In researching this volume I have often been reminded that many of the notions that contemporary sociologists use to describe spirituality or spiritual people were first developed and refined by early twentieth-century sociologists, psychologists, and philosophers who confronted and sought to understand religion's place in secularizing societies. Religious individualism and particular notions of a core spiritual self are thoroughly woven into explanations of religious differentiation, disenchantment, and the privatization of religion. Similar concepts of mysticism and religious experience have shaped and reshaped sociology's understanding of religion's boundaries, and likewise the proper focus for its analysis. A further surprise has been contemporary spiritual practitioners' use of social scientific concepts to describe their own religious worlds. Both groups' understandings of religion in modernity build upon conceptions of secularization and experience that are shaped by shared concerns about the role of religion in modern America. Their answers and understandings are different indeed, but cross-fertilization between them did not end in the era of James.

While these earlier cross-fertilizations demonstrate that social science and spirituality have been actively engaging each other for quite some time, drawing on and sometimes reinforcing each others' conceptions of individual religiosity, these interactions also present a compelling reason to resist telling a simple historical narrative of spirituality that restores to it a lost or concealed past.[4] The puzzle of spirituality in America cannot be solved by locating it within a history it refuses. Notwithstanding the importance of tracing spirituality's pasts, historical narratives disentangle the various tendrils of spiritual practice, ideology and experience, making the object clear yet in the process obscuring the very institutional and theoretical entanglements that give it power. Narrating spirituality in a way that gives it a past and affords it a tradition makes it unrecognizable to those who practice and produce it. And as such, it also renders its generative and entangled practices—those very aspects that allow it to thrive and shape conceptions that are central to American religious and social life—more difficult to observe.

Yet to argue that we should resist historical narrative does not mean that we can turn away from the question of how spiritual practice and concepts or religious experience are produced and reproduced through time. Whether in articulating one's own proper relation to the physical or astral body, in reading and writing about the divine, or in narrating various experiential stories that elide or highlight social ties, contemporary practitioners' daily activities can be placed within a constellation of engagements that we can map and engage through time. Theories of practice are helpful in addressing the ways that spirituality is practiced and produced. Practices have memory. The foregoing chapters demonstrate that the apprehension of "experience itself" is made possible through habits and activities that are ambiguously defined as secular or religious. Various practices, from styles of writing (automatic writing, spirit meditation, "flow writing") to speaking and exercising maintain and carry forward old ideas, even as they are rearticulated in new ways, in new conditions. Or as Bakhtin observes, no meaning is ever lost.[5] This is not a new argument: all manner of cultural products are reproduced in daily practices without our attention to them. Their value is not only in helping us manage local decisions, but also in reproducing the conditions in which such decisions appear possible and ethical.[6]

Coupling a theory of practice to a more open-ended question of the space of religious production (within multiple fields) likewise makes possible a more flexible usage of practice than what "religious" practice generally implies. "Religion" and "religious practice" frequently conjure a variety of related conceptions of intention, belief, and reflexivity developed within the differentiated field of religion. Once religious practice is coupled to a religious field, it follows that conducting religious practice or taking part in religious practice is necessarily within a field of conscious adoption and adherence. We have difficulty talking about religious practice in a way that allows us to talk about its practice in a nonreflexive, nonconscientious way.[7] It appears next to impossible to even imagine a modern person having a religious life that he or she engages or experiences unreflexively or without consciously claiming that position. And so it follows, it is likewise difficult for us to imagine modern people living in a world where the divine is felt and apprehended, where selves are porous, and where enchantments are inescapably present.[8] Yet this is precisely what many metaphysical practices compel us to consider. We find that the genre memories of various practices, embedded within numerous social fields, continue to reproduce (and work on) social life, unevenly making and shaping religious experience, and allowing metaphysicals to find themselves living in worlds that are thoroughly enchanted and populated by spirits, immanently known and unknown. To say the least, these practices seem to run counter to what some argue is secularism's demands for conscious belief that comes in the wake of disenchantment. The further question is the degree to which such enchantments are shaped by a presumption of enchantment's impossibility. With this in mind, we can continue to be surprised and perplexed at the irruptions of the sacred into daily life (or, alternatively continue to argue over whether this is the result of peculiar or necessary brain waves or neuroreceptors[9]) or we can investigate how those irruptions take place and work to locate the institutions and practices that contribute both to their occlusion and to their continuation.

Part of what makes spirituality so alive and vibrant for so many Cantabrigians is the promise that it fully conforms to modern society. Like all things modern, they tell me, it is grounded on verifiable facts, objective truths, or experimental results. It exists in time but also indicates something that is timeless, which is gradually becoming known to them, and to us. Thus, while the "information" or "knowledge" that a metaphysical explorer gains in the astral sphere might not be fully translatable into the mundane realms of daily life, thus requiring spiritual adepts to creatively and consciously expand the religious imaginary, this does not change their sense that they cannot choose to be spiritual. Indeed, choice is not the proper way to view metaphysical realities, just as it is not the proper way to view modernity's verities. One cannot choose to believe that the sun rises in the morning or that the dollar's worth is tied to the workings of international markets. And as my respondents constantly told me, one cannot choose to believe that one is a being of light. People who do not comprehend their true nature, origin, and eventual destination will end up constantly bewildered by what is going on around them, buffeted by forces that they could reasonably expect to understand in part and, if they were fortunate, learn to manipulate. Freedom, then, comes not in escape from the system but in learning how it works through mystical exploration, intensive interpretation, and experiential revelation.

To live within metaphysical projects is to accept the reality of forces that work on everyday life and to learn to interpret things in the world as results of their effects. And while there is no reason for us to collapse the difference between popular sociology's invisible forces ("the state," "the economy") and metaphysical forces ("karma," "energy," "soul clusters"), metaphysical practitioners had no difficulty in doing so. Each system articulates individuals as embedded within systems, social processes, or "forces," and each domain presents moral stories about how these can be changed, resisted, or lived within. Within the metaphysical world the elaborate possibilities never involve escape. Cultivating knowledge about these truths does not lead to an out. The truth does not make you free. But it might make you healthier, and it could even make you happier, at least for a moment.

One night at the mystical discussion group our discussion turned to movies. Eric was starting a mystical movie Web site and had invited everyone who wanted to come to a "mystical movie night" at his house to watch *Waking Life*. After he described the premise of that film, Marcy asked him if he had seen *The Green Mile*, which was out in theaters at the time.

"Not yet," he said.

"It's about a light worker," Marcy said. "You haven't seen it either Cathy? You should. It's a really great movie."

Two nights previously I had seen *Russian Ark* at the art film cinema close to MIT. I rarely went to the movies, and so I was happy that I had one to talk about. The *Russian Ark* also happened to be a movie that I thought that many in the group would enjoy. Since no one had heard of it, I told them that they should make a point to see it, preferably on the big screen, as it was really a movie about music, art, and cinematography. I added that I didn't think it was a mystical movie in the same way that Marcy thought *The Green Mile* was. Its theme was historical.

Eric asked what the movie was about, and I tried to explain it, even though, I said, part of the beauty of the film was that it didn't have a proper plot. In order to describe what the movie was about and why I enjoyed it, I started by giving some background on why it was that I was at the movies at all. My husband Jonathan had read about it in the *Boston Phoenix* and insisted that we go. I agreed, mainly because he told me that it was short (under an hour), and because we already had a babysitter booked. We would go to the movie first and then to a party to which we had been invited. I added that Jonathan either hadn't told me anything about the movie or I hadn't been listening when he did, so I missed the key fact that the movie was filmed in one continuous shot. The movie begins with the voice of the cameraman and a nineteenth-century European narrator who enters the Hermitage from a side entrance. The movie continues as the cameraman and the European travel through the Hermitage's galleries, each threshold revealing a different tableau and era. The movie is subtitled, I added, which contributed to my disorientation.

I explained that I struggled in the first few minutes to figure out what the movie was about, but that soon I gave up and began to concentrate on the beautiful cinematography and music. I was soon completely caught up in its mood, and just decided to let the movie unfold without overthinking it. I described how the movie ends with a ten-minute ballroom scene, with an orchestra playing in the middle conducted by Valery Gergiev. It was an incredible and unexpected visual and auditory experience, I said. I definitely thought that everyone should go see it if they could.

As I finished saying all of this, I noticed the flicker of attention around the room, and I immediately realized that I had been misunderstood. What I wanted to say was that the movie was good, and it made me think about how placing things in different order allows us to think about them differently—a simple point, and not very profound. But something I had said suggested that watching the movie was mystical. Cathy mused that maybe I had been a "Russian noblewoman" in a past life. A bit irritated at this thought, I kept talking, adding another example to try to pull myself out of her—their—interpretations. I said that while I was home by myself the previous week I had put our new recording of Beethoven's Ninth Symphony on the CD player and settled down to read. When the chorale movement began, however, the music intruded into my concentration. It reminded me of T. S. Eliot's phrase, "and you are the music while the music lasts." Perhaps it was the addition of the vocal registers, perhaps it was the distinctively fierce tempo (quite unlike our older, very familiar recording). Whatever the reason, I began to listen more intently and felt surrounded by something that was at once both familiar and new.

I then stopped talking. Silence followed this time. My decision to add more examples had not convinced my audience that watching the movie had not been mystical. In fact, the opposite had occurred. I had placed three events into a single narrative, providing the group with indeterminate connections to explore. As they began to speak again, tying the links ever tighter, my frustration turned back on myself. Why did I continue to be surprised by my own language's capacity to be drawn into their interpretive projects? The people gathered in the room required little effort to hear my words, and my world, as enchanted; it was likewise no stretch on my part to understand how they had come to understand them as such. Our languages were almost the same: both populated by invisible forces that took shape in narratives that marked heretofore unseen relations and connections. Sitting and listening, I considered again the claim I had recently come across in my reading: "We become disenchanted" only when the distinction between the mundane and the magical develops, "and remain so only while it lasts: in its absence."[10]

If this is so, then there is all the more reason to pay attention to the spiritual worlds around us, so that we speak and think more clearly about how various enchantments are linked and shaped together and how the distinctions between us emerge and disappear. Such exchanges require a closer inspection of how the nonsecular remains woven deeply into our language and our habits, and as such challenge any surprise or uncanny feeling we might gain in encountering them. With all of this in mind, we thus necessarily begin an argument with ourselves, one that challenges the deep mystifications of our secularisms.

Notes

INTRODUCTION

1. I resided in Cambridge between 1998 and 2004, and conducted fieldwork between 2001 and 2004, with a concentrated period of full-time research between June 2002 and August 2003. During this time I documented the groups, sites, and businesses where people gathered, shopped, took classes, and participated in spiritual events. I visited as many of these groups as I was able, typically making multiple visits. I participated where it was possible or required, although always identifying myself as an interested researcher (an identification that had repercussions, which I discuss more below). In addition to recording numerous informal conversations with spiritual practitioners, I conducted seventy-seven audiotaped interviews.

2. A few counterexamples include Adrian Ivakhiv, *Claiming Sacred Ground: Pilgrims and Politics at Glastonbury and Sedona* (Bloomington: Indiana University Press, 2001); Jeffrey Kripal, *Esalen and the Religion of No Religion* (Chicago: University of Chicago Press, 2007). In contrast, studies of neo-paganism and witchcraft more frequently employ ethnographic, participant observation methods and thus are much more likely to locate these practices in place. See Sarah Pike, *Earthly Bodies Magical Selves* (Berkeley: University of California Press, 2001); Tanya Luhrmann, *Persuasions of the Witch's Craft: Ritual Magic in Contemporary England* (Cambridge, MA: Harvard University Press, 1989). Neo-paganism and spiritual groups share some common threads and ideas, but are genealogically and theologically distinct in some respects. While the boundaries between these groups are equally fuzzy, recent literature suggests that the distinction

191

holds, broadly speaking. See Michael York, *The Emerging Network: A Sociology of the New Age and Neo-Pagan Movements* (Lanham, MD: Rowman and Littlefield, 1995).

3. For example, Robert Bellah et al., *Habits of the Heart: Individualism and Commitment in American Life* (Berkeley: University of California Press, 1985); Wade Clark Roof, *Spiritual Marketplace: Baby Boomers and the Remaking of American Religion* (Princeton, NJ: Princeton University Press, 1999); Robert Wuthnow, *After Heaven: Spirituality in America since the 1950s* (Berkeley: University of California Press, 1998); Michele Dillon and Paul Wink, *In The Course of a Lifetime* (Berkeley: University of California Press, 2007). Each of these volumes suggests that while religious individualism has been present in American history, it takes on a different, more radical, and widespread shape during the 1960s.

4. My thinking has been expanded by the turn in religious studies to historically informed studies of sacred space (for example, David Chidester and Edward Linenthal, eds., *American Sacred Space* [Bloomington: Indiana University Press, 1995]; Thomas Tweed, *Crossing and Dwelling* (Cambridge, MA: Harvard University Press, 2006). I likewise have been influenced by sociologist Thomas Gieryn's discussion of the epistemological interplay of "field" and "lab" in "City as Truth-Spot: Laboratories and Field-Sites in Urban Studies," *Social Studies of Science* 36 (2006): 5–38. Ultimately, the analysis in this book became more closely associated with Cambridge as a specific "field" and not as a "lab." At the same time, it is arguably the case that the specific field of Cambridge is, along with several other locations in the Americas, a particularly formative one in shaping both academic and lay understandings of religious experience and spirituality.

5. Sydney Ahlstrom calls these traditions "harmonial" in his classic *A Religious History of the American People* (New Haven, CT: Yale University Press, 1974). Ahlstrom includes Spiritualists, Theosophists, Transcendentalists, and New Thought devotees among the groups that believe that "spiritual composure, physical health, and even economic well-being are understood to flow from a person's rapport with the cosmos." Ahlstrom, like later observers, would note that this "vast and highly diffuse religious impulse that cuts across all the normal lines of religious division . . . often shapes the inner meaning of the church life to which people formally commit themselves," 1019–20. Recent scholarship favors a variety of other terms for this tradition, for example, Catherine Albanese's term "metaphysical religion" in *A Republic of Mind and Spirit* (New Haven, CT: Yale University Press, 2007), and Leigh Schmidt's designation of similar groups and trajectories as "mystics" and "ultra-liberal Protestants" in *Restless Souls: The Making of American Spirituality* (San Francisco: HarperSanFrancisco, 2005).

6. Numerous studies abound; many tell the story of developing and chang-

ing histories of new age and occult religions (Joscelyn Godwin, *The Theosophical Enlightenment* [Albany: State University of New York Press, 1994]; Wouter Hanegraaff, *New Age Religion and Western Culture* [Albany: State University of New York Press, 1998]; Christopher H. Partridge, *The Re-enchantment of the West: Alternative Spiritualities, Sacralization, Popular Culture, and Occulture* [London: Clark International, 2004]); American Transcendentalism (Catherine Albanese, *Corresponding Motion: Transcendental Religion and the New America* [Philadelphia: Temple University Press, 1977]; Arthur Versluis, *American Transcendentalism and Asian Religions* [New York: Oxford University Press, 1993]); the ongoing debates between science and religion and their proper boundaries (R. Laurence Moore, *In Search of White Crows* [New York: Oxford University Press, 1977]; Leigh Schmidt, *Hearing Things: Religion, Illusion, and the American Enlightenment* [Cambridge, MA: Harvard University Press, 2000]; Robert C. Fuller, *Alternative Medicine and American Religious Life* [New York: Oxford University Press, 1989]).

A developing body of research seeks to link these histories with mainstream currents in American religious, cultural, and political thought and expression. See, for example, R. Marie Griffith, *Born Again Bodies: Flesh and Spirit in American Christianity* (Berkeley: University of California Press, 2004); Beryl Satter, *Each Mind a Kingdom: American Women, Sexual Purity and the New Thought Movement, 1875–1920* (New York: Oxford University Press, 1999).

7. Ralph Waldo Emerson's Divinity School address is represented in countless texts as a key moment in the emergence of American Transcendentalism, if not (as D. Elton Trueblod wrote in 1939), "a turning point in American life and letters." "The Influence of Emerson's Divinity School Address," *Harvard Theological Review* 32 (1939): 43. On the Sarah Bull salon, see Stephen Prothero, "Hinduphilia and Hinduphobia in U.S. Culture," in *The Stranger's Religion*, ed. Ann Lannestrom (Notre Dame, IN: University of Notre Dame Press, 2004), 13–37. Henry James, *The Bostonians* (New York: Modern Library, 1956).

8. William James gave testimony in an 1898 Massachusetts State House inquiry into whether mind curers should be regulated, arguing against state interference. "It is enough for you as legislators to ascertain that a large number of our citizens, persons as intelligent and well educated as yourself or I, persons who numbers seem daily to increase, are convinced that these healing practices do achieve the results that they claim.'" Quoted in Reuben A. Kessel, "Price Discrimination in Medicine," *Journal of Law and Economics* 1 (1954): 26.

9. Wai Chee Dimock, "A Theory of Resonance," *PMLA* 112 (1997): 1060–71.

10. Scholars of American religion might well be suspicious of the "return" to studying spirituality in Cambridge, after decades of active work to de-

center the New England religious narrative from the history of American religions (see, for example, Harry Stout and D. G. Hart, eds., *New Directions in American Religious History* [New York: Oxford University Press, 1998]). While this iteration of Cambridge's spiritual explorations recapitulate various motifs of New England religiosity (from the Puritans through the Transcendentalists to liberal Protestant experimentalists to secularization) *as* American religion, where highly educated, mostly white, experimentalists take center stage, a return to these spaces also suggests ways to investigate how this centrality is constituted from within the space of spiritual practices. Thus while the claims of spiritual practitioners are frequently that "everything is everything," these claims to universalism are shaped by the parochialisms and geographical specificity of spiritual practice.

11. Even though I keep in mind Robert Sharf's charge that it is "incumbent upon [scholars] to reject the perennialist hypothesis insofar as it anachronistically imposes the recent and ideologically laden notion of religious experience on our interpretations of premodern phenomena," it is nonetheless the case that Cambridge's contemporary spiritual practitioners' understandings of their own metaphysical realities are directly shaped by such perennialist hypotheses. Robert Sharf, "Experience," in *Critical Terms for Religious Studies,* ed. Mark C. Taylor (Chicago: University of Chicago Press, 1998), 98. Unlike scholars of medieval Catholicism, premodern India, or even seventeenth-century New England, scholars of twentieth-century religion engage in religious worlds that have been shaped by perennial and universal views of religious experience from the beginning. There is thus nothing "anachronistic" about the perennial forms of religious experience in Cambridge. As a consequence, it is incumbent to analyze the practices and strategies that develop around such theologies of experience, much as it is necessary to work to signal (if not recover) the ways that these views have shaped our views and visions of "others'" religious experiences. See, for example, Grace Jantzen, *Power, Gender, and Christian Mysticism* (Cambridge: Cambridge University Press, 1995); James Hoopes, *Consciousness in New England: From Puritanism and Ideas to Psychoanalysis and Semiotics* (Baltimore: Johns Hopkins University Press, 1989); Richard King, *Orientalism and Religion* (New York: Routledge, 1999).

12. This research model thus began with an approach similar to the one that I outlined in *Heaven's Kitchen: Living Religion at God's Love We Deliver* (Chicago: University of Chicago Press, 2003), which owes much to the extended case method. Michael Burawoy, "The Extended Case Method," *Sociological Theory* 16 (1988): 5–33; see also Nina Eliasoph and Paul Lichterman, "We Begin with Our Favorite Theory . . . : Reconstructing the Extended Case Method," *Sociological Theory* 17 (1989): 228–34. While in *Heaven's Kitchen* I focused on aspects of discursive practice as well as the space and shape of religion in public life, in this volume the "extended case" presents a unique opportunity to investigate and theorize the uses

of the past (via memory, practice, and institution) within spiritual traditions in America and to theorize the absence of history within sociological studies of spirituality.

13. William H. Sewell Jr., "The Concept(s) of Culture," in *Beyond the Cultural
Turn,* ed. Victoria Bonnell and Lynn Hunt (Berkeley: University of Califor-
nia Press, 1999), 35–61; Ann Swidler, *Talk of Love* (Chicago: University of
Chicago Press, 2001); Courtney Bender, "Things in Their Entanglements"
(lecture, "Exploring the Postsecular Conference," Yale University, New
Haven, CT, April 3–4, 2009).

14. Pamela Klassen and Courtney Bender, "Habits of Pluralism," in *After
Pluralism,* ed. Courtney Bender and Pamela Klassen (New York: Columbia
University Press, 2010); Charles Stewart, "Syncretism and Its Synonyms:
Reflections on Cultural Mixture," *Diacritics* 29 (1999): 40–62.

15. The ways that practices carry history should not imply the "contemporiza-
tion" of the past. As Mikhail Bakhtin argues, "a genre is always the same
and yet not the same, always old and new simultaneously. Genre is reborn
and renewed at every new stage in the development of literature and in
every individual work of a given genre. . . . A genre lives in the present,
but always *remembers* its past, its beginning. Genre is a representative of
creative memory in the process of literary development." *Problems of Dostoevsky's Poetics* (Minneapolis: University of Minnesota Press, 1984), 106.
Genres thus help to produce the circumstances of their own (re)telling,
and also reproduce the types of meaning that are possible to speak of, and
through. See also Jeffrey Olick, "Genre Memories and Memory Genres,"
American Sociological Review 64 (1999): 381–402.

16. David Yamane proposes that sociologists can use narrative approaches to
study religious experiences but nonetheless simultaneously argues that
sociologists and other scholars only have access to narrative *accounts*
expressed post hoc, and never have access to the experiences "themselves." This distinction between experience and account is a "fundamental fact" according to Yamane, who argues that sociologists "must bracket
any claims to apprehending religious experience itself and instead give
our full attention to the primary way people concretize . . . their experiences . . . through narratives." David Yamane, "Narrative and Religious
Experience." *Sociology of Religion* 61 (2000): 175–76. See also Omar McRoberts, "Beyond *Mysterium Tremendum:* Thoughts Toward an Aesthetic Study
of Religious Experience," *Annals of the American Academy of Political and
Social Sciences* 595 (2004): 190–203. James Spickard is critical of Yamane's
distinction and demonstrates in contrast that religious experiences can be
communal and, in those cases, apprehended by sociologists. This is a wor-
thy criticism, but notably (like most other studies of this kind) turns from
the central question posed, namely whether the unavailability of direct
"individual" religious experience is a "fundamental fact." James Spickard,
"Ritual, Symbol, and Experience: Understanding Catholic Worker House

Masses," *Sociology of Religion*, 66 (2005): 337–57. See also Thomas Csordas, "Embodiment as a Paradigm for Anthropology" *Ethos* 18 (1990): 5–47.

17. Sharf, "Experience," 98.

18. Martin Jay, *Songs of Experience: Modern American and European Variations on a Universal Theme* (Berkeley: University of California Press, 2005), 80.

19. Wayne Proudfoot, *Religious Experience* (Berkeley: University of California Press, 1989). See also Jay, *Songs of Experience*, 78–132.

20. Proudfoot, *Religious Experience*, 117–18.

21. Peter Berger, *The Heretical Imperative* (Garden City, NY: Doubleday, 1979), 53–54.

22. Similar criticisms also arise intermittently from the field of psychology itself. See Chris J. Boyatzis, "A Critique of Models of Religious Experience," *International Journal for the Psychology of Religion* 4 (2001): 247–58.

23. While this approach paved the way for stronger analysis of how conversion and experience are shaped within religious communities, sociologists have not turned these conceptual or cultural tools to those very cases of religious experience that appear to occur outside of religious institutions, and instead look at those examples as unusual exceptions that nonetheless reinforce the notion that numinous, noncultural, transhistorical "experience" is a natural category of human experience. This transhistorical experience is most frequently reproduced within survey studies, of which there are numerous examples. Most draw on survey responses to several questions on NORC or related (Gallup) surveys, with wording similar to Andrew Greeley's "Have you ever felt as though you were very close to a powerful spiritual force that seemed to lift you out of yourself?" Andrew Greeley, *The Sociology of the Paranormal: A Reconnaissance* (Beverly Hills, CA: Sage, 1975). Further examples include David Hay and Ann Morisy, "Reports of Ecstatic, Paranormal, or Religious Experience in Great Britain and the United States: A Comparison of Trends," *Journal for the Scientific Study of Religion* 17 (1978): 255–68; William L. MacDonald, "The Effects of Religiosity and Structural Strain on Reported Paranormal Experiences," *Journal for the Scientific Study of Religion* 34 (1995): 366–76; Roger Straus, "The Social-Psychology of Religious Experience: A Naturalistic Approach," *Sociological Analysis* 42 (1981): 157–67.

24. Edward Berryman, "Medjugorje's Living Icons: Making Spirit Matter (for Sociology)," *Social Compass* 48 (2001): 594. As I argue elsewhere, even sociologists who study religious experiences in groups depend upon the existence of nonaffiliated persons' religious experiences as examples of the sociologically inexplicable (nonsocial, nonreducible) aspects of religion. Thus, far from being a category of tertiary interest, the extrasociological existence of religious experiences bolsters sociology of religion's claims to nonreductionism. Religious experience is certainly not the only term to play this role, but it been an important one.

25. Leigh Schmidt, "The Making of Modern 'Mysticism,'" *Journal of the American Academy of Religion* 71 (2003): 273–302.

26. Ibid., 294, 295.

27. Robert Sharf, "Buddhist Modernism and the Rhetoric of Meditative Experience," *Numen* 42 (1995): 228–83.

28. See Ann Taves, *Fits, Trances, and Visions: Experiencing Religion and Explaining Experience from Wesley to James* (Princeton, NJ: Princeton University Press, 1999); Moore, *In Search of White Crows;* Robert Fuller, "American Psychology and the Religious Imagination," *Journal of the History of the Behavioral Sciences* 42 (2006): 221–35; Christopher White, *Unsettled Minds: Psychology and the American Search for Spiritual Assurance, 1830–1940* (Berkeley: University of California Press, 2008).

29. Taves, *Fits, Trances, and Visions,* 6. See also R. Bruce Mullin, *Miracles and the Modern Religious Imagination* (New Haven, CT: Yale University Press, 1996); Richard Ostrander, *The Life of Prayer in a World of Science* (New York: Oxford University Press, 2000).

30. Joachim Wach, *Sociology of Religion* (Chicago: Chicago University Press 1949), 162–65; Ernst Troeltsch, *The Social Teachings of the Christian Church* (Louisville, KY: Westminster John Knox Press, 1992). Notably, Max Weber's concept of "charisma" stands in contrast to these understandings of religious experience. While Wach and Troeltsch suggest that there is "something" in the experience itself that leads to revolutionary or mystical groups, Weber's discussions of charisma signal that a person's "gifts" and "messages" from the divine can only be truly understood as charisma (and not madness or hereticism) if they are accepted by a social group. Thus, Weber notes, while "pure charisma does not recognize any legitimacy other than one which flows from personal strength," the "genuinely charismatic ruler . . . is responsible to the ruled—responsible, that is, to prove that he himself is indeed the master willed by God." *Economy and Society* (Berkeley: University of California Press, 1978), 1114. For another summation of the distinctiveness of Weber's view of charisma in contrast to his contemporaries' "theological" understandings, see David Norton Smith, "Faith, Reason, and Charisma: Rudolf Sohm, Max Weber, and the Theology of Grace," *Sociological Inquiry* 68 (1998): 30–62.

31. Courtney Bender, "Religion and Spirituality: History, Discourse, and Measurement" (paper prepared for the Social Science Research Council, 2006); "Touching the Transcendent: On the Status of Religious Experience in the Sociological Study of Religion," in *Everyday Religion: Observing Modern Religious Lives,* ed. Nancy T. Ammerman (New York: Oxford University Press, 2007), 201–18.

32. Sociologists in the 1960s and 1970s developed various survey instruments to investigate individuals' "peak experiences" and "abnormal experiences," hoping to examine the "social situations [that] are structured to

produce religious experiences among participants." This research criticized "purely" psychological views of religious experience, but nonetheless distinguished experiences borne of participation within religious groups and more "mystical," less culturally rooted experiences. Charles Glock and Rodney Stark, *Religion and Society in Tension* (Chicago: Rand McNally, 1965), 52. Criticizing purely psychological approaches, Glock and Stark state "in such circumstances, it is as irrelevant to seek the causes of such behavior in purely individual terms as it would be to search for a personality syndrome to account for the fact that Roman Catholics typically genuflect when passing in front of an altar."

33. In a discussion of "spiritual parvenus" in *After Heaven,* for example, Robert Wuthnow notes that having an out-of-the-ordinary (peak) experience is typically "not enough" to propel parvenus to join a religious group; rather, in large measure such experiences only remind or suggest to such persons that something "more" exists. The cameo appearance of individual religious experience is particularly notable in Wuthnow's otherwise careful attention to the cultural construction of "spirituality." Here, it emerges as an event that precedes any kind of religious belonging or connection. Examples such as these demonstrate how thoroughly individual religious experience articulated in this naturalistic way shapes sociological analysis of religion. See Wuthnow, *After Heaven,* 134–35. A similar discussion of religious experience appears in Roof, *Spiritual Marketplace,* 175ff.

34. Bellah et al., *Habits of the Heart,* 221, 226. The number of articles and books that take up or critique Sheila-ism, or Bellah's depiction of Sheila, are legion. See, for example, Bruce Greer and Wade Clark Roof, "Desperately Seeking Sheila: Locating Religious Privatism in American Society," *Journal for the Scientific Study of Religion* 31 (1992): 346–52; Melissa Wilcox, "When Sheila's a Lesbian: Religious Individualism among Lesbian, Gay and Transgender Christians," *Sociology of Religion* 63 (2002): 497–513; Robert Fuller, *Spiritual But Not Religious: Understanding Unchurched America* (New York: Oxford University Press, 2001), 159–62; Roof, *Spiritual Marketplace.*

35. Louis Menand, *The Metaphysical Club* (New York: Farrar Straus and Giroux, 2001).

36. Taylor's June 2001 lecture appears to be drawn from several published essays, including primarily "Have We Engaged in a Colossal Misreading of James's *Varieties?" Streams of William James* 5 (2003): 2–6; and "Swedenborgian Roots of American Pragmatism: The Case of D. T. Suzuki," *Studia Swedenborgia* 9 (1995).

37. Taylor argues similarly in his published work for a psychology that is "more phenomenological, more observational, and even more existential kind of science that accommodate[s] the full range of human experience, including psychic phenomena and mystical awakening" (Taylor, "Have We Engaged in a Colossal Misreading?" 6).

38. Eugene Taylor, *Shadow Culture: Psychology and Spirituality in America* (Washington, DC: Counterpoint, 1999).

39. See also Craig Hazen, *The Village Enlightenment: Popular Religion and Science in the Nineteenth Century* (Urbana: University of Illinois Press, 2000).

40. Jeanne Favret-Saada, *Deadly Words: Witchcraft in the Bocage* (Cambridge: Cambridge University Press, 1977), 17.

41. Susan Harding graphically recounts being similarly caught as she "interviews" a senior fundamentalist minister and finds herself transformed in the process of listening from a cultural analyst to a sinner on her way to redemption. *The Book of Jerry Falwell* (Princeton, NJ: Princeton University Press, 2001).

42. The majority of my interview respondents were very well educated (more than half had completed some graduate coursework; all but three held college degrees), of European descent, and predominantly from Christian (Protestant and Catholic) backgrounds. The range of participants in the many classes, courses, and rituals in which I took part shared similar characteristics, so far as I was able to ascertain.

43. As such, they perhaps epitomize what Renato Rosaldo observed some time ago as members of the "postcultural" West, wherein American cultural politics mark those who live through mixtures and hybrids as similarly obscure and uninteresting to anthropology's continued valuation of authentic, nostalgic cultures. Renato Rosaldo, "Ideology, Place, and People without Culture," *Cultural Anthropology* 3 (1988): 78. Other narratives that discuss metaphysicals and spiritual practitioners as lacking culture and history shape them as modern (or postmodern) "primitives" who, lacking telos or a sense of belonging (and hence a sense of responsibility), are unable to participate (or refuse to participate) in political or moral communities. See Eric Wolf, *Europe and the People without History* (Princeton, NJ: Princeton University Press, 1982); Kerwin Lee Klein, "In Search of Narrative Mastery: Postmodernism and the People without History," *History and Theory* 34 (1995): 275–98.

44. Thomas Sugrue, *There Is a River: The Story of Edgar Cayce* (New York: Holt 1942), 12–13.

45. Ibid., 30.

46. Hugo Münsterberg, *Psychology and Life* (Boston: Houghton Mifflin, 1899), 248.

47. White, *Unsettled Minds,* 194–95.

CHAPTER ONE

1. The literature on contemporary spirituality that begins with an individualistic and market-oriented understanding of its organization is extensive. Examples of recent work that finds the ephemeral qualities of contemporary, alternative, or nontraditional spirituality liberatory (or poten-

tially so) include Paul Heelas, *The New Age Movement* (Oxford: Blackwell, 1996). The literature that is explicitly critical is much more extensive and includes Kimberly Lau, *New Age Capitalism: Making Money East of Eden* (Philadelphia: University of Pennsylvania Press, 2000); Richard Cimino and Don Lattin, *Shopping for Faith: American Religion in the New Millennium* (San Francisco: Jossey-Bass, 1998); Lorning M. Danforth, *Firewalking and Religious Healing* (Princeton, NJ: Princeton University Press, 1989). Other books that are a bit more balanced in their approach to this issue yet nonetheless take a similar, individual-centered approach to the topic include Robert Wuthnow, *After Heaven: American Spirituality since the 1950s* (Berkeley: University of California Press, 1998); and Wade Clark Roof, *Spiritual Marketplace: Baby Boomers and the Remaking of American Religion* (Princeton, NJ: Princeton University Press, 1999).

2. I regularly visited the public bulletin-board listings at the Harvest Cooperative, three coffee shops, the Cambridge Public Library, and the Cambridge Center for Adult Education. In addition, I read *Spirit of Change* and *Earthstar,* and searched online "holistic" and "spirituality" listings for New England for other practitioners working in Cambridge. Two spiritual bookstores in Cambridge listed ongoing events on their Web sites. As I began to interview and conduct observations, I asked leaders and participants for names of other possible contacts and groups. In addition, I compared the types of groups and activities that I learned about in Cambridge with printed taxonomies of "new age" religious groups and practices, both to look for what I might have missed and what was missing. These taxonomies include J. Gordon Melton, Jerome Clark, and Aidan Kelly, eds., *New Age Encyclopedia* (Detroit: Gale Research, 1991); and Wouter Hanegraaff, *New Age Religion and Western Culture* (Albany: State University of New York Press, 1998).

3. My focus on alternative health, religious, and arts institutions is not exhaustive of the institutional fields where spirituality is organized; rather, these three fields were most important in Cambridge, and focusing on their intersections presents opportunities to articulate and establish the organizational structure of its production in one location. One might expect various other intersections and entanglements in the lived practice and production of spirituality in other regions and locations (for example, stronger affinities between spiritual groups and psychology in some areas, or more interest and generative interrelationships between "spirituality" and Native American or different Asian religious traditions elsewhere). Likewise, we could certainly begin to map out the varied institutional landscape of spirituality with this in mind, perhaps noting with more clarity the geographic centers and margins of spiritual production in the United States. Future research, including multi-sited studies or analysis of other single locales, should yield further insights into the variation in the ways that spirituality is institutionalized.

4. For example, Eugene Taylor, *Shadow Culture: Psychology and Spirituality in America* (Washington, DC: Counterpoint, 1999); Michael York, *The Emerging Network: A Sociology of the New Age and Neo-Pagan Movements* (Lanham, MD: Rowman and Littlefield, 1995); Colin Campbell, "The Cult, the Cultic Milieu, and Secularization" in *The Cultic Milieu*, ed. Jeffrey Kaplan and Helene Löow (Walnut Creek, CA: Alta Mira Press, 2002), 23. Campbell's discussion of the "cultic milieu" is perhaps the best known articulation of the emergent countercultural views, calling a "cultic milieu" "unorthodox and deviant belief systems together with their practices, institutions and personnel . . . constitutes a unity by virtue of a common consciousness of deviant status, a receptive and syncretistic orientation and an interpenetrative communication structure." Such an approach has been undertaken by Sususmu Shimazono's study of Japanese spiritual practices in "'New Age Movement' or 'New Spirituality Movements and Culture?'" *Social Compass* 46 (1999): 121–33.

5. On the loose boundaries of organizational fields, see Robert Wuthnow, *Loose Connections* (Cambridge, MA: Harvard University Press, 1998). On cultural practice and fields, see Roger Friedland and Robert A. Alford, "Bringing Society Back In: Symbols, Practices, and Institutional Contradictions," in *The New Institutionalism in Organizational Analysis*, ed. Walter W. Powell and Paul J. DiMaggio (Chicago: University of Chicago Press, 1991).

6. Paul DiMaggio and Walter Powell, "The Iron Cage Revisited: Institutional Isomorphism and Collective Rationality," in *New Institutionalism in Organizational Analysis*.

7. Catherine Albanese, "Introduction: Awash in a Sea of Metaphysicals," *Journal of the American Academy of Religion* 75 (2007): 588.

8. Throughout this volume I italicize quotes that I transcribed from taped interviews. All other quotations throughout the volume are paraphrases recorded in my field notes. The names and many identifying features of my respondents have been changed.

9. Courtney Bender, "The Position of the Sacred in Contemporary Alternative Medicine" (unpublished manuscript, Columbia University, 2002).

10. Robert C. Fuller, *Alternative Medicine and American Religious Life* (New York: Oxford University Press, 1989); Ellie Hedges and James A. Beckford. "Holism, Healing, and the New Age," in *Beyond New Age: Exploring Alternative Spirituality*, ed. Steven Sutcliffe and Marion Bowman (Edinburgh: Edinburgh University Press, 2000); R. Marie Griffith, *Born Again Bodies: Flesh and Spirit in American Christianity* (Berkeley: University of California Press, 2004), 69–77; Beryl Satter, *Each Mind a Kingdom: American Women, Sexual Purity, and the New Thought Movement, 1875–1920* (New York: Oxford University Press, 1999), 85–93.

11. These recent developments do not highlight a growing unease with

biomedicine, nor are we witnessing the resurgence of what Paul Starr calls the medical sectarianism of the nineteenth century's largely unregulated health-care market. Paul Starr, *The Social Transformation of American Medicine* (New York: Basic Books, 1982), 93–99. See also Meredith McGuire, *Ritual Healing in Suburban America* (New Brunswick, NJ: Rutgers University Press, 1988).

There is, in fact, no apparent correlation between individuals' dissatisfaction with biomedicine and complementary and alternative medicine (CAM) use. John Astin, "Why Patients Use Alternative Medicine," *Journal of the American Medical Association* 279 (1998): 1548–53. Recent surveys on Americans' participation in alternative and complementary health practices demonstrate that this once truly "alternative" way of thinking about health has become quite mainstream, at least in some respects. The National Health Interview Survey of 2002 found that 35 percent of Americans had used an alternative health therapy within the previous calendar year (this number rises to close to 62 percent when individuals who pray for health reasons are included). Twenty-five percent of Americans using CAM (excluding prayer) do so on the suggestion of a conventional (biomedical) medical professional. Patricia M. Barnes, Eve Powell-Griner, Kim McFann, and Richard L. Nahin, "Complementary and Alternative Medicine Use among Adults: United States, 2002," *Advance Data from Vital and Health Statistics* No. 343 (Hyattsville, MD: Jack R. Anderson National Center for Health Statistics, 2002).

12. These include the diminishing role of government regulation on pharmaceuticals and dietary supplements (Marion Nestle, "Deregulating Dietary Supplements," in *Food Politics* [Berkeley: University of California Press, 2002]), the rise of broad-based patients' rights movements and advocacy groups (Steven Epstein, *Impure Science: AIDS, Activism, and the Politics of knowledge* [Berkeley: University of California Press, 1996]), and the development of governmentally funded research institutes on CAM treatments (for example, Michael H. Cohen, *Complementary and Alternative Medicine: Legal Boundaries and Regulatory Perspectives* [Baltimore: Johns Hopkins University Press, 1998]; and Michael S. Goldstein, "The Emerging Socioeconomic and Political Support for Alternative Medicine in the United States," *Annals of the American Academy of Political and Social Science* 583 [2002]: 44–63).

13. Ted J. Kaptchuk, "Acupuncture: Theory, Efficacy, and Practice," *Annals of Internal Medicine* 136 (2002): 374–83; Daniel C. Cherkin et al., "Characteristics of Licensed Acupuncturists, Chiropractors, Massage Therapists, and Naturopathic Physicians," *Journal of the American Board of Family Practice* 15 (2002): 378–90.

14. Catherine Albanese observes that a particular strain of American metaphysics is linked by fascination with, and belief in, a vitalism developed in the writings and practices of Phineas Parkhurst Quimby, Franz Anton

Mesmer, and Mary Baker Eddy. "The Subtle Energies of the Spirit: Explorations in Metaphysical and New Age Spirituality," *Journal of the American Academy of Religion* 67 (1999): 305–26; and "The Magical Staff: Quantum Healing in the New Age" in *Perspectives on the New Age,* ed. James Lewis and J. Gordon Melton (Albany: State University of New York Press, 1992).

15. Rodney Stark and William Sims Bainbridge, for example, negatively compare client-practitioner social forms with religious communities. "Of Churches, Sects, and Cults: Preliminary Concepts for a Theory of Religious Movements," *Journal for the Scientific Study of Religion* 18 (1979): 117–33.

16. On the institutional organization of private and individual identities and goals, see Paul Lichterman, *The Search for Political Community* (Cambridge: Cambridge University Press, 1997); Kieran Healy, "Embedded Altruism, Blood Collection Regimes, and the European Union's Donor Population," *American Journal of Sociology* 105 (2000): 1633–57.

17. R. Stephen Warner, "The Place of the Congregation in the Contemporary American Religious Configuration," in *American Congregations: New Perspectives in the Study of Congregations,* ed. James Wind and James Lewis (Chicago: University of Chicago Press, 1994); Penny Edgell Becker, *Congregations in Conflict: Cultural Models of Local Religious Life* (New York: Cambridge University Press, 1999). This field's robustness has been further demonstrated in a number of recent studies that show how new entrants form congregations (regardless of their theological predilections) given that they are regulated by similar zoning, financial, and professionalizing pressures. Fenggang Yang and Helen Rose Ebaugh, "Transformations in New Immigrant Religions and Their Global Implications," *American Sociological Review* 66 (2001): 269–88; Patricia M. Y. Chang, "Escaping the Procrustean Bed: A Critical Analysis of the Study of Religious Organizations, 1930–2001," in *Handbook of the Sociology of Religion,* ed. Michele Dillon (Cambridge: Cambridge University Press 2003).

18. Jody Shapiro Davie, *Women in the Presence* (Philadelphia: University of Pennsylvania Press, 1995). For recent survey reports on mainstream religious groups' interests in spiritual development and spiritual growth, see Robert Wuthnow, *All in Sync: How Music and Art Are Revitalizing American Religion* (Berkeley: University of California Press, 2003), chap. 2; and Nancy Ammerman, *Pillars of Faith: American Congregations and Their Partners* (Berkeley: University of California Press, 2005), 23–30.

19. Leigh Schmidt, *Restless Souls: The Making of American Spirituality* (San Francisco: HarperSanFrancisco, 2006); Pamela Klassen, "Textual Healing: Mainstream Protestants and the Therapeutic Text, 1900–1925," *Church History* 75 (2006): 809–48.

20. Michele Dillon and Paul Wink, *In the Course of a Lifetime* (Berkeley: University of California Press, 2007).

21. Several recent studies, for example, have drawn attention to the sheer

number of "arts" activities that happen within local congregations. See, for example, Wuthnow, *All in Sync;* and Mark Chaves, *Congregations in America* (Cambridge, MA: Harvard University Press, 2003). As Robert Wuthnow points out, however, the arts performances that occur in religious organizations are complicated by "distinctive institutional purposes" of both groups, where, for example, church leaders might shy away from focusing on the excellence of a musical performance out of concern that it would draw attention away from its purpose in focusing worshipful behavior (Robert Wuthnow, "Arts Leaders and Religious Leaders: Mutual Perceptions," *Monograph* [2001]: 65). Likewise, conversation among artists in identifying the spiritual in twentieth-century arts (particularly the visual arts) is ongoing (Erika Doss, "Robert Gober's 'Virgin' Installation: Issues of Spirituality in Contemporary American Art," in *The Visual Culture of American Religions,* ed. David Morgan and Salley Promey (Berkeley: University of California Press, 2001).

22. Amei Wallach notes in a preface to a conversation among contemporary artists about "art, religion, and spirituality" that artists seem to draw on several "significant artistic traditions of religious inquiry and transformation." These "traditions" of inquiry notably include Emersonian transcendentalism, Jewish mysticism, and D. T. Suzuki's interpretations of Zen Buddhism ("Art, Religion, and Spirituality: A Conversation with Artists," in *Crossroads: Art and Religion in American Life,* ed. Alberta Arthurs and Glenn Wallach [New York: Norton, 2001], 235). Given the well-documented decoupling of (and consequential antagonisms between) "religion" and "art" that Judith Blau and others (see Blau, "The Toggle Switch of Institutions: Religion and Art in the U.S. in the Nineteenth and Early Twentieth Centuries," *Social Forces* 74 [1996]: 1159–77) argue are responsible for the development of "high culture" in America, it is perhaps not surprising that "mainstream" religious theologies do not appear in Wallach's list of influences: more interesting, however, is the degree to which Wallach identifies the liberal mystical tradition as central to contemporary artists' engagement with the spiritual.

23. The "art worlds" that spiritual practitioners in Cambridge participated within were largely amateur and informal, but nonetheless extremely vibrant and robust: this is little surprise, given that "amateur and semi-amateur active arts participation appears pervasive" nationally. Arthur C. Brooks, "Artists as Amateurs and Volunteers," *Nonprofit Management and Leadership* 13 (2002): 5–15.

24. This number includes all of those yoga teachers that I learned of by word of mouth, through watching and tracking local posters and flyers, and scouring yoga online yoga directories and listings. It does not include teachers who appeared in directories only one time (or for whom I could not locate a last name, as was the case with many local fitness centers' listings). All but four of the yoga teachers who taught in only one site taught

exclusively at the Baron Baptiste Vinayasa Yoga Studio. Baptiste, a nationally known "power yoga" teacher, has a distinctive style of yoga, training program for teachers, and lineage. Of the remaining teachers who teach in only one setting, three have their own studios (one is a "hot" yoga teacher and student of Bikram Choudhory) and devote substantial time to administration and lecturing in addition to local teaching responsibilities.

25. John Dewey, *Experience and Nature* (Baltimore: Waverly Press, 1925), 33.

26. Wuthnow, *All in Sync.*

27. Spirituality groups, unlike "religious" groups, rarely build edifices, legally incorporate as religious entities, or otherwise move beyond the status of amateurism. Those groups that do appear on the horizon often seem to come and go with fads. For example, only a few of the dozens of "neo-Oriental" religious and spiritual organizations in Cambridge that Harvey Cox visited during the mid-1970s still are in operation (and those groups that still exist have clear ties to Asian religious institutions, like the Cambridge Zen Center). Harvey Cox, *Turning East* (New York: Simon and Schuster, 1977).

28. See, for example, Nancy Ammerman, "Religious Identities and Religious Institutions," in *Handbook for the Sociology of Religion,* ed. Michele Dillon (Cambridge University Press, 2003).

29. Ernst Troeltsch, *The Social Teachings of the Christian Churches* (Louisville, KY: Westminster John Knox Press, 1992), 2:800.

30. For an interesting treatment of James's theoretical influence on Troeltsch, which includes extensive quotations from Troeltsch's published memorial review of James's philosophy of religion, see Charles H. Long, "The Oppressive Elements of Religion and the Religions of the Oppressed," *Harvard Theological Review* 69, no. 3 (1976): 379–412. See also Walter E. Wyman Jr., *The Concept of Glaubenslehre: Ernst Troeltsch and the Theological Heritage of Schleiermacher* (Chico, CA: Scholars Press, 1983); and Karl-Fritz Daiber, "Mysticism: Troeltsch's Third Type of Religious Collectivities," *Social Compass* 49 (2002): 329–41.

31. Troeltsch, *Social Teachings of the Christian Churches,* 796–97.

32. Ibid., 799.

33. These "trends" are not inevitable but rather have taken shape historically, often due to the work of various congeries of politically motivated actors who sought to make secular institutions realities. See, for example, Christian Smith, ed., *The Secular Revolution: Power, Interests, and Conflict in the Secularization of American Public Life* (Chicago: University of Chicago Press, 2003); see also David Hollinger, *Science, Jews, and Secular Culture* (Princeton, NJ: Princeton University Press, 1996).

34. Both Weber (rationalization) and Durkheim (differentiation) shaped these views of secularization, defined primarily as the increasing constriction of religious authority in other spheres of life. As several sociologists have noted of late, these ideas were rarely tested, making the theory, as Chris-

NOTES TO PAGES 46–48

tian Smith says, both "uninteresting and unhelpful" (Christian Smith, "Introduction: Rethinking the Secularization of American Public Life," in *The Secular Revolution* [Berkeley: University of California Press, 2003], 14). Others have gone further, questioning the degree to which modern states can be said to work on these principles, noting, as José Casanova does, the apparent "deprivatization" of religion in many modern societies (*Public Religions in the Modern World* [Chicago: University of Chicago Press, 1993]).

35. I am not arguing that we abandon secularization theory whole cloth or that we ignore the real and complex changes that have tended toward the secularization of numerous institutional fields, including medicine and the arts. At the same time, it is increasingly evident that drawing a bright line between the secular and the religious is quite difficult in the American context. As I argue here, doing so all too frequently depends on sociologists' capacity to conjure a disconnected "mystical" individual or spiritual seeker to explain the continued appearance of religious production in these erstwhile secularized spheres. Given that institutional and social change is ongoing, and given that some of the recent shifts remind us that secularization is not a unidirectional, final, or completed process in any institutional field, observing spiritual practice organizationally allows us to ask better questions about what sociologists increasingly view as non-unified, non-unilinear processes of secularization. See Philip Gorski and Ates Altinordu, "After Secularization," *Annual Review of Sociology* 34 (2008): 55–85.

36. Michael Schudson, "The Varieties of Civic Experience," in *The Civic Life of American Religion,* ed. Paul Lichterman and C. Brady Potts (Stanford: Stanford University Press, 2008).

37. The Boston Expo is organized by a regional for-profit group based in western Massachusetts that holds similar expos in Northhampton, Massachusetts; Pittsburgh, Pennsylvania; and Portland, Maine. At the June 2001 and November 2002 Boston expo, about two-thirds of the tables and stands were groups and practitioners from eastern Massachusetts.

38. The Whole Health Expo shares a passing resemblance to (and arguably is a latter-day cousin of) the world's fairs and "exhibitions" tradition that developed in the nineteenth century to exhibit the progress of modern societies; these types of gatherings have greatly interested religion scholars. John Burris, *Exhibiting Religion: Colonialism and Spectacle in International Expositions* (Charlottesville: University of Virginia Press, 2001), 174–75. See also Tomoko Masuzawa, *The Invention of World Religions* (Chicago: University of Chicago Press, 2005); Barbara Kirshenblatt-Gimblett, *Destination Culture: Tourism, Museum, and Heritage* (Berkeley: University of California Press, 1998). These surface resemblances notwithstanding, my journey to the Expo suggested that drawing on the interpretive strategies used by cultural critics to read the Expo would not be particularly fruitful.

CHAPTER TWO

1. Spiritual practitioners' understandings of the sacred move easily between the transcendent and immanent, yet with a decided emphasis on an immanent divine. Throughout this chapter I use the term "divine" to indicate the "god," "universe," or "vital energies" (or a variety of other ideas) that my respondents used to talk about the universal powers that they experienced.

2. For example Robert Wuthnow, *After Heaven: Spirituality in America since the 1950s* (Berkeley: University of California Press, 1998); Wade Clark Roof, *Spiritual Marketplace: Baby Boomers and the Remaking of American Religion* (Princeton, NJ: Princeton University Press, 1999). Very few recent sociological studies of American spirituality use field observation techniques; one exception is work by Kelly Besecke, "Seeing Invisible Religion: Religion as a Societal Conversation about Transcendent Meaning," *Sociological Theory* 23 (2005): 179–96.

3. Peter Bearman and Katherine Stovel, "Becoming a Nazi: A Model for Narrative Networks," *Poetics* 27 (2000): 69–90; Carol Cain, "Personal Stories: Identity Acquisition and Self-understanding in Alcoholics Anonymous," *Ethos* 19 (1991): 210–53; David Smilde, *Reason to Believe* (Berkeley: University of California Press, 2007). Each demonstrates how taking on new cultural or religious identities alters and reorganizes the shape and position of personal ties and associations within one's narrative.

4. Fifty-seven of my seventy-seven interviewees reported a direct religious experience, and all but a handful followed the narrative arc discussed in this chapter. Interviewees frequently interjected such accounts quite early in interviews without prompting.

5. By this logic, some kinds of narration preserve events by erasing them. "The suppressing and the surpassing of the event . . . is a characteristic of discourse itself. . . . If language is a *meinen,* an intending, it is so precisely due to this *Aufhebung* [lifting up] through which the event is cancelled as something merely transient and retained as the same meaning." Paul Ricoeur, *Interpretation Theory: Discourse and the Surplus of Meaning* (Fort Worth: Texas Christian University Press, 1976), 12.

6. Wayne Proudfoot suggests that claims to ineffability and emotional "felt" knowledge work as "protective strategies" against reductive social scientific forms of analysis. *Religious Experience* (Berkeley: University of California Press, 1987).

7. As linguists have noted, "reportable events are almost by definition unusual. They are therefore inherently less credible than non-reportable events. In fact, we might say that the more reportable an event is, the less credible it is. Yet credibility is . . . essential." William Labov, "Speech Actions and Reactions in Personal Narrative," in *Georgetown University Round Table on Languages and Linguistics 1981: Analyzing Discourse: Text and Talk,*

ed. Deborah Tannen (Washington, DC: Georgetown University Press, 1982), 228. With this in mind it is fair to say that any story is oriented not only toward reporting "the facts" but doing so in a way that is contextually credible. As I argue in the book's introduction, interactions between social scientific and religious experiencers are a formative interaction in the articulation of Cambridge practitioners' narrative genres.

8. Like other types of speech, narratives anticipate situational contexts and possible rejoinders, thus building answerability into the story itself. We do so by drawing from past events and interchanges, thus bringing previous, situational expectations into new exchanges. Dorothy Holland, "A Practice Theory of Self and Identity," in *Identity and Agency in Cultural Worlds* (Cambridge: Harvard University Press, 1998), 19–49; and Elinor Ochs and Linda Capps, "A Dimensional Approach to Narrative," in *Living Narrative* (Cambridge: Harvard University Press, 2001), 1–58.

9. See, for example, R. Marie Griffith, *God's Daughters: Evangelical Women and the Power of Submission* (Berkeley: University of California Press, 1997); Smilde, *Reason to Believe.* Here we nonetheless see how important it is to broaden our conception of the social spaces of spiritual practice, given that all too frequently analysis of spiritual practitioners' narratives draws on the narrative itself as evidence of lack of social connectivity. As a consequence the omission of social ties and other cultural and social information within experiential narratives reinforces sociological perceptions that spiritual individualists are not socially "connected."

10. William James, *The Varieties of Religious Experience* (New York: Penguin, 1982), 31. The role that William James and his American and European intellectual circles played in articulating "religious experience" (and the subsequent transformation of that prescriptive and culturally specific view into a descriptive, scientific category) has been the subject of numerous monographs. The best include Ann Taves, *Fits, Trances, and Visions* (Princeton, NJ: Princeton University Press, 1999); Christopher White, *Minds Intensely Unsettled* (Berkeley: University of California Press, 2008).

11. White writes that James drew substantially on the work of the first "survey" of religious experience conducted by his student Edwin Starbuck, and that the lines between scholarly investigation and pastoral interest of eliciting (proper) experiences was much disputed by James and his colleagues. White speculates that we might see James's excess of experiential examples as an attempt to "elicit emotional responses or somehow give off traces of their intensity." Christopher White, "A Measured Faith: Edwin Starbuck, William James, and the Scientific Reform of Religious Experience," *Harvard Theological Review* 101 (2008): 443.

12. White, *Minds Intensely Unsettled,* 137. See also Edwin Starbuck, "A Study of Conversion," *American Journal of Psychology* 8 (1897): 268–308, which includes a copy of his questionnaire.

13. On the distinction between narrative and descriptive clauses, see Roberto

Franzosi, "Narrative Analysis—Or Why (and How) Sociologists Should Be Interested in Narrative," *Annual Review of Sociology* 24 (1998): 529. Franzosi's "descriptive" clause shares some relation to what Labov and Waletsky call "free clauses." Both are clauses or bits of information that can be inserted in multiple positions within a narrative without changing the development of its temporally articulated claims. William Labov and J. Waletsky, "Narrative Analysis: Oral Versions of Personal Experience," in *Essays on the Verbal and Visual Arts* (Seattle: University of Washington Press, 1967). Of course, the further point here is that even "descriptive" or "free" clauses become embedded within the narrative's moral arc: see Gary Saul Morson, *Narrative and Freedom* (New Haven, CT: Yale University Press, 1996); Michael Bernstein, *Foregone Conclusions: Against Apocalyptic History* (Berkeley: University of California Press, 1994).

14. See Donald Braid, "Personal Narrative and Experiential Meaning," *Journal of American Folklore* 109 (1996): 5–30.

15. Susan Harding writes that "generative belief, belief that indisputably transfigures you and your reality, comes only through speech" (*The Book of Jerry Falwell* [Princeton, NJ: Princeton University Press, 2001], 60). While this strong claim has been criticized by others who focus on embodiment and ritual (see, for example, Tanya Luhrmann, "Metakinesis: How God Becomes Intimate in Contemporary U.S. Christianity," *American Anthropologist* 106 [2004]: 518–28), the larger point that can be drawn is that speech is likewise embodied practice, often ritualized. The turn to focus on speaking as experiencing should not suggest a collapse of experience into words, but rather an expansion of our understanding of speech into the practices (always embodied and social) that shape ways of speaking, and what speech can convey and to whom.

16. Steven Katz, "Mysticism and the Interpretation of Sacred Scripture," in *Mysticism and Sacred Scripture,* ed. Steven Katz (Oxford: Oxford University Press, 2000), 56.

17. Bobbi Parish, *Create Your Personal Sacred Text: Develop and Celebrate Your Spiritual Life* (New York: Broadway Books, 1999), xii-xiv.

18. Ochs and Capps, *Living Narrative.*

19. Julia Cameron, *The Artist's Way: A Spiritual Path to Higher Creativity* (New York: Tarcher Putnam, 1992) 10–11, 15–16 (emphasis in original).

20. Ibid., 118.

21. André LeBlanc, "The Origins of the Concept of Dissociation: Paul Janet, His Nephew Pierre, and the Problem of Post-hypnotic Suggestion," *History of Science* 34 (2001): 57–69; June Downey and John Anderson, "Automatic Writing," *American Journal of Psychology* 27 (1915): 161–95; W. Koutstaal, "Skirting the Abyss, A History of Experimental Explorations of Automatic Writing in Psychology," *Journal of the History of the Behavioral Sciences* 28 (1992): 5–27.

Ann Taves notes that scholarly fascination with writing crossed the (sometimes blurry) divide between psychological and parapsychological investigations, wherein some claimed that automatic writing provided evidence for no extraconscious (or "external" consciousness), where others claimed the contrary. Ann Taves, "The Fragmentation of Consciousness and *The Varieties of Religious Experience:* William James's Contribution to a Theory of Religion," in *William James and a Science of Religions,* ed. Wayne Proudfoot (New York: Columbia University Press, 2004).

22. Hammond's rules form the preface to a volume of messages that he reports he received from his dead sister using just these techniques. Charles Hammond, *Light from the Spirit World: Comprising a Series of Articles on the Condition of Spirits* (Rochester, NY, 1852).

23. Michael Brown, *The Channeling Zone* (Cambridge, MA: Harvard University Press, 1997).

24. Stein researched and coauthored two papers on automatic writing in the late 1890s, based on research conducted in William James's and Hugo Münsterberg's laboratories. Stein's investigations into writing automatically have since been the subject of some debate. Literary scholar and historian Barbara Will argues that Stein imagined and privileged genius as the "surplus" of the normal mechanics of writing, and that genius was possible as a type of detached observation of writing as the process occurred. This view is consistent with some of the findings published in the two papers coauthored while at Harvard. See Barbara Will, "Gertrude Stein, Automatic Writing and the Mechanics of Genius," *Forum for Modern Language Studies* 37, no. 2 (2001): 169–75.

25. Ralph Waldo Trine, *In Tune with the Infinite* (New York: Dodd, Mead, 1897), 159, 163, 174 (emphasis added).

26. Jane Revere Burke, *The One Way* (New York: Dutton, 1922), xv–xx. Burke published several volumes recounting messages of recently departed luminaries of the likes of Mark Twain, William James, and Andrew Jackson Davis. One reviewer drolly reported, "a reader who is familiar with James' writings might wonder why his famous literary style does not appear in his messages from the spirit world." R. C. Scarf, Book Review, *American Journal of Psychology* 47 (1935): 186.

27. Burke, *The One Way,* xii.

28. These writing forms reemerged in the 1960s and 1970s in the field of composition and education, popularized first by Peter Elbow in *Writing without Teachers* (New York: Oxford University Press, 1963), which subsequently influenced other manuals including Natalie Goldberg's guide to journaling, writing, and meditation *Writing Down the Bones: Freeing the Writer Within* (New York: Shambhala, 1986).

29. The value of analyzing spirituality as sets of historically viable practices becomes particularly clear when we observe a case where spiritual writing practices are viewed ahistorically. As an example, Catherine Brekus com-

pares early American Puritans' diaries with contemporary spiritual journals. The former are filled with the private worries of individuals never assured of their salvation. These diaries "always involved an anguished confrontation with the corrupt self," and was always a process of "mourning" although also a "powerful means of grace." Brekus contrasts Puritan practices with contemporary spiritual writings and argues that she has observed a "shift" in American culture from the deeply troubled personal interrogations to the relentlessly cheery yet empty platitudes of today's writers. This critique hinges on a sense that contemporary spirituality is unmoored from any religious past and caters to thoroughly self-focused secular, consumerist selves.

If, in contrast, we view contemporary spiritual journaling not as a "new" practice borne of the 1960s but rather as linked to (if not continuous with) metaphysical writing practices developed through the twentieth century, we might think differently of representations of contemporary journaling as evidence for atrophying Protestant practices denatured by a secular therapeutic. We might, as in the case of the writings of Julia Cameron, detect or ponder a set of longer lasting theological projects, where writing becomes enchanted space to meet the divine. Such an observation positions contemporary writing practices on a different theological footing when contrasted with various past Puritan practices. The point here of course is not to "redeem" contemporary spiritual practices but rather to place both past and present practices within a similar social-religious and theological space. Catherine Brekus, "'A Place to Go to Connect with Yourself': A Historical Perspective on Journaling" (Chicago: Martin Marty Center Religion and Culture Web Forum, 2004), 6, 8; Brekus, "Writing as a Protestant Practice: Devotional Diaries in Early New England," in *Practicing Protestants: Histories of Christian Life in America, 1630–1965,* ed. Laurie Maffly-Kipp and Leigh Schmidt (Baltimore: Johns Hopkins University Press, 2006).

30. While the dual processes of writing and interpreting frequently took place in the confines of spiritual practitioners' private journals, experiential events were frequently discussed and interpreted in various group settings, and it was in such settings that I frequently witnessed the elaboration of multiple interpretations held in place through dialogue. I provide numerous examples in other chapters.

31. Elizabeth Owens, *Discover Your Spiritual Life: Illuminate Your Soul's Path* (St. Paul, MN: Llewellyn Worldwide, 2004), 177.

32. Julie Tallard Johnson, *Spiritual Journaling: Writing Your Way to Independence* (Rochester, VT: Bindu Books 2006), 141–42.

33. Squire Rushnell, *When God Winks at You: How God Speaks Directly to You Through the Power of Coincidence* (Nashville, TN: Thomas Nelson Books, 2006), 10.

34. Owens, *Discover Your Spiritual Life,* 47–48.

35. Gary Saul Morson, *Narrative and Freedom* (New Haven, CT: Yale University Press, 1996), 110.

CHAPTER THREE

1. M. Merleau-Ponty, *The Phenomenology of Perception* (London: Routledge, 1962), 148.
2. Swami Vivekananda, *Raja Yoga* (Calcutta: J. N. Dey, 1959), 53 (originally published in 1897).
3. There are many ways to talk about metaphysical relations between body, mind, and spirit, yet it is important nonetheless to note that Cambridge's metaphysicals talk about their bodies in ways that mark a slight departure from recent scholarship emphasizing metaphysicals as privileging "mind over matter." Catherine Albanese, "The Magical Staff: Quantum Healing in the New Age," in *Perspectives on the New Age,* ed. James Lewis and J. Gordon Melton (Albany: State University of New York Press, 1992); Albanese, "The Aura of Wellness: Subtle-Energy Healing and New Age Religion," *Religion and American Culture* 10 (2000): 29–55; Jay Johnston and Ruth Barcan, "Subtle Transformations: Imagining the Body in Alternative Health Practices," *International Journal of Cultural Studies* 9 (2006): 25–44; Judith Fadlon, "Meridians, Chakras, and Psycho-Neuro-Immunology: The Dematerializing Body and the Domestication of Alternative Medicine," *Body and Soul* 10 (2004): 69–86; Steven Sutcliffe and Marion Bowman, eds., *Beyond New Age* (Edinburgh: Edinburgh University Press, 2000); Michael Brown, *The Channeling Zone* (Cambridge, MA: Harvard University Press, 1997); Donald Meyer, *The Positive Thinkers: Religion as Pop Psychology from Mary Baker Eddy to Oral Roberts* (New York: Pantheon, 1980).

 Scholarly preoccupation with spiritual health and healing and other "mental" sciences of psychology and pop psychology have turned attention directly to the various energetic bodies that metaphysicals cultivate. These various works make evident that a whole, "healed" body is both the goal and the technological apparatus necessary for connecting with the divine. But a shift from the physical to the energetic body is not a matter of replacing one body with another or escaping the demands of the flesh by clinging to spiritual forms. As R. Marie Griffith demonstrates, New Thought claims for mental and spiritual perfection (eschewing bodily perfection) nonetheless often returned to the physical body in the development of new procedures for perfecting the mind. As she argues, the legacy of the New Thought movement is its "passion for the flesh at the core of the mind-over-matter scheme of causation: the craving for a perfectible, eternal, living, breathing disciplined yet sensual body" (*Born Again Bodies: Flesh and Spirit in American Christianity* [Berkeley: University of California Press, 2004], 18). With this in mind, we can likewise ask in this chapter how metaphysicals' current obsession with disciplinary projects of relaxation and attunement give shape to the astral or invisible body, and likewise to the flesh.

4. In so doing, they follow in a long line of writers and practitioners who view the body as hooked up to a flowing energy source. William Walker Atkinson, for example, writes, "The man who thinks that all is evil is apt to see much evil, and will be brought into contact with others who will seem to prove his theory. And the man who looks for good in everything and everybody will be likely to attract to himself the things and people corresponding to his thought. . . . You will be able to carry this idea more clearly if you will think of the Marconi wireless instruments, which receive the vibrations only from the sending instrument which has been attuned to the same key, while other telegrams are passing through the air in near vicinity without affecting the instrument. The same law applies to the operations of thought." Atkinson, *Thought Vibration or the Law of Attraction in the Thought World* (Chicago: New Thought, 1908), 7. Ralph Waldo Trine's best-selling volume makes similar claims for the links between modern energetic technologies and the "laws" of the "Spirit of Infinite Life," which are "creating, working, ruling through the agency of great immutable laws and forces that run through all the universe, that surround us on every side." Trine, *In Tune with the Infinite* (New York: Dodd, Mead, 1921), 11; also Vivekananda, *Raja Yoga,* 61.

    The metaphorical promise of energetic fields was likewise the inspiration for many liberal Protestants. Quaker mystic Rufus Jones similarly described the relationship between an individual and God through technological metaphors. Reflecting on a long-distance call that failed to properly connect, he encourages readers to imagine themselves as technological devices and move toward closer connection with God: "Here is where most of us fail in this other sphere—this inner wireless sphere—we are poor transmitters. We make the connection, we receive the gift of grace. . . . We absorb and accumulate what we can, but we transmit little of all that comes to us. . . . We need on the one hand to listen deeper, to get further in beyond the tensions and the noises, but on the other hand we need to be more radio-active, better transmitters of the grace of God." *Spiritual Energies* (New York: Macmillan, 1922), 64.

5. T. J. Jackson Lears's discussions of turn-of-the-century "creators of the therapeutic ethos" resonate quite strongly with the practices of twenty-first-century metaphysicals. Both "offered harmony, vitality, and the hope of self-realization. . . . One might seek wholeness and security through careful management of personal resources; or one might pursue emotional fulfillment and endless 'growth' through intense experience. These approaches were united by several assumptions: an implicit nostalgia for the vigorous health allegedly enjoyed by farmers, children, and others 'close to nature'; a belief that expert advice could enable one to recover that vigor without fundamental social change; and a tacit conviction that

self-realization was the largest aim of human existence." "Salvation to Self-realization: Advertising and the Therapeutic Roots of the Consumer Culture, 1880–1930," in *The Culture of Consumption: Critical Essays in American History, 1880–1980,* ed. Richard Wightman Fox and T. J. Jackson Lears (New York: Pantheon Books, 1983).

6. Albanese argues that Leadbeater's book provided the "lingua franca" of the new esoteric and experiential view of the etheric double, and chronicles the ways that his ideas and articulation was passed through a variety of writers. Albanese, *A Republic of Mind and Spirit* (New Haven, CT: Yale University Press, 2006), 453–57.

7. Charles Leadbeater, *The Chakras: A Monograph,* 2nd ed. (Madras, India: Theosophical Publishing House, 1938), 12.

8. Leadbeater developed his philosophical understanding of chakras from his Theosophical interests and engagement with Sanskrit texts. His book moves quickly into philosophical discussion of the seven levels of bodies (of which the physical body is only one) that each spirit-soul inhabits through its progression in multiple lives. He draws liberally from Sanskrit texts and lards his text with Sanskrit terminology. That said, Leadbeater's repeatedly articulated purpose is to extract the scientific laws of the chakras, explaining that while the Sanskrit texts have identified the chakra system, his clairvoyant experiences demonstrated to him that the chakras are a universal, nonculturally-specific reality.

9. Just as Leadbeater argued that the Sanskrit texts held truths that science would later determine were universally true, so later metaphysical experimenters took a page from Leadbeater's own book and jettisoned his "Victorian" sensibilities about the lower and higher chakras as elite cultural baggage that had muddled the "true" scientific views of chakras that modern science could obtain. Rosalyn Bruyere, for example, touts both her individual experiences and scientific experiments concerning chakras in "an eight-year research study on the human electromagnetic field conducted at UCLA" to bolster her positions. While she draws liberally from Leadbeater and gives him some credit, she nonetheless dismisses his book as steeped in his own cultural views, rather than a truly "scientific" perspective. Complaining that his interpretation "split the body in two halves" higher and lower, "it is not surprising to find a group of upper-class Victorian British gentry deciding that emotionalism was bad. They were validating a position they already held and they visited India collecting data to support their belief." Rosalyn Bruyere, *Wheels of Light* (New York: Simon and Schuster, 1989), 58.

10. The group's fascination with the "fifth chakra" nonetheless suggested that Cambridge's metaphysicals were not merely interested in the local diagnoses that these auras and stories might illuminate. In interchanges like this, metaphysicals demonstrated their desire to place themselves in a hierarchy where each person is located according to their dominant

chakra, whether "lower" (associated gross motor and organ functions and brute emotions), "middle," (oriented to human interactions), or "higher" (indicating spiritual interactions are dominant).

11. Nineteenth-century Spiritualists' fascination with technologies and their uses to contact the dead or prove their presence is chronicled in a number of interesting books. The telegraph and the telephone and other similar innovations captured the imagination of ways that time and space might be collapsed or brought together, not just within this plane but also within the "astral" planes as well. Furthermore, experimentation and the development of electricity led to a steady development of metaphoric and theological interpretations of the divine as the supreme, immanent energetic forces that humans connected to, much as an individual telephone receiver or device "tapped into" the currents that ran through a wire. Technology and science provided ample room for claims that the realities of the astral world had been "proved" and, likewise, ample space for imagining new types of spiritual connection, movement, and communication. See, for example, Leigh Schmidt, *Hearing Things: Religion, Illusion, and the American Enlightenment* (Cambridge, MA: Harvard University Press, 2000); Avital Ronell, *The Telephone Book: Technology, Schizophrenia, Electric Speech* (Lincoln: University of Nebraska Press, 1989); Robert S. Cox, *Body and Soul* (Charlottesville: University of Virginia Press, 2003), 87–88.

12. Teachers nonetheless also noted that it was often difficult for people to stick with yoga long enough to begin to see its benefits, and that classes provided regularity and encouragement, as well as correction if necessary. Likewise, teachers told me, a good yoga teacher was necessary for learning how to do more difficult poses properly.

13. Many of the independent yoga teachers I talked with drove home the difficulties of properly relaxing and finding the proper attitude toward yoga by comparing their teaching with popularized yoga taught in health clubs by teachers of dubious expertise. Yoga teachers used this popularity to underscore the precariousness of the true value of yoga for Americans, who misunderstood and appropriated "everything" for self-satisfying but empty ends. This in turn opened up the possibility for critique of Americans' interest in bodily perfection by presenting a different way to imagine the body's "natural" beauty as well perhaps by suggesting a discourse about bodily perfection that focuses less on the body as "seen" than the body as "felt."

14. B. K. S. Iyengar, *Light on Yoga* (New York: Schocken Books, 1976), 422–24.

15. Erich Schiffman, *Yoga: The Spirit and Practice of Moving into Stillness* (New York: Simon and Schuster, 1996), 297 (italics in original).

16. Yoga teachers' emphasis that sleep might also be overtaken with anxiety stands in great contrast to the writings of Ralph Waldo Trine and other New Thought writers who also emphasized the power of relaxation or (in this case "attunement"). Compare Trine's comments on sleep, which in

some ways mirror yoga teachers' interests in the effects of relaxation in liberating the higher self, but that diverge when it comes to interest in locating true restfulness. Trine says, "The soul needs no rest, and while the body is at rest in sleep the soul life is active the same as when the body is in activity." The body and its organs hinder the true sight, in other words, but sleep, necessary for the body's repair, enables the soul, imbued with its own modes of perception, consciousness, and presence, to soar. "When we are not deriving information through outward avenues of sensation, we are receiving instruction through interior channels of perception." Trine, *In Tune with the Infinite,* 119–20, 123.

17. Michel Foucault, *Discipline and Punish* (New York: Vintage, 1977).
18. Elizabeth de Michelis uses the term "modern yoga" to indicate the forms of yoga that took root in America and in Europe in the nineteenth and twentieth centuries (*A History of Modern Yoga* [New York: Continuum, 2001]; see also Joseph Alter, *Yoga in Modern India* [Princeton, NJ: Princeton University Press, 2004]). Alter investigates yoga's reshaping in light of Indian national projects in the early twentieth century. These authors and others make clear that the process of creating an ancient tradition of "yoga" that was apprehendable for modern (Indian and American-European) audiences required a condensation and reshaping of a variety of loosely organized lineages, teachers, histories, and texts. See, for example, Hugh Urban, *Tantra: Sex, Secrecy, Politics, and Power in the Study of Religion* (Berkeley: University of California Press, 2003); and Sarah Strauss, *Positioning Yoga: Balancing Acts across Cultures* (New York: Berg, 2005).
19. The meetings between James and Vivekananda are noted in passing in both Mark Singleton, "Salvation through Relaxation: Proprioceptive Therapy and Its Relationship to Yoga," *Journal of Contemporary Religion* 20 (2005): 289–304, and Stephen Prothero, *American Jesus: How the Son of God Became a National Icon* (New York: Farrar Straus Giroux, 2003), 269. Sarah Bull's house was the home of the Cambridge Conferences on metaphysical and comparative religion. Bull was a devotee of Vivekananda and gained great notoriety upon her death, leaving the majority of her estate to the fledgling Vedanta Society. Her daughter successfully contested the will in 1911; it was voided largely because of the testimony of Bull's "psychic gymnastics," including "mystic meditations," magnetic healing, strange breathing techniques, and various "raja yoga" love rites, all of which suggested that Sarah Bull was under the sway of insanity or of the "psychic conspiracy" of Hindu swamis. Stephen Prothero recounts the trial in "Hindophobia and Hinduphilia in U.S. Culture," in *The Stranger's Religion,* ed. Ann Lannstrom (Notre Dame, IN: University of Notre Dame Press, 2004), 14–15.
20. Vivekananda's explanation of yoga to Indian audiences in contrast evoked a "a revered precolonial past [offering] not only ideas and practices, but

also heroes and success stories that could be applied to the rising national project." Strauss, *Positioning Yoga,* 13.

21. Ibid., 13–14.

22. James notes this practice antedates "theologies and is independent of philosophies" yet "is capable of entering into closest marriage with every speculative creed." James, *The Varieties of Religious Experience* (New York: Penguin, 1982), 289.

23. Annie Payson Call, *Power through Repose* (Boston: Little, Brown, 1900), 17, 20–21 (originally published in 1851).

24. Mark Singleton observes, "Ironically (since Vivekananda arguably derived many of his theories from James in the first place), the Swami and his work subsequently become James' own authority on yoga and James quotes him whenever he speaks or writes about such matters." Singleton, "Salvation through Relaxation," 299.

25. Ibid., 299–300. Elizabeth de Michelis concurs: "It is obvious [from passages in *Raja Yoga*] that both Vivekananda and his audiences were deeply engaged in forms of alternative medicine, in healing and in related occultistic concerns. . . . Various forms of Harmonialism, Metaphysical belief and mesmeric practice were widespread in the USA at the time. These ideas surely played a part in inspiring Vivekananda to select" Sanskritic elements that matched these already understood concepts. *History of Modern Yoga,* 151–52.

26. For example, Theos Bernard, *Hatha Yoga* (New York: Columbia University Press, 1944); Paul Brunton, *Search for Secret India* (New York: Rider, 1934) both exemplify works by American scholar-adventurers who claimed to bring Asian truths to the United States. Their experiences and eyewitness accounts in India and Nepal established and reinforced their claims to authority and authenticity. Despite the commonplace understanding that these texts are cut from the same orientalist cloth as the texts that preceded them, they nonetheless remain valuable reminders that desire for authenticity is hardly new, and that authenticity is frequently brokered in relation to criticisms that preceding forms and philosophies were insufficient in this regard.

27. Jess Stearn, *Yoga, Youth, and Reincarnation* (New York: Doubleday, 1965), 31.

28. Ibid., 28.

29. Ibid., 10. On the "Omnipotent Oom," also known as Pierre Bernard (and uncle of Theos Bernard), see Urban, *Tantra.*

30. Stearn contrasts Moore's yoga style with that of her boyfriend, the astrologer Louis Acker. Acker is portrayed as a lug-headed, petulant oaf who nonetheless possesses formidable occult powers, including great abilities at both yoga and astrology. At the same time he is also a forgetful hulk who passes his days by pushing large boulders around Moore's farm and making clouds evaporate, merely for the fun of it. Acker's character repre-

sents a deformed yoga that focuses only on gaining superhuman abilities. It is nonetheless (or perhaps because of this) unfocused and undisciplined. Stearn, clearly enamored with his "pretty guru," is irritated by the attraction that Moore feels for the virile Acker, and can barely express his glee when an ancient Concord resident dismisses Acker's ability to make clouds dematerialize as child's play and warns him to stop, lest all of Concord's gardens wither in a drought.

31. Stearn, *Yoga, Youth, and Reincarnation,* 22, 293–94.

32. Harvey Cox, *Turning East: The Promise and Peril of the New Orientalism* (New York: Simon and Schuster, 1977) 10–11.

33. Cox lists nine of the fifty "neo-Orientalist" groups in Cambridge and Boston by name. Of these, six are no longer organizationally present in Cambridge or Boston, and one has significantly diminished presence. Two thrive: the Cambridge Zen Center and the "Dances for Universal Peace." Cox mentions in addition "dozens of smaller, less stable groups" as well (*Turning East,* 9–11). At least one of those groups emerged as the Cambridge Insight Meditation Center, a vipassana meditation and Buddhist center formally incorporated in 1985 after meeting in an ad hoc fashion for a decade. CIMC's history is chronicled in Wendy Cadge, *Heartwood: The First Generation of Theravada Buddhism in America* (Chicago: University of Chicago Press, 2005).

34. Robert S. Cox reports that Nathaniel Hawthorne pleaded with his fiancée, Sophia, to avoid mesmerism, "for the 'sacredness of an individual is violated by it,' and there would be an 'intrusion into the holy of holies'" (*Body and Soul,* 41).

35. As we will see in the following chapter, the question of what kinds of spirits or entities (or memories) caused metaphysicals to have information about themselves or others surfaced occasionally and was an issue of debate for respondents. Regardless of whether they thought that the astral beings that circulated in the world were ghosts or ascended astral beings, or traces or shards of other soul clusters, they nonetheless agreed on their existence.

36. Avery Gordon, *Ghostly Matters: Haunting in the Sociological Imagination* (Minneapolis: University of Minneapolis Press, 1997).

37. Robert Orsi, *Between Heaven and Earth: The Religious Worlds We Make and the Scholars Who Study Them* (Princeton, NJ: Princeton University Press, 2004), 73–74.

CHAPTER FOUR

1. Studying the practices and discursive uses of past life belief among American mystics veers from recent focus on past life beliefs as *beliefs* that "settle" individuals' philosophical conundrums about life after death. The degree to which mystics say that belief in past lives solves certain modern

issues is noteworthy, but emphasis on past life as an idea does little to enliven our understanding of how these practices are lived. In particular, it does little to demonstrate how unsettling and complicated experiences of past lives can be. Two representative papers that focus on the philo-sophical uses of past lives include Tony Walter and Helen Waterhouse, "A Very Private Belief: Reincarnation in Contemporary England," *Sociology of Religion* 60, no. 2 (1999): 187–97; Tony Walter, "Reincarnation, Modernity, and Identity," *Sociology* 35 (2000): 21–38.

2. As Eric Hirsch and Charles Stewart note, "the distribution of the Western notion of history is actually far from uniform even in the heartland of the West." "Introduction; Ethnographies of Historicity," *History and Anthro-pology* 16 (2005): 266. See also Susan Harding, *The Book of Jerry Falwell* (Princeton, NJ: Princeton University Press, 2001), 228–46.

3. See, for example, Dorothy Holland, "Figured Worlds," in *Identity and Agency in Cultural Worlds* (Cambridge, MA: Harvard University Press, 1998).

4. Michael Lambek, *The Weight of the Past* (New York: Palgrave, 2003); Joan W. Scott, "Fantasy Echo: History and the Construction of Identity," *Critical Inquiry* 27 (2001): 284–304.

5. The turn to historicity also fruitfully engages the field of collective memory in which sociologist Jeffrey Olick argues "there is no such thing as memory; there is only the activity of remembering." Remembering is structured, but only insofar as remembering takes place within an ongo-ing "response to a [dialogic] partner and to a history of such responses." Jeffrey Olick, *In the House of the Hangman: The Agonies of German Defeat, 1943–1949* (Chicago: University of Chicago Press, 2005), 19–20. See also Kerwin Lee Klein, "On the Emergence of Memory in Historical Discourse," *Representations* 69 (2000): 127–50.

6. The place of the imaginary or "unreal" social agent provocatively ad-dressed by Dipesh Chakrabarty, *Provincializing Europe: Postcolonial Thought and Historical Difference* (Princeton, NJ: Princeton University Press, 2000). See also Robert Orsi, *Between Heaven and Earth* (Princeton, NJ: Princeton University Press, 2004).

7. See, for example, John Caughey, *Imaginary Social Worlds: A Cultural Approach* (Lincoln: University of Nebraska Press, 1984). Caughey asks sociologists to pay more attention to imaginary worlds, particularly those that are lived through aesthetic and religious representations, arguing that we can learn much from attending to these social worlds we in-habit in dreams, literature, fantasy, and storytelling. Yet Caughey sees a sharp distinction between the imagined and real worlds. Imaginary "other times and places" of our fantasies and nightmares have their own temporal reality, pacing, and cognitive style. Nonetheless, they remain "other." Caughey includes religious worlds in his analysis, and notes that "spirit relations" and other relations with the divine are "imaginary social

relationships" (20). Whereas the self can imaginatively become "other" in these worlds, these other selves do not and indeed cannot consequentially play out within daily life: if individuals become too attuned to the tempo of imaginary worlds, both social order and the self are threatened (30). Compare this to Bruno Latour's recent expansion of the notion of agency to effectively include spirits, inanimate objects, and other "things" in *Reassembling the Social* (New York: Oxford University Press, 2005).

8. David Carr, *Time, Narrative, and History* (Bloomington: Indiana University Press, 1986), 116.

9. Cathy's several iterations of the same story for different ends highlights the degrees to which personal stories and vignettes can be used to "generate a multiplicity of partial selves," such that "selves evolve in the time frame of a single telling as well as in the course of many tellings that eventually compose a life." Elinor Ochs and Linda Capps, "Narrating the Self," *Annual Review of Anthropology* 25 (1996): 25. See also James L. Peacock and Dorothy Holland, "The Narrated Self: Life Stories in Process," *Ethos* 21 (1993): 367–84.

10. This conversation about how to interpret Cathy's experiences and what they mean replayed a nineteenth-century debate between Swedenborgian-influenced thinkers who argued that reincarnation does not exist and Theosophists and New Thought personalities who accepted reincarnation. Swedenborgians argued that past life beliefs are the result of relations with spirits; tap into the "internal" consciousness of the collective, spirit- and angel- populated heavens; and are misrecognized as one's own ego's memories. The Swedenborgian view of the subconscious or unconscious arguably filtered into Frederic Myers's and other prominent psychical researchers' views of the collective subconscious. See Ann Taves, *Fits, Trances, and Visions* (Princeton, NJ: Princeton University Press, 1999), 253–55; Leigh Schmidt, *Hearing Things: Religion, Illusion, and the American Enlightenment* (Cambridge, MA: Harvard University Press, 2000), 202–21.

11. The missteps and misrecognitions may also suggest traces of Cathy's previous interpretations and evaluations of the meanings of her own experiences. Interview materials like these often carry traces of what Mikhail Bakhtin calls the dynamics of their development, that is, a "feeling for the historical and social concreteness of a living discourse as well as its relativity, a feeling for its participation in historical becoming." "Discourse in the Novel," in *The Dialogic Imagination* (Austin: University of Texas Press, 1981), 331.

12. For example, Joan Grant and Denys Kelsey, *Many Lifetimes* (Alpharetta, GA: Ariel Press, 1967); Edith Fiore, *You Have Been Here Before: A Psychological Look at Past Lives* (New York: Coward, McCann and Geoghagan, 1978); Morris Netherton and Nancy Shiffrin, *Past Lives Therapy* (New York: Morrow, 1978); Christine Yarbro, *Messages from Michael: The Remarkable True Story of a Link between Two Worlds* (New York: Simon and Schuster, 1979).

13. Brian Weiss remains a fixture on the new age and spirituality lecture circuit, teaching others (including Cathy) to use hypnotherapy in past life regression. His most recent book presents "evidence" that it is possible to conduct future life progressions. Brian Weiss, *Same Soul Many Bodies: Discover the Healing Power of Future Lives through Progression Therapy* (New York: Free Press, 2004). In this book and other writings, Weiss suggests that "time" as we know it is best understood as a grid filled with parallel "lives" rather than as a linear unfolding of past present and future.

14. Brian Weiss, *Many Lives, Many Masters* (New York: Simon and Schuster, 1988), 35.

15. Gina Cerminara, *Many Mansions* (New York: Sloane, 1950); Morey Bernstein, *The Search for Bridey Murphy* (Garden City, NY: Doubleday, 1956); Thomas Sugrue, *There Is a River* (New York: Holt, 1942).

16. Cerminara, *Many Mansions,* 26–35.

17. Ibid., 37.

18. While most American writers whom I have encountered state that souls enter a space and time "beyond" life after death and before reincarnating, they differ considerably on what happens during that time and what its purpose is. James van Praagh, an ordained Spiritualist minister with his own nationally syndicated television show, tells his readers that this space is heaven, and that heaven is what a person makes it. "A newly arriving spirit will gravitate to the particular level of the astral world that corresponds to the frequency of its astral body's vibration." In heaven, "souls can create their own home, learn skills, live desires, let go of old habits, before reincarnating." *Reaching to Heaven: A Spiritual Journey through Life and Death* (New York: Dutton, 1999), 47–48, 57–59.

19. Carl T. Jackson, *The Oriental Religions and American Thought: Nineteenth-Century Explorations* (Westport, CT: Greenwood, 1981); and "The New Thought Movement and the Nineteenth Century Discovery of Oriental Philosophy," *Journal of Popular Culture* 9, no. 3 (1975): 523–48. Spiritualists made numerous statements rejecting and accepting reincarnation belief through the early part of the twentieth century, finally rejecting it in 1930. J. Stillson Judah, *The History and Philosophy of the Metaphysical Movement in America* (Philadelphia: Westminster Press, 1967); George Lawton, *The Drama of Life after Death: A Study of the Spiritualist Religion* (New York: Holt, 1932) 153–54. Theosophy's interpretation of reincarnation is chronicled in Joscelyn Godwin, *The Theosophical Enlightenment* (Albany: State University of New York Press, 1994).

20. See Stephen Prothero, "From Spiritualism to Theosophy: 'Uplifting' a Democratic Tradition," *Religion and American Culture* 3 (1993): 197–216. Metaphysicals frequently argued about the trajectory of a soul's progression. In the case of reincarnation, Spiritualists in the United States strongly rejected Blavatsky's reincarnationist view, and took her perspective on karma as evidence that Theosophy was better suited for

environments (such as India) that "remained through all these centuries in a nearly stagnant, semi-barbarous condition, the victims of ignorance, superstition . . . and physical degradation" rather than in advanced countries such as the United States. A. E. Newton, quoted in R. Lawrence Moore, *In Search of White Crows* (New York: Oxford University Press, 1977), 228.

21. Godwin, *The Theosophical Enlightenment,* 340.

22. Edward Maitland and Anna Kingsford, *The Perfect Way, or, the Finding of Christ,* 3rd English ed. with revisions (New York: Lovell, 1890), ix.

23. Jackson, "The New Thought Movement," 531.

24. Charles B. Newcomb, *Discovery of a Lost Trail* (Boston: Shepard and Lee, 1900), 110. Lest Newcomb's readers be hopelessly disappointed by this revelation of the laws of karma, he notes in characteristic New Thought fashion that "when we are willing to assume our rightful attitude toward one another we will find this freedom can be achieved to-day. There is no more reason for our present suffering than will exist a hundred or a thousand years from now."

25. Tyner quoted in Jackson, "The New Thought Movement," 532; Allen Kardec, *Spiritualist Philosophy: The Spirits' Book* (New York: Arno Press, 1976), 79 (originally published in 1875; italics in original). While human progress is the main theme in these texts, the authors frequently draw a contrast with "Indian" ideas of transmigration between species in order to consider the "animality" of human nature. For example, Maitland and Kingsford suggest at one moment that perhaps man can "redescend" into animal form if "he lose his spirit, and become again animal" thus descending and becoming "altogether gross and horrible," concluding that "Man's own wickedness is the creator of his evil beasts." *The Perfect Way,* 46.

26. Yogi Ramacharaka, *Mystic Christianity or the Inner Teachings of the Master* (Chicago: Yogi Publication Society, 1907), 15.

27. Ibid., 55, 267.

28. Maitland and Kingsford, *The Perfect Way,* 23–24.

29. Helena Petrova Blavatsky, *Karma and Reincarnation* (Los Angeles: The Theosophical Company, n.d.), 10 (italics in original).

30. Swedenborg apparently viewed stories of past life recollections as experiences with angels and spirits that had been misrecognized. Sounding a similar refrain in his highly influential tome, *Human Personality,* psychologist and philosopher Frederic Myers suggested that such "memories" were drawn from a collective subconscious (similar to the oversoul), noting "sometime it occurred to [the ancients] a recollection as it were of things which they never saw nor heard, and it came to pass because spirits flowed from their own memory into ideas of thought." Myers's explanation of déjà vu experiences, he said, were related to our participation in a broader subconscious. "[I]f we conceive all personality as a unity instead of a plu-

rality, then the myriads of beings are merely its multiple self projections." Quoted in a review of Myers's *Human Personality,* by Albert Edmunds, "FHW Myers, Swedenborg and Buddha," *Proceedings of the American Society for Psychical Research* 8 (1914): 280.

31. Kardec, *Spiritualist Philosophy,* 89.

32. Catherine Albanese, "On the Matter of Spirit: Andrew Jackson Davis and the Marriage of God and Nature," *Journal of the American Academy of Religion* 60 (1992): 1–17.

33. Kardec, *Spiritualist Philosophy,* 159.

34. Maitland and Kingsford, *The Perfect Way,* 308–9.

35. Newcomb, *Discovery of a Lost Trail,* 18–19.

36. Kardec, *Spiritualist Philosophy,* 163.

37. Neal Vahle, *The Unity Movement: Its Evolution and Spiritual Teachings* (Philadelphia: Templeton Foundation Press, 2002); Charles Braden, *Spirits in Rebellion: The Rise and Development of New Thought* (Dallas: Southern Methodist University Press, 1964).

38. Charles Fillmore, *The Essential Charles Fillmore: Collected Writings of a Missouri Mystic* (Unity Village, MI: Unity Books, 1999), 392.

39. Sugrue, *There Is a River;* Cerminara, *Many Mansions.*

40. J. Gordon Melton, "Edgar Cayce and Reincarnation: Past Life Readings as Religious Symbology," *Syzygy: Journal of Alternative Religion and Culture* 3 (1994): 39–50.

41. Yarbo, *Messages from Michael.*

42. Kardec, *Spiritualist Philosophy,* 84.

43. "Soul clusters" share quite a bit with other types of religious practices that reimagine the family and its proper relations. Western mystical visions of soul connections invert the relationships of kinship rebirth identified in several reincarnation traditions by Gananath Obeyesekere in *Imagining Karma: Ethical Transformation in Amerindian, Buddhist, and Greek Rebirth* (Berkeley: University of California Press, 2002).

44. Cerminara, *Many Mansions,* 191.

45. Drawing on literary critic J. Hollis Miller's notion of the "complex word," Francesca Polletta states that while stories are supposed to explain, they always fail, thus requiring more stories. "The impossibility of a conclusive meaning calls for more stories, which recapitulate the dilemma but differently. All stories both explain and fail to explain." Francesca Polletta, "Contending Stories: Narratives in Social Movements," *Qualitative Sociology* 21 (1998): 428.

46. While in the previous chapter I note how many experiences require or mark a shift from a skeptical self to a fully experiencing body, past life narratives, particularly those that take place in the context of hypnosis, suggest another set of embodiments, including embodied skepticism. Cathy's most skeptical voice was her own "narrator's voice" that spoke *while she was under hypnosis.* Cathy had taught herself self-hypnosis for

labor, and knew very well that it was possible to "suggest" memories, states of being, and somatic experiences that were effectively real. Cathy's skeptical self speaks most clearly, chiding her(self) for speaking with a fake German accent.

This second narrating self, organized against skepticism (including her own) is only one of several that Cathy maintains. The process of her "making sense" of the story thus unfolds through gaining information and perspectives that are only possible by embodying different positions, each of which has the ability or legitimacy to author (authorize) the information that she receives. This process is far from seamless. Cathy's stories leave questions hanging in the space between Prague (where she "saw" her client as a young girl) and Berlin (where she became Max). The experiences that blur spaces and times and do not belong to any particular position or gaze are potentially the most difficult, given that they resonate with various symbolic suggestions but are not fully realizable in any "historical" sense within any of the multiple positions Cathy embodies.

47. See Sarah Gray Thompson, "Do You Remember Your Previous Lives' Language in Your Present Incarnation?" *American Speech* 59, no. 4 (1984): 240–50. In a contrasting view, Akhil Gupta argues that in contemporary India souls take on more of the character of "commodities," without particular characteristics. Akhil Gupta, "The Reincarnation of Souls and the Rebirth of Commodities: Representations of Time in 'East' and 'West,'" *Cultural Critique* 22 (1992): 187–211.

48. Where many commentators have noted the tendency of past life regressors to claim a famous persona and commented on the "narcissism" involved (for example, Melton, "Edgar Cayce and Reincarnation"), the interest in claiming a "real" rather than "fantastic" past life suggests another explanation. Real past figures, and famous ones no less, present the possibility that regressors can link their "memories" with various documented details.

CHAPTER FIVE

1. Sara M. Pike observes similar conversations and engagements about the "politics of cultural appropriation" among contemporary neo-pagan communities in the United States, where issues of how and to what degree one can draw upon or claim native traditions in particular are of constant concern. Sara M. Pike, *Earthly Bodies, Magical Selves: Contemporary Pagans and the Search for Community* (Berkeley: University of California Press, 2001), 123–25.

2. Mikhail Bakhtin, *The Dialogic Imagination* (Austin: University of Texas Press, 1981), 85. Bakhtin emphasizes a constructionist perspective on chronotopes. "Here we employ the Kantian evaluation of the importance of these forms [time and space] in the cognitive process, but differ from

Kant in taking them not as 'transcendental' but as forms of the most immediate reality." Insofar as Bakhtin emphasizes subjectivities shaped through shared chronotopic views, his work shares similarity with phenomenologists including Alfred Schutz, Thomas Luckmann, and Peter Berger. Nonetheless, Bakhtin's emphasis on the distinction between "literary" chronotopes and the chronotopic articulations within daily social life presents an opportunity to inquire sociologically into the spaces that are opened up not only via ritual and remembrance but also through literature and literary practices and the interplay between the literary, the fantastic, and the social. Sumathi Ramaswamy's investigation of the "lost land" of Lemuria as a motif in occult literature, scientific theorizing, nation building, and new age fantasy provides an excellent example. Sumathi Ramaswamy, *The Lost Land of Lemuria: Fabulous Geographies: Catastrophic Histories* (Berkeley: University of California Press, 2004).

3. Nation, race, and religion are tied together in rituals, histories, narratives, and practices, as well as through legal claims to land, self-governance, and the like. In other words, religious groups continue to claim territories, contest others' claims, and establish diasporic imaginaries that constantly unsettle and challenge material and political narratives of nation and people. In numerous cases we see that living religious chronotopes and the claims to authority and authenticity that they engender can refigure political and cultural claims to land, political voice, and personhood. Edward Linenthal and David Chidester, *American Sacred Space* (Bloomington: Indiana University Press, 1995); Henry Goldschmidt and Elizabeth McAlister, eds., *Race, Nation, and Religion in the Americas* (New York: Oxford University Press, 2004); Peter van der Veer, ed., *Nation and Migration: The Politics of Space in South Asian Diaspora* (Philadelphia: University of Pennsylvania Press, 1995); Genevieve Zubrzycki, *The Crosses of Auschwitz: Religion and Nationalism in Post-Communist Poland* (Chicago: University of Chicago Press, 2006).

4. Bakhtin's distinction between "literary" and "real" (everyday life) chronotopes gives rise to a view of a creative interaction *between* them. "There is a sharp and categorical boundary line between the actual world as source of representation and the world represented in the work. We must never forget this, we must never confuse . . . the represented world with the world outside the text (naïve realism); nor must we confuse the author-creator of a work with the author as a human being (naïve biographism); nor confuse the listener or reader of multiple and varied periods, recreating and renewing the text, with the passive listener or reader of one's own time (which leads to dogmatism and evaluation). All such confusions are methodologically impermissible. But it is also impermissible to take this categorical boundary line as something absolute and impermeable. . . . However forcefully the real and represented world resist fusion, however immutable the presence of that categorical boundary line between them,

they are nevertheless indissolubly tied up with each other and find themselves in continual mutual interaction; uninterrupted exchange goes on between them." Bakhtin, *The Dialogic Imagination,* 254.

This view has been particularly useful for scholars who have sought to figure the relationships between various "types" of time and space imagined, envisioned, and lived in religious and subaltern cultures as, for example, in Michael Lambek's investigations of the interleaving of "historical" and "mythic" time in Madagascar spirit mediumship (*The Weight of the Past: Living with History in Mahajanga, Madagascar* [New York: Palgrave, 2002]). Srinivas Aravamudan similarly reads for "interruptive as well as mimetic outcomes" in reading the history and fiction of South Asian gurus' encounters with the West (*Guru English: South Asian Religion in a Cosmopolitan Language* [Princeton, NJ: Princeton University Press, 2006], 222).

5. Notwithstanding real social changes within American society in the last half-century, social conditions do not in necessarily prompt people to understand their places in the world as similarly rootless and mobile. So, while various scholars have considered the homelessness of contemporary spiritual practitioners as a condition that propels spiritual seeking, we might in this case consider how contemporary spiritual practice articulates those very conditions, being as much active as responsive in shaping these chronotopes. See, for example, Wade Clark Roof, *Spiritual Marketplace: Baby Boomers and the Remaking of American Religion* (Princeton, NJ: Princeton University Press, 1999), 59–76; Robert Wuthnow, *After Heaven: Spirituality in America since the 1950s* (Berkeley: University of California Press, 1998), 1–19.

6. Sumathi Ramaswamy notes that "narratives of loss are about a transition from homogeneity to differentiation, from the originary fullness of autonomy to a degraded condition. . . . These narratives suffer from a yearning for unity with the homogeneous past, a desire for the closure of difference." *The Lost Land of Lemuria,* 7.

7. Arjun Appadurai, *Modernity at Large* (Minneapolis: University of Minnesota Press, 1996), 77.

8. Svetlana Boym, *The Future of Nostalgia* (New York: Basic Books, 2001), 8.

9. Barbara Sellers-Young observes that the Americanized form of belly dance was built on a "romanticization of the Near East and . . . a general movement of increased awareness and acceptance of the female body" ("Raks el Sharki: Transculturation of a Folk Form," *Journal of Popular Culture* 26 [1992]: 142).

10. Laura Donaldson writes on the appropriation and refashioning of Native American religious traditions under the gaze of pan-feminist spirituality in "On Medicine Women and White Shame-ans: New Age Native Americanism and Commodity Fetishism as Pop Culture Feminism," *Signs: Journal of Women in Culture and Society* 24 (1999): 677–98.

11. Robert S. Cox, *Body and Soul: A Sympathetic History of American Spiritualism*

(Charlottesville: University of Virginia Press, 2003), 231; Catherine Albanese, *A Republic of Mind and Spirit* (New Haven, CT: Yale University Press, 2006), 246–50; Gauri Viswanathan, *Outside the Fold: Conversion, Modernity, and Belief* (Princeton, NJ: Princeton University Press, 1998), 198–99. Viswanathan's discussion of Annie Besant's interest in theories of racial evolution suggests further that race theories and progressive "universalism" were far from antithetical causes. As Viswanathan observes, Besant's emphasis on spiritual and historical progress was linked to a view that "racial evolution would produce superhuman agents endowed with the capacity to transform others and so promote social change" (*Outside the Fold,* 186).

Metaphysical practitioners are not the only religious people to articulate racialized narratives with geographical tinges. Henry Goldschmidt's interrogation of Jewish and black communities in Brooklyn, New York, notes how narratives of "chosenness" intertwine race and religion in various narratives of historical agency. Henry Goldschmidt, *Race and Religion among the Chosen Peoples of Crown Heights* (New Brunswick, NJ: Rutgers University Press, 2006), 224–33. Respondents in Cambridge are clearly shape shifting and grafting different sorts of identities and narratives of agency, race, and becoming than are Goldschmidt's Lubavitchers and black Israelites. Nonetheless, similar methods obtain, setting the focus on what these claims (and occasional contests) over these designations enact and suggest, and the imaginative and social worlds that they help to form.

12. Charles W. Leadbeater, *The Astral World: Its Scenery, Inhabitants, and Phenomena* (New York: Cosimo Classics, 2005).

13. Tomoko Masuzawa outlines the development of a tradition of "world religions" that imbricates religious progress and race in *The Invention of World Religions* (Princeton, NJ: Princeton University Press, 2005). Masuzawa is relatively silent on the various traditions that fall outside of this emergent rubric, however, noting only in passing that the religious taxonomies of theosophical and other occult distinctions are "atypical" (ibid., 74n5).

14. Thus where Benedict Anderson writes that "nationalism . . . parts company with the Great Religions" because "Heaven harbors no nations, and the dead are no use to nationalism in so remote a sequestration," he is invoking a particular set of Christian theologies about the afterlife that are quite different from those marked out by Spiritualism, Theosophy, and other metaphysical theologies. "The Goodness of Nations," in *Nation and Religion,* ed. Peter van der Veer (Princeton, NJ: Princeton University Press, 1999), 198.

15. Much like the "lost" lands of Lemuria, the esoteric planet Vulcan was posited by nineteenth-century astronomers to account for and explain observed anomalies in Mercury's orbit, and once having entered into popular consciousness and fascination never fully departed. So, just as paleo-biologists later abandoned theories dependent on catastrophic lost

continents to account for evolutionary spread of animal species, so physicists (in this case, Einstein) determined a better explanation for Mercury's wobble and abandoned the "search" for this etheric planet. Nonetheless these other lands and their scientific provenance continue to surface. Robert Fontenrose, "In Search of Vulcan," *Journal for the History of Astronomy* 4 (1973): 145–58.

16. Alex Owen argues that "in occult practice the exploration of 'vast unknown continents' [of the mind] was intimately bound up with the exercise of the willed imagination. Whether undertaken in the waking or the sleep state, Astral Travel was predicated on the Adept's ability to both create and control the experience" (*The Place of Enchantment: British Occultism and the Culture of the Modern* [Chicago: University of Chicago Press, 2004], 179).

17. Leadbeater, *The Astral World*, 6–7.

18. Swami Panchadasi, *Astral Worlds: Its Scenes, Dwellers, and Phenomena* (Chicago: Advanced Thought, 1915), 36.

19. Kurt Leland, *Otherwhere: A Field Guide to Nonphysical Reality for the Out-of-Body Traveler* (Charlottesville, VA: Hampton Roads, 2001).

20. Leland, *Otherwhere*, 42.

21. Leland thus follows in an occult path noted by Alex Owen, who writes, "Occultists' acknowledgement that in effect occult reality is created in knowable form by the fictionalizing mind serves only to signal once again the extreme modernity of the magical enterprise. It did nothing to detract from a belief in the higher truths and a verifiable occult 'real' revealed in those visionary deeps. This remained, after all, enchantment, albeit in demonstrably modern mode." Owen, *The Place of Enchantment*, 184. See also Gauri Viswanathan, "Secularism in a Framework of Heterodoxy," *PMLA* 123 (2008): 465–76.

22. See Adrian Ivakhiv, "Nature and Self in New Age Pilgrimage," *Culture and Religion* 4 (2004): 93– 118; Ivakhiv, *Claiming Sacred Ground: Pilgrims and Politics in Glastonbury and Sedona* (Bloomington: Indiana University Press, 2001).

23. Craig Calhoun, "'Belonging' in the Cosmopolitan Imaginary," *Ethnicities* 3 (2003): 532. Calhoun does not suggest where (or even if) the practices of these social imaginaries might be located or if they either extend beyond or envelop social locations and identities that muddle along, outside of the rarefied realms of political discourse and public philosophy.

24. Bryan S. Turner, "Cosmopolitan Virtue, Globalization, and Patriotism," *Theory Culture and Society* 19 (2002): 57.

25. Svetlana Boym, *The Future of Nostalgia*, 17.

26. Jeffrey Kripal ends his volume *Esalen: America and the Religion of No Religion* by asking rhetorically if we are ready to embrace America as mysticism, or "more specifically, can we revision 'America' not as a globally hated imperial superpower, not as a 'Christian nation' obsessed with made

and arrogant apocalyptic fantasies abroad and discriminatory 'family values' at home, not as a monster consumer of the world's ever-dwindling resources, but as a universal human ideal yet to be fully realized, as a potential yet to be actualized, as an empty and so creative space far more radical and free than the most patriotic or religiously right among us have dared to imagine?" He continues, asking at the end, "Are we ready for a radically American mysticism, for an 'America' *as* mysticism?" ([Chicago: University of Chicago Press, 2007], 463–64, 466).

CONCLUSION

1. Philip Gorski and Ates Altinordu, "After Secularization?" *Annual Review of Sociology* 34 (2008): 55–85.
2. As I argue in a recent essay, this taken-for-grantedness is embedded within the methods that sociologists use to study religion. The very question of religion (its location and thereby its definition) is frequently answered even before the research begins; it is the question that is answered on the way to some other more important question. Courtney Bender, "Things in Their Entanglements" (paper presented at "Exploring the Postsecular Conference," Yale University, New Haven, CT, April 3–4, 2009).
3. Talal Asad, *Formations of the Secular* (Stanford: Stanford University Press, 2003).
4. Dipesh Chakrabarty, *Provincializing Europe: Postcolonial Thought and Historical Difference* (Princeton, NJ: Princeton University Press, 2000).
5. "At any moment in the development of the dialogue there are immense, boundless masses of forgotten contextual meanings, but at certain moments of the dialogue's subsequent development along the way they are recalled and invigorated in renewed form (in a new context). Nothing is absolutely dead: every meaning will have its homecoming festival." Mikhail Bakhtin, *Speech Genres and Other Late Essays* (Austin: University of Texas Press, 1996), 170; Wai Chee Dimock, "A Theory of Resonance," *PMLA* 112 (1997): 1060–71.
6. Pierre Bourdieu, *The Logic of Practice* (Stanford: Stanford University Press, 1990).
7. Courtney Bender, "Practicing Religion," in *Cambridge Companion to the Study of Religion,* ed. Robert Orsi (New York: Cambridge University Press, forthcoming).
8. Charles Taylor, *A Secular Age* (Cambridge, MA: Harvard University Press, 2007).
9. Current examples in this genre include the research of cognitive psychologist Pascal Boyer and neuroscientist Richard Davidson. The degree to which these studies align spirituality with the secular are evident furthermore within the "new atheists" literature, some of which argues that spirituality in the form of meditation is not inimical to atheism. See,

for example, Sam Harris, *The End of Faith* (New York: Norton, 1996). The ongoing interest among scientists to contextualize or mark spirituality or religion as something other than cultural and historical, and to locate it within the body or the neurons, can play both ways (both for and against secular claims). See, for example, Ann Taves, *Fits, Trances, and Visions: Experiencing Religion and Explaining Experience from Wesley to James* (Princeton, NJ: Princeton University Press, 1999); Christopher White, *Unsettled Minds: Psychology and the American Search for Spiritual Assurance, 1830–1940* (Berkeley: University of California Press, 2008); Robert C. Fuller, "American Psychology and the Religious Imagination," *Journal of the History of the Behavioral Sciences* 42 (2006): 221–35.

10. Mark A. Schneider, *Culture and Enchantment* (Chicago: University of Chicago Press, 1993), ix.

Bibliography

Ahlstrom, Sydney. *A Religious History of the American People.* New Haven, CT: Yale University Press, 1974.

Albanese, Catherine. "The Aura of Wellness: Subtle-Energy Healing and New Age Religion." *Religion and American Culture* 10 (2000): 29–55.

———. *Corresponding Motion: Transcendental Religion and the New America.* Philadelphia: Temple University Press, 1977.

———. "Introduction: Awash in a Sea of Metaphysicals." *Journal of the American Academy of Religion* 75 (2007): 582–88.

———. "The Magical Staff: Quantum Healing in the New Age." In *Perspectives on the New Age,* edited by James Lewis and J. Gordon Melton, 68–84. Albany: State University of New York Press, 1992.

———. *Nature Religion in America.* Chicago: University of Chicago Press, 1990.

———. *A Republic of Mind and Spirit.* New Haven, CT: Yale University Press, 2006.

———. "The Subtle Energies of Spirit: Explorations in Metaphysical and New Age Spirituality." *Journal of the American Academy of Religion* 67 (1999): 305–26.

Alter, Joseph. *Yoga in Modern India.* Princeton, NJ: Princeton University Press, 2004.

Ammerman, Nancy. *Pillars of Faith: American Congregations and Their Partners.* Berkeley: University of California Press, 2005.

———. "Religious Identities and Religious Institutions." In *Handbook for the Sociology of Religion,* edited by Michele Dillon, 207–24. Cambridge: Cambridge University Press, 2003.

Anderson, Benedict. "The Goodness of Nations." In *Nation and Religion,* edited by Peter van der Veer, 195–203. Princeton, NJ: Princeton University Press, 1999.

Appadurai, Arjun. *Modernity at Large.* Minneapolis: University of Minnesota Press, 1996.

Asad, Talal. *Formations of the Secular.* Stanford: Stanford University Press, 2003.

Astin, John. "Why Patients Use Alternative Medicine," *Journal of the American Medical Association* 279 (1998): 1548–53.

Atkinson, William Walker. *Thought Vibration or the Law of Attraction in the Thought World.* Chicago: New Thought, 1906.

——— [Swami Panchadasi, pseud.]. *Astral Worlds: Its Scenes, Dwellers, and Phenomena.* Chicago: Advanced Thought, 1915.

——— [Yogi Ramacharaka, pseud.]. *The Hindu-Yogi Science of Breath.* Chicago: Yogi Publication Society, 1903.

——— [Yogi Ramacharaka, pseud.]. *Mystic Christianity or the Inner Teachings of the Master.* Chicago: Yogi Publication Society, 1907.

Bakhtin, Mikhail. *The Dialogic Imagination.* Austin: University of Texas Press, 1981.

———. "The Problem of Speech Genres." In *Speech Genres and Other Late Essays,* 60–102. Austin: University of Texas, 1986.

———. *Problems of Dostoevsky's Poetics.* Minneapolis: University of Minnesota Press, 1984.

———. *Speech Genres and Other Late Essays.* Austin: University of Texas Press, 1986.

———. "Toward a Methodology for the Human Sciences." In *Speech Genres and Other Late Essays,* 159–72.

Barnes, Patricia M., Eve Powell-Griner, Kim McFann, and Richard L. Nahin. "Complementary and Alternative Medicine Use among Adults: United States, 2002." In *Advance Data from Vital and Health Statistics,* No. 343. Hyattsville, MD: Anderson National Center for Health Statistics, 2002.

Barthes, Roland. "From Work to Text." In *Image, Music, Text,* 154–64. New York: Hill and Wang, 1977.

Bearman, Peter, and Katherine Stovel. "Becoming a Nazi: A Model for Narrative Networks." *Poetics* 27 (2000): 69–90.

Becker, Penny Edgell. *Congregations in Conflict: Cultural Models of Local Religious Life.* New York: Cambridge University Press, 1999.

Bellah, Robert, et al. *Habits of the Heart: Individualism and Commitment in American Life.* Berkeley: University of California Press, 1985.

Bender, Courtney. "American Reincarnations: What the Many Lives of Past Lives Tell Us about Contemporary Spirituality." *Journal of the American Academy of Religion* 75 (2007): 589–614.

———. *Heaven's Kitchen: Living Religion at God's Love We Deliver.* Chicago: University of Chicago Press, 2003.

———. "(How) Does God Speak Back?" *Poetics* 36 (2008): 476–92.

———. "Religion and Spirituality: History, Discourse, and Measurement." New York: Social Science Research Council, 2006.

———. "Things in Their Entanglements." Paper presented at the "Exploring the Post-Secular" Conference, Yale University, April 3–4, 2009.

———. "'Touching the Transcendent': Rethinking Religious Experience in the Sociological Study of Religion." In *Everyday Religion: Observing Religion in Modern Lives,* edited by Nancy Ammerman, 201–18. New York: Oxford University Press, 2007.

Berger, Peter. *The Heretical Imperative.* Garden City, NY: Doubleday, 1979.

Bernard, Theos. *Hatha Yoga.* New York: Columbia University Press, 1944.

Bernstein, Michael. *Foregone Conclusions: Against Apocalyptic History.* Berkeley: University of California Press, 1994.

Bernstein, Morey. *The Search for Bridey Murphy.* Garden City, NY: Doubleday, 1956.

Berryman, Edward. "Medjugorje's Living Icons: Making Spirit Matter (for Sociology)." *Social Compass* 48 (2001): 593–610.

Besecke, Kelly. "Seeing Invisible Religion: Religion as a Societal Conversation about Transcendent Meaning." *Sociological Theory* 23 (2005): 179–96.

Blau, Judith. "The Toggle Switch of Institutions: Religion and Art in the U.S. in the Nineteenth and Early Twentieth Centuries." *Social Forces* 74 (1996): 1159–77

Blavatsky, Helena Petrova. *Karma and Reincarnation.* Los Angeles: The Theosophical Company, n.d.

Bowman, Marion. "More of the Same? Christianity, Vernacular Religion and Alternative Spirituality in Glastonbury." In *Beyond New Age,* edited by Marion Bowman and Steven Sutcliffe, 83–104. Edinburgh: Edinburgh University Press, 2000.

Boyatzis, Chris J. "A Critique of Models of Religious Experience." *International Journal for the Psychology of Religion* 4 (2001): 247–58.

Boym, Svetlana. *The Future of Nostalgia.* New York: Basic Books, 2001.

Braid, Donald. "Personal Narrative and Experiential Meaning." *Journal of American Folklore* 109 (1996): 5–30.

Brekus, Catherine. "A Place to Go to Connect with Yourself: A Historical Perspective on Journaling." University of Chicago Divinity Center, Martin Marty Center Religion and Culture Web Forum, 2004. http://divinity.uchicago.edu/martycenter/publications/webforum/022004/.

———. "Writing as a Protestant Practice: Devotional Diaries in Early New England." In *Practicing Protestants: Histories of Christian Life in America, 1630–1965,* edited by Laurie Maffly-Kipp and Leigh Schmidt, 19–34. Baltimore: Johns Hopkins University Press, 2006.

Brooks, Arthur C. "Artists as Amateurs and Volunteers." *Nonprofit Management and Leadership* 13 (2002): 5–15

Brown, Michael. *The Channeling Zone: American Spirituality in an Anxious Age.* Cambridge, MA: Harvard University Press, 1997.

Brunton, Paul. *The Secret Path: A Technique of Spiritual Self-Discovery for the Modern World.* New York: Rider, 1934.

Bruyere, Rosalyn. *Wheels of Light*. New York: Simon and Schuster, 1989.

Buell, Lawrence. *Emerson*. Cambridge, MA: Belknap Press, 2004.

Burawoy, Michael. "The Extended Case Method." *Sociological Theory* 16 (1988): 5–33.

Burke, Jane Revere. *The One Way*. New York: Dutton, 1922.

Burris, John. *Exhibiting Religion: Colonialism and Spectacle in International Exposi-tions*. Charlottesville: University of Virginia Press, 2001.

Cadge, Wendy. *Heartwood: The First Generation of Theravada Buddhism in America*. Chicago: University of Chicago Press, 2005.

Cain, Carole. "Personal Stories: Identity Acquisition and Self-Understanding in Alcoholics Anonymous." *Ethos* 19 (1991): 210–53.

Calhoun, Craig. "'Belonging' in the Cosmopolitan Imaginary." *Ethnicities* 3 (2003): 531–53.

Call, Annie Payson. *Power through Repose*. Boston: Little, Brown, 1900. First published 1891 by Roberts Brothers.

Cameron, Julia. *The Artist's Way: A Spiritual Path to Higher Creativity*. New York: Tarcher Putnam, 1992.

Campbell, Colin. "The Cult, the Cultic Milieu, and Secularization." In *The Cultic Milieu: Oppositional Subcultures in an Age of Globalization*, edited by Jeffrey Kaplan and Heléne Lööw, 12–25. Walnut Creek, CA: AltaMira Press, 2002.

Carr, David. *Time, Narrative, and History*. Bloomington: Indiana University Press, 1986.

Casanova, José. *Public Religions in the Modern World*. Chicago: University of Chicago Press, 1993.

Caughey, John. *Imaginary Social Worlds: A Cultural Approach*. Lincoln: University of Nebraska Press, 1984.

Cerminara, Gina. *Many Mansions*. New York: Sloane Associates, 1950.

Chakrabarty, Dipesh. *Provincializing Europe: Postcolonial Thought and Historical Difference*. Princeton, NJ: Princeton University Press, 2000.

Chang, Patricia M. Y. "Escaping the Procrustean Bed: A Critical Analysis of the Study of Religious Organizations, 1930–2001." In *Handbook of the Sociology of Religion*, edited by Michele Dillon, 123–36. Cambridge: Cambridge University Press, 2003.

Chaves, Mark. *Congregations in America*. Cambridge, MA: Harvard University Press, 2003.

Cherkin, Daniel C., Richard A. Deyo, Karen J. Sherman, L. Gary Hart, Janet H. Street, Andrea Hrbek, Elaine Cramer, Bruce Milliman, Jennifer Booker, Robert Mootz, James Barassi, Janet R. Kahn, Ted J. Kaptchuk, and David M. Eisenberg. "Characteristics of Licensed Acupuncturists, Chiropractors, Massage Therapists, and Naturopathic Physicians." *Journal of the American Board of Family Practice* 15 (2002): 378–90.

Chidester, David, and Edward Linenthal, eds. *American Sacred Space*. Bloomington: Indiana University Press, 1995.

Christy, Arthur. *The Orient in American Transcendentalism.* New York: Octagon Books, 1964. First published 1932 by Columbia University Press.

Cimino, Richard, and Don Lattin. *Shopping for Faith: American Religion in the New Millennium.* San Francisco: Jossey-Bass, 1998.

Cohen, Michael H. *Complementary and Alternative Medicine: Legal Boundaries and Regulatory Perspectives.* Baltimore: Johns Hopkins University Press, 1998.

Cox, Harvey. *Turning East: The Promise and Peril of the New Orientalism.* New York: Simon and Schuster, 1977.

Cox, Robert S. *Body and Soul: A Sympathetic History of American Spiritualism.* Charlottesville: University of Virginia Press, 2003.

Csordas, Thomas. "Embodiment as a Paradigm for Anthropology." *Ethos* 18 (1990): 5–47.

———. *The Sacred Self.* Berkeley: University of California Press, 1984.

Daiber, Karl-Fritz. "Mysticism: Troeltsch's Third Type of Religious Collectivities." *Social Compass* 49 (2002): 329–41.

Danforth, Lorning. *Firewalking and Religious Healing.* Princeton, NJ: Princeton University Press, 1989.

Davie, Jody Shapiro. *Women in the Presence.* Philadelphia: University of Pennsylvania Press, 1995.

de Certeau, Michel. *The Practice of Everyday Life.* Berkeley: University of California Press, 1984.

Dennett, Daniel. *Breaking the Spell, Religion as a Natural Phenomenon.* New York: Viking, 2006.

Dewey, John. *Experience and Nature.* Chicago: Open Court, 1925.

Dillon, Michele, and Paul Wink. *In the Course of a Lifetime.* Berkeley: University of California Press, 2007.

DiMaggio, Paul. "Constructing an Organizational Field as a Professional Project: U.S. Art Museums, 1920–1940." In *The New Institutionalism in Organizational Analysis,* edited by Walter W. Powell and Paul J. DiMaggio, 267–92. Chicago: University of Chicago Press, 1991.

DiMaggio, Paul, and Walter Powell. "The Iron Cage Revisited: Institutional Isomorphism and Collective Rationality." In *The New Institutionalism in Organizational Analysis,* edited by Walter W. Powell and Paul J. DiMaggio, 1–40. Chicago: University of Chicago Press, 1991.

Dimock, Wai Chee. "A Theory of Resonance." *Proceedings of the Modern Language Association* 112 (October 1997): 1060–71.

Donaldson, Laura. "On Medicine Women and White Shame-ans: New Age Native Americanism and Commodity Fetishism as Pop Culture Feminism." *Signs: Journal of Women in Culture and Society* 24 (1999): 677–98.

Doss, Erika. "Robert Gober's 'Virgin' Installation: Issues of Spirituality in Contemporary American Art." In *The Visual Culture of American Religions,* edited by David Morgan and Salley Promey, 129–45. Berkeley: University of California Press, 2001.

Downey, June, and John Anderson. "Automatic Writing." *American Journal of Psychology* 27 (1915): 161–95.

Eden, James. *Energetic Healing: The Merging of Ancient and Modern Medical Practices.* New York: Plenum Press, 1993.

Edmunds, Albert. "FHW Myers, Swedenborg and Buddha." *Proceedings of the American Society for Psychical Research* 8 (1914): 253–85.

Elbow, Peter. *Writing without Teachers.* New York: Oxford University Press, 1963.

Eliasoph, Nina, and Paul Lichterman. "We Begin with Our Favorite Theory . . . : Reconstructing the Extended Case Method." *Sociological Theory* 17 (1989): 228–34.

Eliot, T. S. "The Dry Salvages." In *Four Quartets.* 1943. Reprint, San Diego: Harcourt Brace Jovanovich, 1971.

Epstein, Steven. *Impure Science: AIDS, Activism, and the Politics of Knowledge.* Berkeley: University of California Press, 1996.

Fadlon, Judith. "Meridians, Chakras and Psycho-Neuro-Immunology: The Dematerializing Body and the Domestication of Alternative Medicine." *Body and Soul* 10 (2004): 69–86.

Favret-Saada, Jeanne. *Deadly Words: Witchcraft in the Bocage.* Cambridge: Cambridge University Press, 1980.

Fontenrose, Robert. "In Search of Vulcan." *Journal for the History of Astronomy* 4 (1973): 145–58.

Foucault, Michel. *Discipline and Punish.* New York: Vintage, 1977.

Franzosi, Roberto. "Narrative Analysis—Or Why (and How) Sociologists Should Be Interested in Narrative." *Annual Review of Sociology* 24 (1998): 517–54.

Friedland, Roger, and Robert A. Alford. "Bringing Society Back In: Symbols, Practices, and Institutional Contradictions." In *The New Institutionalism in Organizational Analysis,* edited by Walter W. Powell and Paul J. DiMaggio. Chicago: University of Chicago Press, 1991.

Fuller, Robert C. *Alternative Medicine and American Religious Life.* New York: Oxford University Press, 1989.

———. "American Psychology and the Religious Imagination." *Journal of the History of the Behavioral Sciences* 42 (2006): 221–35.

———. *Spiritual But Not Religious: Understanding Unchurched America,* New York: Oxford University Press, 2001.

Geertz, Clifford. *The Interpretation of Cultures.* New York: Basic Books, 1973.

Gieryn, Thomas. "City as Truth-Spot: Laboratories and Field-Sties in Urban Studies." *Social Studies of Science* 36 (2006): 5–38.

Glock, Charles, and Rodney Stark. *Religion and Society in Tension.* Chicago: Rand McNally, 1965.

Godwin, Joscelyn. *The Theosophical Enlightenment.* Albany: State University of New York Press, 1994.

Goldberg, Natalie. *Writing Down the Bones: Freeing the Writer Within.* New York: Shambhala, 1986.

Goldschmidt, Henry. *Race and Religion among the Chosen Peoples of Crown Heights*. New Brunswick, NJ: Rutgers University Press, 2006.

Goldschmidt, Henry, and Elizabeth McAlister, eds. *Race, Nation, and Religion in the Americas*. New York: Oxford University Press, 2004.

Goldstein, Michael S. "The Emerging Socioeconomic and Political Support for Alternative Medicine in the United States." *Annals of the American Academy of Political and Social Science*. 583 (2002): 44–63.

Gordon, Avery. *Ghostly Matters: Haunting and the Sociological Imagination*. Minneapolis: University of Minnesota Press, 1997.

Gorski, Philip, and Ates Altinordu. "After Secularization." *Annual Review of Sociology* 34 (2008): 55–77.

Greeley, Andrew. *The Sociology of the Paranormal: A Reconnaissance*. Beverly Hills, CA: Sage, 1975.

Greenblatt, Stephen. "The Touch of the Real." In *Practicing New Historicism*, edited by Catherine Gallagher and Stephen Greenblatt, 20–48. Chicago: University of Chicago Press, 2000.

Greenhouse, Carol J. *Praying for Justice: Faith, Order, and Community in an American Town*. Ithaca, NY: Cornell University Press, 1986.

Greer, Bruce, and Wade Clark Roof. "Desperately Seeking Sheila: Locating Religious Privatism in American Society." *Journal for the Scientific Study of Religion* 31 (1992): 346–52.

Griffith, R. Marie. *Born Again Bodies: Flesh and Spirit in American Christianity*. Berkeley: University of California Press, 2004.

———. *God's Daughters: Evangelical Women and the Power of Submission*. Berkeley: University of California Press, 1997.

Gupta, Akhil. "The Reincarnation of Souls and the Rebirth of Commodities; Representations of Time in 'East' and 'West.'" *Cultural Critique* 22 (1992): 187–211.

Hall, David. "Review Essay: What Is the Place of 'Experience' in Religious History?" *Religion and American Culture* 13 (2003): 241–50.

Hammond, Charles. *Light from the Spirit World: Comprising a Series of Articles on the Condition of Spirits*. 2nd ed. Rochester, NY: Dewey, 1852.

Hanegraaff, Wouter. *New Age Religion and Western Culture*. Albany: State University of New York Press, 1998.

Harding, Susan. *The Book of Jerry Falwell*. Princeton, NJ: Princeton University Press, 2001.

Hay, David, and Ann Morisy. "Reports of Ecstatic, Paranormal, or Religious Experience in Great Britain and the United States: A Comparison of Trends." *Journal for the Scientific Study of Religion* 17 (1978): 255–68.

Hazen, Craig. *The Village Enlightenment: Popular Religion and Science in the Nineteenth Century*. Urbana: University of Illinois Press, 2000.

Healy, Kieran. "Embedded Altruism: Blood Collection Regimes and the European Union's Donor Population." *American Journal of Sociology* 105 (2000): 1633–57.

Hedges, Ellie, and James A. Beckford. "Holism, Healing, and the New Age." In *Beyond New Age: Exploring Alternative Spirituality*, edited by Steven Sutcliffe and Marion Bowman, 169–87. Edinburgh: Edinburgh University Press, 2000.

Heelas, Paul. *The New Age Movement*. Oxford: Blackwell, 1996.

Herberg, Will. *Protestant Catholic Jew*. Chicago: University of Chicago Press, 1960.

Hirsch, Eric, and Charles Stewart. "Introduction; Ethnographies of Historicity." *History and Anthropology* 16 (2005): 261–74.

Holland, Dorothy, Debra Skinner, William Lachiotte, and Carol Cain. *Identity and Agency in Cultural Worlds*. Cambridge, MA: Harvard University Press, 1998.

Hollinger, David. *Science, Jews, and Secular Culture*. Princeton, NJ: Princeton University Press, 1996.

Hoopes, James. *Consciousness in New England: From Puritanism and Ideas to Psychoanalysis and Semiotics*. Baltimore: Johns Hopkins University Press, 1989.

Hufford, David. *The Terror that Comes in the Night*. Philadelphia: University of Pennsylvania Press, 1982.

Ivakhiv, Adrian. *Claiming Sacred Ground: Pilgrims and Politics at Glastonbury and Sedona*. Bloomington: Indiana University Press, 2001.

———. "Nature and Self in New Age Pilgrimage." *Culture and Religion* 4 (2004): 93–118.

Iyengar, B. K. S. *Light on Yoga*. New York: Schocken Books, 1976.

Jackson, Carl T. "The New Thought Movement and the Nineteenth Century Discovery of Oriental Philosophy." *Journal of Popular Culture* 9, no. 3 (1975): 523–48.

———. *The Oriental Religions and American Thought: Nineteenth-Century Explorations*. Westport, CT: Greenwood, 1981.

James, Henry. *The Bostonians*. New York: Modern Library, 1956.

James, William. *The Varieties of Religious Experience*. New York: Penguin, 1982. First published 1902 by Longmans, Green.

Jantzen, Grace. *Power, Gender, and Christian Mysticism*. Cambridge: Cambridge University Press, 1995.

Jay, Martin. *Songs of Experience: Modern American and European Variations on a Universal Theme*. Berkeley: University of California Press, 2005.

Johnson, Julie Tallard. *Spiritual Journaling: Writing Your Way to Independence*. Rochester, VT: Bindu Books, 2006.

Johnston, Jay, and Ruth Barcan. "Subtle Transformations: Imagining the Body in Alternative Health Practices." *International Journal of Cultural Studies* 9 (2006): 25–44.

Jones, Rufus. *Spiritual Energies in Daily Life*. New York: MacMillan, 1922.

Judah, J. Stillson. *The History and Philosophy of the Metaphysical Movement in America*. Philadelphia: Westminster Press, 1967.

Kaptchuk, Ted J. "Acupuncture: Theory, Efficacy, and Practice." *Annals of Internal Medicine* 136 (2002): 374–83.

Kardec, Allan [Hippolyte Leon Denizard Rivail, pseud.]. *Spiritualist Philosophy: The Spirits' Book.* New York: Arno Press, 1976. First published 1875 by Colby and Rich.

Katz, Stephen. "Mysticism and the Interpretation of Sacred Scripture." In *Mysticism and Sacred Scripture,* edited by Steven Katz, 7–67. New York: Oxford University Press, 2000.

Keane, Webb. "Religious Language." *Annual Review of Anthropology* 26 (1997): 47–71.

Kessel, Reuben A. "Price Discrimination in Medicine." *Journal of Law and Economics* 1 (1954): 20–53.

King, Richard. *Orientalism and Religion: Postcolonial Theory, India, and the "Mystic East."* New York: Routledge, 1999.

Kirshenblatt-Gimblett, Barbara. *Destination Culture: Tourism, Museum, and Heritage.* Berkeley: University of California Press, 1998.

Klassen, Pamela. "Textual Healing: Mainstream Protestants and the Therapeutic Text, 1900–1925." *Church History* 75 (2006): 809–49.

Klassen, Pamela, and Courtney Bender. "Habits of Pluralism." In *After Pluralism: Reimagining Models of Interreligious Engagement,* edited by Courtney Bender and Pamela Klassen. New York: Columbia University Press, 2010.

Klein, Kerwin Lee. "In Search of Narrative Mastery: Postmodernism and the People without History." *History and Theory* 34 (1995): 275–98.

———. "On the Emergence of Memory in Historical Discourse." *Representations* 69 (2000): 127–50.

Koutstaal, Wilma. "Skirting the Abyss: A History of Experimental Explorations of Automatic Writing in Psychology." *Journal of the History of the Behavioral Sciences.* 28 (1992): 5–27.

Kripal, Jeffrey. *Esalen: America and the Religion of No Religion.* Chicago: University of Chicago Press, 2007.

Labov, William. "Speech Actions and Reactions in Personal Narrative." *In Georgetown University Round Table on Languages and Linguistics 1981: Analyzing Discourse, Text and Talk,* edited by Deborah Tannen. Washington DC: Georgetown University Press, 1982.

Labov, WIlliam, and J. Waletsky. "Narrative Analysis: Oral Versions of Personal Experience." In *Essays on the Verbal and Visual Arts,* 12–44. Seattle: University of Washington Press, 1967.

Lambek, Michael. *The Weight of the Past.* New York: Palgrave, 2003.

Lau, Kimberly. *New Age Capitalism: Making Money East of Eden.* Philadelphia: University of Pennsylvania Press, 2000.

Lawless, Elaine. "Rescripting Their Lives and Narratives: Spiritual Life Stories of Pentecostal Women Preachers." *Journal of Feminist Studies in Religion* 7 (1991): 53–71.

Lawton, George. *The Drama of Life after Death: A Study of the Spiritualist Religion.* New York: Holt, 1932.

Leadbeater, Charles. *The Astral World: Its Scenery, Inhabitants, and Phenomena.* New York: Cosimo Classics, 2005.

———. *The Chakras: A Monograph.* Madras, India: Theosophical Publishing House, 1938.

Lears, T. J. Jackson. "From Salvation to Self-realization: Advertising and the Therapeutic Roots of the Consumer Culture, 1880–1930." In *The Culture of Consumption: Critical Essays in American History, 1880–1980,* edited by Richard Wightman Fox and T.J. Jackson Lears, 1–38. New York: Pantheon Books, 1983.

LeBlanc, Andre. "The Origins of the Concept of Dissociation: Paul Janet, His Nephew Pierre, and the Problem of Post-hypnotic Suggestion." *History of Science* 34 (2001): 57–69.

Leland, Kurt. *Otherwhere: A Field Guide to Nonphysical Reality for the Out-of-Body Traveler.* Charlottesville, VA: Hampton Roads, 2001.

Lichterman, Paul. *The Search for Political Community.* Cambridge: Cambridge University Press, 1997.

Long, Charles H. "The Oppressive Elements of Religion and the Religions of the Oppressed." *Harvard Theological Review* 69, no. 3 (1976): 379–412.

Luhrmann, Tanya. "Metakinesis: How God Becomes Intimate in Contemporary U.S. Christianity." *American Anthropologist* 106 (2004): 518–28.

———. *Persuasions of the Witch's Craft: Ritual Magic in Contemporary England.* Cambridge, MA: Harvard University Press, 1989.

MacDonald, William L. "The Effects of Religiosity and Structural Strain on Reported Paranormal Experiences." *Journal for the Scientific Study of Religion* 34 (1995): 366–76.

Maitland, Edward, and Anna Kingsford. *The Perfect Way, or, the Finding of Christ.* New York: Lovell, 1890.

Masuzawa, Tomoko. *The Invention of World Religions.* Princeton, NJ: Princeton University Press, 2005.

———. "Troubles with Materiality: The Ghost of Fetishism in the Nineteenth Century." *Comparative Studies in Society and History* 42 (2000): 242–67.

McCutcheon, Russell. *Manufacturing Religion.* New York: Oxford University Press, 2003.

McGuire, Meredith. *Ritual Healing in Suburban America.* New Brunswick, NJ: Rutgers University Press, 1988.

McRoberts, Omar. "Beyond *Mysterium Tremendum:* Thoughts Toward an Aesthetic Study of Religious Experience." *Annals of the American Academy of Political and Social Sciences* 595 (2004): 190–203.

Melton, J. Gordon. "Edgar Cayce and Reincarnation: Past Life Readings as Religious Symbology." *Syzygy: Journal of Alternative Religion and Culture* 3 (1994): 39–50.

Melton, J. Gordon, Jerome Clark, and Aidan Kelly, eds. *New Age Encyclopedia*. Detroit: Gale Research, 1991.

Menand, Louis. *The Metaphysical Club*. New York: Farrar Straus and Giroux, 2001.

Merleau-Ponty, M. *The Phenomenology of Perception*. London: Routledge, 1962.

Meyer, Donald. *The Positive Thinkers: Religion as Pop Psychology from Mary Baker Eddy to Oral Roberts*. New York: Pantheon, 1980.

Michelis, Elizabeth de. *A History of Modern Yoga*. New York: Continuum, 2001.

Moore, R. Lawrence. *In Search of White Crows*. New York: Oxford University Press, 1977.

Morson, Gary Saul. *Narrative and Freedom*. New Haven, CT: Yale University Press, 1996.

Mullin, R. Bruce. *Miracles and the Modern Religious Imagination*. New Haven, CT: Yale University Press, 1996.

Münsterberg, Hugo. *Psychology and Life*. Boston: Houghton Mifflin, 1899.

Naharo, Master, and Gail Radford. *The Complete Reiki Course*. Hod Hosharon, Israel: Astrolog, 2001.

Nestle, Marion. *Food Politics*. Berkeley: University of California Press, 2002.

Newcomb, Charles B. *Discovery of a Lost Trail*. Boston: Shepard and Lee, 1900.

Obeyesekere, Gananath. *Imagining Karma: Ethical Transformation in Amerindian, Buddhist, and Greek Rebirth*. Berkeley: University of California Press, 2002.

Ochs, Elinor, and Linda Capps. *Living Narrative*. Cambridge, MA: Harvard University Press, 2001.

———. "Narrating the Self." *Annual Review of Anthropology* 25 (1996): 19–43.

Olick, Jeffrey. "Genre Memories and Memory Genres." *American Sociological Review* 64, no. 3 (1999): 381–402.

———. *In the House of the Hangman: The Agonies of German Defeat, 1943–1949*. Chicago: University of Chicago Press, 2005.

Orsi, Robert. *Between Heaven and Earth: The Religious Worlds People Make and the Scholars Who Study Them*. Princeton, NJ: Princeton University Press, 2004.

Ostrander, Richard. *The Life of Prayer in a World of Science*. New York: Oxford University Press, 2000.

Owen, Alex. *The Place of Enchantment: British Occultism and the Culture of the Modern*. Chicago: University of Chicago Press, 2004.

Owens, Elizabeth. *Discover Your Spiritual Life: Illuminate Your Soul's Path*. St. Paul, MN: Llewellyn Worldwide, 2004.

Parish, Bobbi. *Create Your Personal Sacred Text: Develop and Celebrate Your Spiritual Life*. New York: Broadway Books, 1999.

Partridge, Christopher H. *The Re-enchantment of the West: Alternative Spiritualities, Sacralization, Popular Culture, and Occulture*. Vol. 1. London: Clark International, 2004.

Patton, Kimberly, and John Stratton Hawley, eds. *Holy Tears*. Princeton, NJ: Princeton University Press, 2005.

Peacock, James, and Dorothy Holland. "The Narrated Self: Life Stories in Process." *Ethos* 21 (1993): 367–84.

Pelletier, Kenneth. *The Best Alternative Medicine: What Works? What Does Not?* New York: Simon and Schuster, 2000.

Pike, Sarah. *Earthly Bodies Magical Selves.* Berkeley: University of California Press, 2001.

Polletta, Francesca. "Contending Stories: Narratives in Social Movements." *Qualitative Sociology* 21, no. 4 (1998): 419–46.

Porterfield, Amanda. *The Transformation of American Religion: The Story of a Late Twentieth-Century Awakening.* New York: Oxford University Press, 2001.

Prothero, Stephen. *American Jesus: How the Son of God Became a National Icon.* New York: Farrar, Strauss and Giroux, 2003.

———. "Hindophobia and Hindophilia in U.S. Culture." In *The Stranger's Religion,* edited by Ann Lannstrom, 13–37. Notre Dame, IN: University of Notre Dame Press, 2004.

———. *The White Buddhist.* Bloomington: Indiana University Press, 1996.

Proudfoot, Wayne. *Religious Experience.* Berkeley: University of California Press, 1985.

Radway, Janice. *Reading the Romance.* Chapel Hill: University of North Carolina Press, 1991.

Ramaswamy, Sumathi. *The Lost Land of Lemuria: Fabulous Geographies, Catastrophic Histories.* Berkeley: University of California Press, 2004.

Ricoeur, Paul. *Interpretation Theory: Discourse and the Surplus of Meaning.* Fort Worth: Texas Christian University Press, 1976.

Ronell, Avital. *The Telephone Book: Technology, Schizophrenia, and Electric Speech.* Lincoln: University of Nebraska Press, 1989.

Roof, Wade Clark. *Spiritual Marketplace: Baby Boomers and the Remaking of American Religion.* Princeton, NJ: Princeton University Press, 1999.

Rosaldo, Renato. "Ideology, Place, and People without Culture." *Cultural Anthropology* 3 (1988): 77–87.

Rushnell, Squire. *When God Winks at You: How God Speaks Directly to You through the Power of Coincidence.* Nashville, TN: Thomas Nelson Books, 2006.

Satter, Beryl. *Each Mind a Kingdom: American Women, Sexual Purity, and the New Thought Movement, 1875–1920.* New York: Oxford University Press, 1999.

Scarf, R. C. "Book Note: 'The One Way.'" *American Journal of Psychology* 47 (1935): 186.

Schiffman, Erich. *Yoga: The Spirit and Practice of Moving into Stillness.* New York: Simon and Schuster, 1996.

Schmidt, Leigh Eric. *Hearing Things: Religion, Illusion, and the American Enlightenment.* Cambridge, MA: Harvard University Press, 2000.

———. "The Making of Modern 'Mysticism.'" *Journal of the American Academy of Religion* 71 (2003): 273–302.

———. *Restless Souls: The Making of American Spirituality.* San Francisco: Harper-SanFrancisco, 2006.

Schneider, Mark A. *Culture and Enchantment.* Chicago: University of Chicago Press, 1993.

Schudson, Michael. "The Varieties of Civic Experience." In *The Civic Life of American Religion,* edited by Paul Lichterman and C. Brady Potts, 23–47. Stanford: Stanford University Press, 2008.

Scott, Joan W. "Fantasy Echo: History and the Construction of Identity." *Critical Inquiry* 27, no. 2 (2001): 284–304.

Sellers-Young, Barbara. "Raks el Sharki: Transculturation of a Folk Form." *Journal of Popular Culture* 26 (1992): 141–52.

Sewell, William H., Jr. "The Concept(s) of Culture." In *Beyond the Cultural Turn,* edited by Victoria Bonnell and Lynn Hunt, 35–61. Berkeley: University of California Press, 1999.

Sharf, Richard. "Buddhist Modernism and the Rhetoric of Meditative Experience." *Numen* 42 (1995): 228–83.

———. "Experience." In *Critical Terms for Religious Studies,* edited by Mark C. Taylor, 94–116. Chicago: University of Chicago Press, 1998.

Shimazono, Susumu. "'New Age Movement' or 'New Spirituality Movements and Culture?'" *Social Compass* 46 (1999): 121–33.

Singleton, Mark. "Salvation through Relaxation: Proprioceptive Therapy and Its Relationship to Yoga." *Journal of Contemporary Religion* 20 (2005): 289–304.

Smilde, David. *Reason to Believe.* Berkeley: University of California Press, 2007.

Smith, Christian. "Introduction: Rethinking the Secularization of American Public Life." In *The Secular Revolution: Power, Interests, and Conflict in the Secularization of American Public Life,* edited by Christian Smith, 1–95. Chicago: University of Chicago Press, 2003.

———, ed. *The Secular Revolution: Power, Interests, and Conflict in the Secularization of American Public Life.* Chicago: University of Chicago Press, 2003.

Smith, David Norton. "Faith, Reason, and Charisma: Rudolf Sohm, Max Weber, and the Theology of Grace." *Sociological Inquiry* 68 (1998): 30–62.

Snell, Merwin-Marie. "Modern Theosophy in Its Relation to Hinduism and Buddhism." *Biblical Culture* 5, no. 4 (1895): 258–65.

Somers, Margaret. "The Narrative Constitution of Identity: A Relational and Network Approach." *Theory and Society* 23 (1994): 605–49.

Somers, Margaret, and Gloria Gibson. "Reclaiming the Epistemological 'Other': Narrative and the Social Constitution of Identity." In *Social Theory and the Politics of Identity,* edited by Craig Calhoun, 37–99. Oxford: Blackwell, 1994.

Spickard, James. "Ritual, Symbol, and Experience: Understanding Catholic Worker House Masses." *Sociology of Religion* 66 (2005): 337–57.

Starbuck, Edwin. "A Study of Conversion." *American Journal of Psychology* 8 (1897): 268–308.

Stark, Rodney, and William Sims Bainbridge. "Of Churches, Sects, and Cults: Preliminary Concepts for a Theory of Religious Movements." *Journal for the Scientific Study of Religion* 18 (1979): 117–33.

Starr, Paul. *The Social Transformation of American Medicine.* New York: Basic Books, 1982.

Stearn, Jess. *Yoga, Youth, and Reincarnation.* New York: Doubleday, 1965.

Stewart, Charles. "Syncretism and Its Synonyms: Reflections on Cultural Mixture." *Diacritics* 29 (1999): 40–62.

Stout, Harry, and D. G. Hart, eds. *New Directions in American Religious History.* New York: Oxford University Press, 1997.

Straus, Roger. "The Social-Psychology of Religious Experience: A Naturalistic Approach." *Sociological Analysis* 42 (1981): 157–67.

Strauss, Sarah. *Positioning Yoga: Balancing Acts across Cultures.* New York: Berg, 2005.

Sugrue, Thomas. *There Is a River.* New York: Holt, 1942.

Sullivan, Winnifred Fallers. *Prison Religion.* Princeton, NJ: Princeton University Press, 2009.

———. "The Way We Live Now: Religion Unbound." In *After Pluralism,* edited by Pamela Klassen and Courtney Bender. New York: Columbia University Press, forthcoming.

Sutcliffe, Steven. *Children of the New Age.* London: Routledge, 2003.

Sutcliffe, Steven, and Marion Bowman, eds. *Beyond New Age: Exploring Alternative Spirituality.* Edinburgh; University of Edinburgh Press, 2000.

Swidler, Ann. *Talk of Love.* Chicago: University of Chicago Press, 2001.

Taves, Ann. *Fits, Trances, and Visions: Experiencing Religion and Explaining Experience from Wesley to James.* Princeton, NJ: Princeton University Press, 1999.

———. "The Fragmentation of Consciousness and the Varieties of Religious Experience: William James's Contribution to a Theory of Religion." In *William James and a Science of Religions,* edited by Wayne Proudfoot, 48–72. New York: Columbia University Press, 2004.

Taylor, Charles. *A Secular Age.* Cambridge, MA: Harvard University Press, 2007.

———. *Sources of the Self.* Cambridge, MA: Harvard University Press, 1989.

Taylor, Eugene. "Have We Engaged in a Colossal Misreading of James's *Varieties?*" *Streams of William James* 5 (2003): 2–6.

———. *Shadow Culture: Psychology and Spirituality in America.* Washington, DC: Counterpoint, 1999.

———. "Swedenborgian Roots of American Pragmatism: The Case of D. T. Suzuki." *Studia Swedenborgia* 9 (1995).

Thompson, Sarah Gray. "Do You Remember Your Previous Lives' Language in Your Present Incarnation?" *American Speech* 59 (1984): 240–50.

Travis, Trysh. "It Will Change the World if Everyone Reads This Book: New Thought Religion in Oprah's Book Club." *American Quarterly* 59 (2007): 1017–41.

Trine, Ralph Waldo. *In Tune with the Infinite.* New York: Dodd, Mead, 1921.

Troeltsch, Ernst. *The Social Teachings of the Christian Churches.* Louisville, KY: Westminster John Knox Press, 1992.

Trueblood, D. Elton. "The Influence of Emerson's Divinity School Address." *Harvard Theological Review* 32 (1939): 41–56

Turner, Bryan S. "Cosmopolitan Virtue, Globalization, and Patriotism." *Theory, Culture, and Society* 19 (2002): 45–65.

Tweed, Thomas. *Crossing and Dwelling.* Cambridge, MA: Harvard University Press, 2006.

Urban, Hugh. *Tantra: Sex, Secrecy, Politics, and Power in the Study of Religion.* Berkeley: University of California Press, 2003.

Vahle, Neal. *The Unity Movement: Its Evolution and Spiritual Teachings.* Philadelphia: Templeton Foundation Press, 2002.

Van der Veer, Peter, ed. *Nation and Migration: The Politics of Space in South Asian Diaspora.* Philadelphia: University of Pennsylvania Press, 1995.

Van Praagh, James. *Reaching to Heaven: A Spiritual Journey through Life and Death.* New York: Dutton, 1999.

Versluis, Arthur. *American Transcendentalism and Asian Religions.* New York: Oxford University Press, 1993.

Viswanathan, Gauri. *Outside the Fold: Conversion, Modernity, and Belief.* Princeton, NJ: Princeton University Press, 1998.

———. "Secularism in the Framework of Heterodoxy." *PMLA* 123, no. 2 (2008): 465–76.

Vivekananda, Swami. *Raja Yoga.* Calcutta: Dey, 1959.

Wach, Joachim. *Sociology of Religion.* Chicago: University of Chicago Press, 1949.

Wallach, Amei. "Art, Religion, and Spirituality: A Conversation with Artists." In *Crossroads: Art and Religion in American Life,* edited by Alberta Arthurs and Glenn Wallach. New York: Norton, 2001.

Walter, Tony. "Reincarnation, Modernity, and Identity." *Sociology* 35 (2000): 21–38.

Walter, Tony, and Helen Waterhouse. "A Very Private Belief: Reincarnation in Contemporary England." *Sociology of Religion* 60 (1999): 187–97.

Warner, Michael. *Publics and Counterpublics.* New York: Zone Books, 2002.

Warner, R. Stephen. "The Place of the Congregation in the Contemporary American Religious Configuration." In *American Congregations: New Perspectives in the Study of Congregations,* edited by James Wind and James Lewis, 54–99. Chicago: University of Chicago Press, 1994.

Weber, Max. *Economy and Society.* Berkeley: University of California Press, 1978.

Weiss, Brian. *Many Lives, Many Masters.* New York: Simon and Schuster, 1988.

———. *Same Soul, Many Bodies: Discover the Healing Power of Future Lives through Progression Therapy.* New York: Free Press, 2004.

White, Christopher. *Unsettled Minds: Psychology and the American Search for Spiritual Assurance, 1830–1940.* Berkeley: University of California Press, 2008.

Whorton, James. *Nature Cures: The History of Alternative Medicine in America*. New York: Oxford University Press, 2002.

Wilcox, Melissa. "When Sheila's a Lesbian: Religious Individualism among Lesbian, Gay, and Transgender Christians." *Sociology of Religion* 63 (2002): 497–513.

Will, Barbara. "Gertrude Stein, Automatic Writing, and the Mechanics of Genius." *Modern Language Studies* 37 (2001): 169–75.

Wolf, Eric. *Europe and the People without History*. Princeton, NJ: Princeton University Press, 1982.

Wuthnow. Robert. *After Heaven: Spirituality in America since the 1950s*. Berkeley: University of California Press, 1998.

———. *All in Sync: How Music and Art Are Revitalizing American Religion*. Berkeley: University of California Press, 2003.

———. "Arts Leaders and Religious Leaders: Mutual Perceptions." In *Crossroads: Art and Religion in American Life*, edited by Alberta Arthurs and Glenn Wallach, 31–70. New York: Norton, 2001.

———. *Loose Connections*. Cambridge, MA: Harvard University Press, 1998.

Wyman, Walter E., Jr. *The Concept of Glaubenslehre: Ernst Troeltsch and the Theological Heritage of Schleiermacher*. Chico, CA: Scholars Press, 1983.

Yamane, David. "Narrative and Religious Experience." *Sociology of Religion* 61 (2000): 2.

Yang, Fenggang, and Helen Rose Ebaugh. "Transformations in New Immigrant Religions and Their Global Implications." *American Sociological Review* 66 (2001): 269–88.

Yarbo, Chelsea Quinn. *Messages from Michael: The Remarkable True Story of a Link between Two Worlds*. Chicago: Playboy Press, 1979.

York, Michael. *The Emerging Network: A Sociology of the New Age and Neo-Pagan Movements*. Lanham, MD: Rowman and Littlefield, 1995.

Zaleski, Carol. *Otherworld Journeys*. New York: Oxford University Press, 1987.

Index

acupuncture, 25, 27–29, 50, 56, 93

Albanese, Catherine, 202–3n14, 214n6

alternative health: biomedicine, 26–28, 202n11; centers and clinics, 6, 54; groups, 48, 49; histories of, 26; increasing mainstream acceptance of, 27, 202n11; outreach to mainstream health communities, 51; patient-led activist groups, 26, 202n12; spirituality and, 25–30, 183. *See also* energy; healing

America: absence of culture, 181; cosmopolitanism of, 180–81; as mysticism, 181, 228–29n26; nostalgia and, 181; religious history of, 46

American Society for Psychical Research, 135

angels, 132

Artist's Way, The (Cameron), 32, 76–77, 80–81, 211n29

Asia: influence on American spiritual practitioners, 86, 95, 106–12, 205n27, 217n26; as "mystical East," 109, 112; philosophical texts of, 10, 97–98, 133; religions of, 4, 112, 200n3, 205n27. *See also* India

astral: beings, 132, 218n35; bodies (*see under* bodies); exploration, 157, 170–72, 186, 228n16; geographies, 166–72; matter, 98; planes, 133, 151, 165, 168–70,

215n11; planets, 168–69; realms, 98, 134, 169–72, 221n18

Astral Plane, The (Leadbeater), 165

Astral Worlds (Panchadasi), 171

astrology, esoteric, 21, 32, 35, 52, 150, 167–68

Atkinson, William Walker: *Astral Worlds,* 171; as Swami Panchadasi, 171; *Thought Vibration or the Law of Attraction in the Thought World,* 213n4; as Yogi Ramacharaka,134–35

Atlantis, 137, 168

auras, 49, 98–99, 112–13, 214n10

automatic writing, 78–80, 128, 185, 209–10n21, 210n24, 210n26

Bailey, Alice, 32, 167, 168

Bakhtin, Mikhail: on chronotopes, 156–57; *The Dialogic Imagination,* 220n11, 224–25n2, 225–26n4; on genre, 195n15; on practice, 185

Bellah, Robert, *Habits of the Heart,* 12, 198n34

belly dance, 39, 56–57, 155–56, 163–64, 226n9

Benson, Herbert, 15

Berger, Peter: Bakhtin and, 225n2; *The Heretical Imperative,* 9

Bernstein, Morey, *The Search for Bridey Murphy,* 131–32

Bible, the: mysticism in, 135; symbolic numbers in, 53

American spirituality—with its focus on individual meaning, experience, and exploration—is usually thought to be a product of the postmodern era. But, as *The New Metaphysicals* makes clear, contemporary American spirituality has historic roots in the nineteenth century and a great deal in common with traditional religious movements. To explore this world, Courtney Bender combines research into the history of the movement with fieldwork in Cambridge, Massachusetts—a key site of alternative religious inquiry from Emerson and William James to today. Through her ethnographic analysis, Bender discovers that a focus on the new, on progress, and on the way spiritual beliefs intersect with science obscures the historical roots of spirituality from its practitioners and those who study it alike.

"Truly distinctive and distinguished. Bender captures the subtlety of the religious voices, practices, and struggles of those she terms contemporary metaphysicals living amid shifting economic realities, modern assumptions about science and progress, and related entanglements. This is a remarkable book simply for recording these fascinating practitioners and helping readers understand their categories of practice and experience in all their complexity. But her work does far more than merely record; it offers a compelling examination of how we may think anew about these categories and the people—metaphysicals and scholars alike—for whom they matter."
R. Marie Griffith, Harvard Divinity School

"In this rich ethnography of the varieties of contemporary spirituality in William James's hometown of Cambridge, Massachusetts, Courtney Bender shows—hopefully once and for all—how wrong James was to say that religion is the experience of individuals in their solitude. In a series of beautifully rendered life stories she brings spirituality down to earth and discloses what is most deeply at stake for Americans in being 'spiritual but not religious.' *The New Metaphysicals* promises fundamentally to change how we think not only about contemporary American spirituality but also how we understand what we mean by 'religion.'"
Robert A. Orsi, Northwestern University

"The classic ethnographic impulse is to challenge our scholarly understandings by observing everyday understandings in action. In *The New Metaphysicals* Courtney Bender instead reveals their complex mutual constitution in our common and standard portrayals of American mysticism as without history or structure. Bender's brilliant use of the tools of practice theory conveys a sense of long-term yet loose structure. Her thick yet elegant descriptions of the institutions, discourses, and practices that create contemporary American mysticism provide a model for the study of religious traditions. And her reassertion of a more structured and culture-full version of practice theory is a must-read for ethnographers of any subject."
David Smilde, University of Georgia

Courtney Bender is associate professor of religion at Columbia University and the author of *Heaven's Kitchen: Living with Religion at God's Love We Deliver*, also published by the University of Chicago Press.

The University of Chicago Press
www.press.uchicago.edu

ISBN-13: 978-0-226-04280-0
ISBN-10: 0-226-04280-4

9 780226 042800

90000